Avian Nutrition

by

Robert G. Black

Previously published as:
Avian Nutrition 2nd edition Copyright 1999
Nutrition of Finches and Other Cage Birds Copyright 1981

Avian Publications
6380 Monroe St NE
Minneapolis MN 55432

Bruce Burchett, Publisher
www.avianpublications.com
bruce@avianpublications.com
Phone & fax 763-571-8902

ISBN 0-910335-04-4

Printed in the USA

DEDICATION

This book is dedicated with thanks
to the researchers whose perseverance and dedication
uncovered the knowledge and information
presented in these pages.

And to the countless birds and animals
whose deprivation and sacrifice enabled us
to bring to light and understanding
these hidden mysteries of the nutritional process.

ACKNOWLEDGEMENTS

The author wishes to express his sincere appreciation to all of those over the years who have purchased and read the first edition of this book, *Nutrition of Finches and Other Cage Birds*, and have heeded the advice and information offered here to the permanent benefit of their birds. The first edition sold out many years ago, but the continued interest expressed in the book and the many requests for it from dedicated breeders and fanciers convinced me to publish the second edition as *Avian Nutrition*, and now seems the right and proper time for the compilation and publication of this third edition.

My special thanks also go to John Wilson of San Francisco, California, for his gentle badgering and insistence that it was time for a serious return to the field of aviculture, and also to Bob Clark of Hereford, Texas, Carol Heesen of Riverbank, California, Roy Beckham of San Jose, California, and Darrell Horst of Woodland, California, for including my publications in their own successful websites.

CONTENTS

PART III – THE MINERALS AND OTHER NUTRITIONAL ELEMENTS

FOREWORD

The study of nutrition is an intimidating pursuit. The more one learns about nutrition, the more complicated and incomprehensible it seems. The complex interactions of all of the necessary nutrients in their cooperation to provide the necessities of biological life to a living organism are completely mystifying. We have no scientifically supported idea yet why most of these chemical compounds act as they do, or what governs their actions and use by the body. We can only describe what happens in the body, not what motivates it to happen. Only one religious philosophy has even explained this process to my satisfaction. That is the teaching of the Rosicrucian Fellowship headquartered in Oceanside, California.

The study of nutrition is a very new science. Though the earliest nutritional reference I have encountered dates from around 2700 B. C. from a treatise on herbal medicine during the reign of the legendary Chinese emperor Shen-nung, it was only in 1931 that vitamin C, ascorbic acid, was definitely isolated and identified. Virtually all detailed knowledge of nutrition and nutritional requirements is a product of the twentieth century. Though such knowledge may have been known to the most advanced of ancient and prehistoric civilizations, as evidenced by their few remaining artifacts, any records of such knowledge have been totally and probably irretrievably lost. Since recent human history indicates that at least fifty years are required for the widespread acceptance of any new discovery, we can be sure that most of the nutritional discoveries of the last few decades will not be totally accepted and utilized for many more years. Nevertheless, all of the information that I could locate is presented in this volume for your information and use.

Our current knowledge of nutrition represents only a very small part of what there is to learn. We have barely touched the surface of potential nutritional knowledge. Much of what is presumed to be true today will undoubtedly be proven false at some time in the future. Yet, slowly, but surely, the knowledge of what maintains life is expanded, to the benefit of all who will learn and put that knowledge to use. Regardless of what discoveries should come in the future, the 1930's, a time of economic disaster, will always be looked upon as the golden age of nutritional discovery.

As mountainous and unending as the study of nutrition may be, at some point, a student must fall back, consolidate his knowledge, and begin teaching others something of what he has learned. I have reached that point. Should all writers wait until they felt confident in every aspect of their subject, no writing would ever be done. One person can never know everything about any subject, no matter how specialized. We can, at best, only chip away at our ignorance and try to drag others, kicking and screaming all the way, into our field of knowledge.

Most of the writing thus far on avian nutrition has been so generalized or full of inaccuracies as to be almost useless. What few books have delved deeply into the nutritional requirements of birds have been so extremely technical as to be almost incomprehensible to the average reader. Virtually no research has been done on the specific nutritional requirements of any bird of avicultural interest, though the Department of Avian Sciences of the University of California, Davis, is making a good start. Most of the information offered in this volume for wild birds maintained in captivity must be inferred from the study of domestic fowl and laboratory animals. This is regrettable, but unavoidable. To make matters worse, even knowledgeable veterinarians and researchers still parrot outdated avicultural literature in attributing a problem as common, disastrous, and preventable as eggbinding to cold weather and wet nests, when it is totally and completely a symptom of nutritional deficiency.

Very little of the information presented in this volume is the result of my personal research and experimentation, yet the information gleaned from the research on poultry and laboratory animals has invariably proven to be 100% accurate when applied to the birds maintained and bred by aviculturists. When my personal experience has led to the conclusion expounded, this is clearly stated. Most of the following information comes from the books listed in the Bibliography, and I am most deeply indebted to these authors and their publishers for the wealth of nutritional information contained in their works.

It is indeed unfortunate, however, that the most knowledgeable authorities have written no book comparable to this for the use of the average breeder of cage birds. Their writing has been primarily for medical and nutritional journals, and the resulting information definitely has not filtered down to the breeder and amateur aviculturist. Untold millions of birds in captivity have died over the last century solely as a result of this lack of the known and available nutritional information.

I must honestly acknowledge that I am certainly not the most qualified to write this book. My gift is in finding, reading, digesting, organizing and presenting the known material in common terms for the use of the average bird fancier. My formal training is in International Affairs and Linguistics. My vocational training has been in management, teaching, horticulture, and aviculture. Nutritional study has always been a very peripheral part of my fields of interest. Nevertheless, the need for this information is so great that I plowed into it full force, and you are reading the result.

Nutrition is the key to aviculture.
It is the most important factor for success
in maintaining and breeding cage birds.
All other conditions are secondary.
No aviculturist can expect to succeed
unless the nutrition of the birds
is of paramount consideration.

Robert G. Black

PART ONE

NUTRITION BASICS

"There is no information, no food, no knowledge,
and no experience that will serve you better for the future
than the knowledge of nutrition."

CHAPTER 1

INTRODUCTION TO NUTRIENTS

Most of our knowledge of the nutrition of birds is the result of studies done in human nutrition or in the nutrition of rats, mice, chickens, and guinea pigs for information leading to further useful knowledge of human nutrition. The original work that has been done with birds is mostly in reference to the nutrition of chickens and other domestic fowl. Original research available on any birds other than domestic fowl has been very rare and sporadic in nature. As a consequence, though the needs of any particular bird for any specific nutrient may not be absolutely and finally proven, if humans, rats, and chickens need that nutrient, all logic and experience will point to its need by all birds, in addition. Many nutritionists will not accept this concept, but in order to have anything to say specifically on the nutrition of cage birds, the author has been forced to make this extension of knowledge into unproven areas. Based upon the known unity of all nature with respect to biological functioning, there is full justification for extending this knowledge into the field of aviculture and cage bird feeding.

In discussing the subject of nutrition of cage birds, it is imperative to begin at a basic level. Even so, words unfamiliar to the average reader must be used occasionally and will be explained as completely as possible. This will assure that no one is left behind hopelessly confused in what is admittedly a confusing subject. Also, the glossary defines all terms used in this book relating to nutrition and the other subjects covered in this work. The glossary provides an instant and ready reference for any term that may be unfamiliar to the reader or that the reader may have missed in the initial reference to it in the text.

Everyone is aware that food contains nutrients that are necessary for life and growth. Any statement beyond this will run into ignorance, heated debate, disbelief, and even ridicule. What comes as a particular surprise to many is the fact that the exact same nutrients that are necessary for people are also necessary for birds. Consequently, this volume is directed to the bird breeder's nutrition as much as it is directed to the nutrition of the birds. Nutrition is universal for humans, animals, and birds Though these warm-blooded bodies all live and function using the same nutrients, some species are able to synthesize some of these vital compounds internally and do not need to have the nutrient supplied in their normal diets.

The primary task of any aviculturist is to provide food to the birds that are maintained and to know what constitutes suitable food for each of the species kept. Without access to the food, the birds certainly cannot eat it and begin the nutritional process. Empty feed dishes and forgotten rations serve no purpose. To the contrary, they assure the eventual death of the birds from starvation. In addition, the food of one species may be a disaster for another species that is not equipped by nature to digest it.

Yet, the specific nutrients required will be the same for all birds. Some will get these nutrients from seeds, some from insects, some from fruit, and some from flesh and carrion. Nevertheless, the basic nutrients needed and ingested are the same for all avian species. Only the quantities of each nutrient needed at the different stages of life will vary from species to species, as well as among individuals within the same species. As previously mentioned, some species are able to synthesize some of the nutrients their bodies need internally, and thus do not need to have them supplied in the diet.

Consumption of the food is the next requirement. As elementary as it may sound in the writing and the reading, food must be eaten to perform the wonders of life and growth. The birds must eat the food you provide, and you must provide foods that will be eaten. A food not consumed is not a food at all, but merely a complex combination of chemical compounds. Any food offering left untouched by the birds is worse than nothing. It may provide a breeding ground for fungi and bacteria, and it is money totally wasted, since few of the items that we feed our birds are free. Money thrown away cannot go to purchase foods that the birds will eat. Also, food uneaten is time wasted in the purchase, in the preparation, and in the provision.

Contrary to human experience, taste does not seem to play a primary role in the food consumption of birds. The energy level of the diet seems to be of primary importance in determining food intake in most birds. Nevertheless, as anyone who has ever maintained a canary, a parakeet, or a finch will confirm, birds do have definite likes and dislikes where taste is concerned in the food supply. In order to maintain and raise birds successfully, the breeder must cater to these specific preferences on the part of individual birds and strains of birds and must supply foods that are acceptable to the birds.

Birds are much like people in that they will seldom try anything new and unfamiliar. If you want to introduce some birds to a new, highly nutritious food that all of your others are eating and love, here is a simple, safe, and effective method. First, remove all other food from the birds' cage. Place a small amount of the desirable new food in the cage, thus enforcing a fast on the birds. Fasting is a healthful process, enabling the bodies of the birds to eliminate toxins and wastes. Fasting also is an aid to healing, freeing the body's metabolism from digestion to rebuilding the damaged tissues. It should not be confused with starvation. The enforced fast should last a maximum of eight hours for the smallest finches, sixteen hours for a larger bird, such as a cardinal or bullfinch, and may go for several days in large parrots. Longer than these periods of fasting will begin starvation, which is to be avoided under any circumstances.

Usually, the birds will test the newly offered food within a few hours, as they get hungry and find nothing else to eat. If they have gone the full period mentioned above without touching the new food, return their normal diet at least two hours before nightfall so that they will not be without food in the crop for the night. The next morning, take away all food again, leaving only the new offering. In my experience, by the third day they will be cleaning up a fairly large portion of the new food each morning. When it is gone, return all normal rations for the rest of the day, plus a little more of the new food. By the fifth or sixth day, most birds will be eating the new food regularly, and you have succeeded. The author has found from experience that small finches will be eating a new food in three hours, Java Rice Birds and Budgerigars in 12 hours, and conures in 48 hours.

During this process, never take away the birds' water, and be sure to watch them closely for signs of distress. If a bird still will not eat the new food when anything else is available, it simply does not consider the new offering palatable and won't eat it voluntarily under any circumstances. In that situation, you are well advised to give up and feed something else of comparable nutritional value that the birds will consume willingly and in adequate quantities.

Once the birds have tested and accepted the new food, you can include it as a part of their normal diet with the assurance that they will now accept it as a part of their regular diet. Keep in mind that different foods require a different variety of enzymes and hormones for thorough digestion, proper assimilation and utilization by the body. If the bird's body is not already producing these substances in adequate quantity, it will require a few days for the body to shift gears, so to speak, in order to handle the new foods properly. For this reason, do not force an entirely new diet on your birds all at once, or you are asking for major problems in the form of digestive upset, diarrhea, and even serious illness. Give the birds' bodies a chance to adapt to any new foods that you choose to include in their diets.

Once a food is eaten, the next necessity is digestion. Digestion is a complex process of chemical breakdown from whole foods to basic nutrients. Food passes from the beak into the esophagus, and then into the crop, which is also called the diverticulum. The crop serves as a food storage area, and food moves from the crop through the lower esophagus to the proventriculus. The proventriculus is the true glandular stomach, and may also be called the forestomach. Hydrochloric acid and digestive enzymes pour into the food mass at the proventriculus, and this creates a highly acid mixture which then passes into the gizzard.

Before complete digestion can take place, food must be broken down into the tiniest of particles, literally into a mush. Humans accomplish this by chewing their food. Seed eating birds have a gizzard for the same purpose. The gizzard is a very powerful muscle that grinds seeds against each other, against its horny lining, and against gravel or grit the bird has consumed. As the food is ground into finer particles, the hydrochloric acid and digestive enzymes picked up in the proventriculus further break down the food particles.

Food then moves into the duodenum, the first section of the small intestine, where it is mixed with enzymes from the pancreas which can digest proteins, fats, and carbohydrates. Since the duodenum cannot tolerate this highly acid mixture, and the pancreatic enzymes will not function in an acid environment, the duodenum must release antacids and alkalis into the food mass to neutralize the acidity. Bile is also added from the liver, and the bile emulsifies the fats and oils found in the food into fine particles. The small intestine then completes the digestive process by breaking down all of the food particles into their basic, microscopic constituents.

This process of digestion can vary greatly, depending upon the variety of bird and its diet. Should any link in this chain of food breakdown occur, subsequent absorption into the bloodstream will be impossible and the bird will starve to death, regardless of the quantity of food consumed. Many nutritional deficiencies and diseases will halt the function of one of these necessary components of the digestive process, thus rendering the entire system useless.

Absorption is the next necessary step before the avian body can make use of the food that has been consumed. The crucial importance of the proper absorption of nutrients cannot be overemphasized. Absorption takes place molecule by molecule through the membrane of the intestinal wall, and any substance which interferes with this absorption will prevent the bird from getting the nutritional benefit of the food consumed. Nutrients that the digestive system cannot absorb, regardless of the reason for non-absorption, are simply passed through the rest of the digestive tract and eliminated.

The mechanism by which the intestinal wall rejects or accepts a molecule for absorption is largely unknown. Yet, we do know that this selectivity occurs.

Calcium, for example, is usually absorbed, but when calcium is attached to the oxalic acid molecule, such as raw spinach contains, the resulting molecule is completely unabsorbable. Minerals are absorbed much more readily when they are chelated. Chelation is the attachment of a mineral element to an amino acid molecule, or to another compound, such as ascorbic acid, or vitamin C. This example may be getting a bit ahead of the proper order for explanation, but such examples are necessary to illustrate the complexity of the absorptive process.

Occasionally, a substance harmful to the body may be absorbed. These harmful items that will do positive damage to the cells of the body are what we call poisons or toxins. Lest we consider this overly bizarre, keep in mind that no life form or function is absolutely perfect, or biological life would last forever. The lungs, for example, will absorb carbon monoxide into the bloodstream many times more rapidly than they will absorb oxygen.

Many things can interfere with proper absorption. Any poison, toxin or foreign bacteria which invade the digestive tract and set up a reaction in the form of diarrhea will wash the nutrients through the digestive system so rapidly that they will not be in contact with the intestinal wall long enough to be absorbed. Also, any sticky substance which coats the lining and plugs up the absorptive surface will prevent absorption.

Also, there are a wide variety of harmful microorganisms whose presence and toxic by-products can cause the total shutdown of the avian digestive system. Acclimating any birds to your local conditions is a matter of controlling the microorganisms they are exposed to and feeding them a balanced diet that is high in complete protein, as well as all of the vital vitamins and minerals they need. Birds as tiny as the waxbills have very limited body reserves when illness strikes, and for this reason, a sick finch almost invariably dies. Any harmful bacteria that they pick up can infect and shut down their digestive tracts, and these harmful microorganisms will result in any finch's death in short order. The birds must have time to develop an immunity to these harmful bacteria.

You can give them the time they need to develop their immunity to unfamiliar microorganisms by treating their drinking water with one drop of a common household sodium hypochlorite bleach to each four ounces of water. This will kill all harmful microorganisms in the water and in the digestive tract when the birds drink the water, without harming the birds in the least. Use this treatment for three days if some birds are sick, but only for one day as a preventative treatment. The chlorine will kill any of the bacteria or other microorganisms present and will give the bird a chance to develop an immunity to them. This immunity can be developed from just the presence of dead microorganisms very rapidly. After all, this is the way most human inoculations and vaccines work. Chlorine is one of the substances that will destroy vitamin E on contact however, so don't use any chlorine treatment on a constant basis.

I have found this simple treatment nearly 100% effective in preventing sickness in newly acquired birds. In cities where the water is already heavily chlorinated, this treatment may not be necessary. Taking birds as small as finches for veterinary care, however, is simply never cost effective. The sick bird will be dead before any culture can be made or any effective antibiotic prescribed. Though many individuals in the past have ridiculed this chlorine treatment as at best useless and at worst dangerous to the birds, I feel sure that they haven't even tried this treatment for themselves on birds that were obviously ill. I have used it for many years, and stand solidly behind this recommendation for any new birds added to your collection or to your breeding areas. Despite the many aviculturists who are not in favor of this treatment, when you cut down to the bottom line, it is this: the treatment works.

The smaller molecules, such as those of the simple sugar glucose, are more easily absorbed than the very large and complicated molecules of a substance such as vitamin B_{12} or cobalamin. For this reason, an over-abundance of glucose from carbohydrate foods may be undesirable and fattening, while an excess of cobalamin may be desirable to ensure the minimum absorption for optimal health. Never forget that eating does not mean absorption. The eating of a food is only the first step in the nutritive process.

Once a nutrient has been absorbed into the bloodstream, it will circulate until it is taken out by a cell through the membrane of the cell wall for use as a fuel for energy, a building block for cell growth and replacement, or storage for future use. How each cell can identify its various nutritional needs and selectively withdraw them from the bloodstream is a complete mystery.

The physical and chemical processes by which the body uses the nutrients absorbed for growth and energy are referred to as metabolism. Metabolism varies greatly from individual to individual, even within the same species. This will be covered more fully in the discussion of biochemical individuality. We are all familiar with people who are cold even in temperatures of eighty degrees Fahrenheit, and others who frolic in short sleeves at fifty degrees in perfect comfort. These differences are the result of a slower or faster rate of metabolism, in this case the burning of food for heat energy, in particular. See the section on iodine for a more thorough discussion on the subject of the production of body heat.

Such differences in metabolism bear little correlation to the amount of food consumed. The successful absorption of the nutrients, by contrast, definitely and strongly affects the rate of use, since nutrients not in the bloodstream certainly cannot be withdrawn and metabolized. Age will often result in slower metabolism, with any lack of nutrients in the diet further harming the body's digestion, absorption, circulation and general metabolism.

There can be no such thing as perfect nutrition at the cell level. Each cell needs a set supply of each individual nutrient, but is totally dependent upon what the blood supply brings it. This supply, in turn, depends on what has been absorbed, which depends upon the efficiency of digestion, which also depends on the nutrients available in the food supply, and so forth. As a consequence, every cell operates continually at what we may refer to as a less than optimal level of nutrition. Sometimes inadequately supplied with a nutrient, at other times oversupplied, it is a wonder at times that any cell continues to function to the use and benefit of the total organism.

All nutrients in the body's metabolism work together to supply the formula for life in each bird and in each of its cells. No nutrient performs its functions alone, but in concert. Since the nutrients occur together in foods, a deficiency of one vitamin, for example, will surely mean that others are also deficient. This interaction of nutrients is one logical argument against the use of single, synthetically produced vitamin supplements. In nature, no vitamin occurs alone, but always in association with other vitamins, minerals, and other food factors. They are found together, consumed together, and work together in the body. A single nutrient in supplement form may not work as well in the body because it upsets this natural balance. It does seem that the biological activity of artificially synthesized vitamins is less than that of the natural compounds, for reasons that are not yet clear. However, this lowered biological activity may well be because of the lack of other nutritional factors that would occur in the same foods with this vitamin in nature. Nevertheless, chemically, down to the last atom, an artificially synthesized vitamin is identical to its counterpart that is found in nature.

Biochemical individuality is a term that seems calculated to frighten away anyone not having a Ph. D. degree. Yet, it simply says in concise form that every individual is different in its body chemistry and its metabolism from every other individual. Everyone easily recognizes that species are quite different in appearance, and may have different body characteristics and differing needs for nutrients. It is also easy to see that outwardly individuals within a species are different. In birds, colors, personality, size, behavior, and even physical shape readily can be seen to be different in members of the same species. Yet, the greatest differences are not external, but within the body and its biochemistry. Dr. Roger J. Williams has written extensively on this subject, and I highly recommend his published works on the subject of biochemical individuality.

Dr. Williams has shown that within an average population of ten individuals in one species, the normal requirement for nutrients will vary greatly in all of those individuals. The unusual members of the sampling will be one that requires far less of a nutrient than the others for normal, healthy life, and one other that will require far more than the others. On the same nutrient amount, most individuals will be perfectly healthy, but one may suffer and die from a severe deficiency.

This proven concept of biochemical individuality effectively shatters any rationale in the Food and Drug Administration's Recommended Daily Allowances for individuals. Neither human beings nor birds are nearly so uniform as the Government would have us believe. There is simply no such thing as an 'average' bird, any more than there is an 'average' human being. Our individual needs for a nutrient can vary a hundred-fold.

This individuality concept must be kept in mind when you observe your birds. Almost everyone has had the experience of owning ten birds of a species and seeing one die for no apparent reason, while all others remain in perfect health, all receiving exactly the same care and diet. The biochemical individuality of the birds is the reason. The one that has died is the individual with a far higher requirement for one of the vital nutrients, a requirement that your diet could not provide. This high requirement, if not filled, can also make any bird more susceptible to the invading disease microorganisms that are found everywhere, in any case of a deficiency of that nutrient.

This whole area of biochemical individuality is without a doubt nature's method for insuring the survival of a species. Though one specific individual may have an extremely high requirement for one nutrient, it may have a corresponding extremely low requirement for another, or it may synthesize the needed nutrient internally. Therefore, if major disaster should occur in the food supply, with a huge drop in the availability of some nutrients, numerous individuals are sure to survive to perpetuate the species because of their very low body requirement for the nutrients that are in short supply. True, most individuals in the species may die from malnutrition in such a case, but the few will always survive to replenish the species.

To illustrate this from my own experience, I once purchased a dozen Fischer's Lovebirds, *Agapornis fischeri*, in beautiful condition and vibrant health. They were truly the nicest Fischer's Lovebirds I have ever seen. Within a few weeks, trouble began to show up – puffiness, erratic actions, lack of muscle control, and eventual death. These lovebirds were on the same diet as I had always fed to lovebirds, finches, doves, cardinals, quail, and psittacines. All other birds around them were in good health and breeding, yet one by one, all but two of the Fischer's Lovebirds died.

The symptoms left no doubt that they were suffering from a severe nutritional deficiency. This strain, all raised by one breeder, obviously had a very high requirement for a particular nutrient that my own diet was not supplying in sufficient quantity. I was unable to track down which nutrient they required in such quantity. The remaining two lovebirds proved to be both hens, apparently without this high nutrient requirement. These two hens proceeded to build a nest and lay dozens of infertile eggs. Both remained in perfect health on my standard avian diet for many months, yet in time, they also began to show the same deficiency symptoms and they also eventually died. Had a male been available, however, these hens would have had the time to raise several clutches of youngsters to preserve the species. This unfortunate occurrence illustrates the usefulness of the biochemical individuality within each individual for the preservation of a species during times of nutrient shortage.

A commonly known human example of this phenomenon is evident in the history of sailing ships of the centuries before 1900. At that time, scurvy or acute vitamin C deficiency was the scourge of the seas and the dread of every sailor. The cause and cure were completely unknown and the fear of scurvy rode the waves on every vessel afloat. Sea voyages might last three to six months or more without the ship touching land. After the first few weeks at sea on navy or merchant marine rations, the first men would become ill with scurvy. These were the unusual individuals on the high side of the requirement for vitamin C. At the end of six months, many men would have died, with most of the rest left ill with scurvy. And yet, a few always survived the longest voyage with no touch of scurvy, obviously those individuals with such an extremely low requirement for vitamin C that they could go for months in perfect health with virtually no intake at all. Some writers have suggested that these few individuals could actually synthesize their own vitamin C, and this is certainly a reasonable concept that deserves extensive study. One suspects that the men who became captains of their ships after many sea voyages were among these few, since only they could survive so long under conditions of severe dietary vitamin C deficiency, enabling them to get the needed experience on the sea.

In a chilling and sobering statistic, Irwin Stone in his book *The Healing Factor*, recounts the now famous voyage of Ferdinand Magellan in 1519. Magellan set sail with a fleet of five ships on his voyage of circumnavigation of the earth. Three years later, he returned to Spain in triumph, but with only one ship and only 18 members of his original crews. The rest had all been lost, hundreds of men, primarily to scurvy. I highly recommend Stone's book as by far the best I have encountered on the subject of vitamin C or ascorbic acid.

There are undoubtedly as many different diets for birds as there are aviculturists. The very fact that birds successfully breed on such a wide variety of dietary offerings testifies to the fact that nutrients are widespread in food products and that the diets are nutritionally complete for the birds that are breeding successfully. However, many of the minor and major problems in the breeding attempts are the direct result of deficiencies in one or more of the required nutrients. As previously stated and well worth repeating, if there is a deficiency of one nutrient, there must surely be deficiencies of others, also.

I shudder at the frequent recommendations of canary fanciers to withhold egg food, greens or other special foods during non-breeding periods, when the hen is sitting, or at times when feeding the young. And yet, this practice does recognize the fact that there is a decided difference in nutritional needs from merely maintaining a bird in good health to breeding the same bird. The maintenance diet needs only sufficient protein and other nutrients for repair and replacement of damaged cells and feathers, while the breeding diet requires far more protein and other nutrients for the proper development of a clutch of eggs and the young birds from a fertilized egg to independent maturity within a few weeks. Egg laying and molting will increase the protein requirement, though not nearly to such an extent as feeding a clutch of nestlings.

The birds instinctively recognize this change in requirements and always consume more high protein foods when molting, and far more high protein foods when feeding nestlings. There is no need for the aviculturist to attempt to regulate this intake in any way. Any bird on a balanced, nutritious diet will never overeat of any one item at any time. In this respect, the birds exhibit far more good sense than most people do. You can safely feed your birds all they will clean up of any food if they are in good health and breeding.

As an example, there are many references in avicultural writings concerning limiting mealworms in avian diets. In my breeding of birds relishing these, the Brazilian Red-crested Cardinals, *Paroaria coronata*, I have fed the standard mealworms, *Tenebrio molitor*, free choice at all times. While they are feeding young, never in my memory have I lost a nestling or adult from malnutrition. With the delicate finches, I offered the Lesser Mealworm, *Alphitobius diaperinus*, free choice. The number they will consume in a day in feeding a growing nest of youngsters is unbelievable, yet I have never noticed the slightest bad effect from this practice. Quite the contrary, as the fertility, hatchability, and young fledged in both the Cardinals and finches all represented 100% of the eggs laid. As a result, I tend to look with suspicion upon any recommendation to limit either of the varieties of mealworm. However, there is little doubt that a bird starved for live insect food may overeat of the mealworms, but the bird is still unlikely to overeat to the point of illness.

As a further example of the nutritional value of the Lesser Mealworms, *Alphitobius diaperinus*, a baby martin not more than three days old fell out of the martin house in my front yard. This baby was so young that pinfeathers were not yet beginning to show on the wings. Fortunately, my experience with birds and their nutrition was at the stage were I felt confident in raising it. As the Purple Martin, *Progne subis*, is a completely insectivorous avian species, this presented quite a challenge. My high-protein egg mix was serving all of the insectivorous finches very well, so the egg mix and the Lesser Mealworms became the exclusive diet for this baby. With the required warmth supplied by a small 7-watt bulb, I fed the baby whenever possible with the mashed, hard-boiled egg and the Lesser Mealworms. The baby seemed to develop normally, its eyes opened, pinfeathers sprouted, and eventually the baby was practicing with its new wings. This healthy young martin became a fledgling, and as it was in the garage with my other cage-bred birds, it began flying around the garage for practice and exercise. After a few days of this, I decided it was old enough to be on its own, so I opened the garage door and allowed this young martin to fly out and join the flock in the front yard that contained other young fledglings in juvenile plumage. This hand-raised fledgling instantly joined the other martins and was indistinguishable from the other fledglings as they soared around the area. Though its diet of only two items had been very limited, it had obviously contained every nutrient that a young martin needs for growth and development in full health.

Another challenge appeared later in the form of six tiny nestling Least Terns, *Sterna antillarum*. The personnel at a landfill project had found and rescued them, and a friend who knew of my success with birds directed these babies to me. Here was something completely new in my experience with birds, since the digestive system of a seabird is designed for a diet quite different from that of finches or the psittacine species. The local fish market had lots of inexpensive fish that I was able to slice into very tiny strips, but fish meat alone would not have all of the nutrients that the baby terns needed for their health, growth, and development. A little of the mashed, hard-boiled egg would be a good substitute, but the main part of their diet would have to be fish to prepare them for a free life. The problem of sufficient vitamins and minerals was solved by sprinkling Vionate® on the pieces of fish, and the baby terns were happy to accept this along with a little of the egg mix. They appeared to grow normally (How would I know what was normal? I'm no ornithologist, and had never even seen a live tern before!), they feathered out, and made a great show of testing their new wings in their small holding area. They seemed to be in perfect health on this substitute diet, and after about two weeks of flying around the garage and eating the fish on their own, they appeared to be as ready for release to freedom as they would ever be. They are marvelous, graceful flyers, and these youngsters when released were soon high in the air and out of sight, and appearing to be heading instinctively in the direction of the nearby seashore.

Any bird that is starved for a certain nutrient or food item may possibly overeat of an item containing the needed nutrients before the craving is satisfied. This is a particular danger with two items: grit and salt, for an excess of either may be fatal. Therefore, use extreme care to give only very small quantities of either grit or salt when you know a bird has been suffering from the lack of these items in its diet. An excess of grit consumed will usually be excreted without impacting in the gizzard or intestines, but salt is a greater danger.

Though it is vital for avian life, a large amount all at once will overwhelm the body's ability to excrete the excess. Avian kidneys cannot eliminate salt as easily as can the kidneys of mammals, and birds that consume an excess of salt may die before the body can excrete the excess amount.

For the record, in order to satisfy those who will at this point be wondering if I really practice what I preach, you are hereby informed that all of my birds, from Gouldian Finches to quail, receive the same diet year-round, breeding or not. They consume far less during their non-breeding periods and totally govern their own intake of the various foods I supply. The birds are never forcefully rested, but choose their own rest periods from breeding as they feel the need for the rest period. To reiterate the point, the birds are not as foolish as most aviculturists seem to think. Their instincts represent far more knowledgeable guidance than we as aviculturists can provide.

A breeding diet must not only contain a greater percentage of protein, but also increased amounts of the vitamins and especially the minerals and elements necessary to support the rapid and sustained growth in the nestlings. The last thing that is needed is increased carbohydrate intake. Carbohydrates contribute nothing to growth – they are the energy foods, and nestlings do not need much energy, since this is supplied in large part by the parental brooding.

For this reason, mixing high carbohydrate foods with high protein items as nestling foods is a very ill-advised practice. Such high carbohydrate items as bread crumbs and cereals dilute the protein content in a food such as egg. The little protein in the cereal grains is incomplete and of no value for growth, so it is utilized for energy. Consequently, the parent birds are forced to eat and feed large quantities of carbohydrates which are at best useless to the nestling, and at worst may supplant the protein beyond the minimum necessary for life and growth, thus causing their death from protein deficiency. You may refer to the chapter on protein for a complete discussion of protein values and the need for complete proteins in avian nutrition.

Many aviculturists have a problem with their birds becoming too fat. In every case that I have seen thus far, the total mixing of high-protein and high carbohydrate foods is the reason for this. The birds feel an instinctive need for the protein, but the only way they can get it is to eat the mixture with the high carbohydrate content. This gives the birds an excess and unneeded amount of carbohydrates in their diet. Since all of these carbohydrates cannot be used for the body's energy needs, the excess and remainder will be stored as fat. A prolonged period of this forced feeding of excess carbohydrates will result in a fat bird.

The craving for other nutrients that are inextricably mixed with the carbohydrates will also cause birds to become fat, as they are forced to eat the excess carbohydrates to get the other nutrients that their bodies are craving.

Trace elements and salt are items that some species need more than others, since they evolved in areas where these items are richly supplied in the diet. See the chapter on trace elements for detailed information on this aspect of nutrition.

In nature, no species exists on a diet of totally dead matter. Even the carrion eaters are consuming vast quantities of living bacteria and other microorganisms that are breaking down the decaying bodies. Any diet devoid of living material with only cooked or preserved foods will be a diet missing some vital ingredients. Though the prepared commercial mixtures are well balanced generally and a blessing of convenience for the breeder, they are not complete diets. The deficiencies show up in constant feather plucking and cannibalism by the birds confined to such diets. Only by eating living tissue can they satisfy the craving for nutrient items that are as yet unidentified, but are missing in the commercial mixtures.

As an experiment, I once purchased fifty baby chicks to raise, giving them the standard, commercial chick starters and growers. As I expected, after a few days, three of the young chicks in the group began to fall behind the others and began appearing listless and inactive. This was to me the classic appearance of the effects of biochemical individuality in action in these individual chicks. I then separated the three sickly chicks and gave them only the high-protein egg mix that I recommend so highly. They ate large amounts of this for three days, caught up with their peers, and became as healthy and active as the others. Their higher needs for some nutrient had been satisfied by the egg mix, but not by the commercial chick starter. All fifty of the chicks were raised to the pullet stage and then given away to someone who had room to keep fifty chickens! There were no losses in this group of fifty chicks, but there certainly would have been without my intervention at the crucial time to supply the extra nutrition to the three chicks that were showing signs of illness.

For a number of years, a strong debate has existed among aviculturists and bird breeders as to the necessity for grit in the diet for the various species of birds maintained in captivity. Obviously, the softbills don't need it at all. Any seed eating bird traditionally has been provided with grit, apparently as a knowledge holdover from the time when every home had a pen of chickens, and the chickens were always in need of grit.

My own feeling after more than forty-five years of keeping birds of one kind or another is that grit is a definite necessity for any bird that swallows its seeds whole, without husking them. In other words, all doves, pheasants, quail and other gallinaceous birds need a ready supply of grit. However, my own experimentation indicates that this is not necessary for those birds that husk their seed. This would include all finches and the seed-eating psittacine birds. I have maintained Society Finches, *Lonchura striata*, Zebra Finches, *Taeniopygia guttata*, Gouldian Finches, *Chloebia gouldiae*, Red-cheeked Cordon Bleus,

Uraeginthus bengalus, Green Singing Finches, *Serinus mozambicus*, Star Finches, *Neochmia ruficauda*, Cutthroat Finches, *Amadina fasciata*, and Strawberry Finches, *Amandava amandava*, in perfect health for extended periods of six months or more with no grit. Several of these species have been bred to the third generation without the presence of any grit in their diet. This would confirm my theory and indicate that grit is not necessary for any bird that shells its seed before swallowing it.

For Americans used to the English system of measurement in pounds and ounces, the use of weight measurements in nutrition will need a short explanation. The standard metric system is now being taught in most American schools, so the younger generations should have no trouble with this. Older readers may not be as familiar with the metric system of measurements. Many of the nutrients are needed only in microscopic quantities, and the metric system is ideally suited for the measurement of those tiny amounts. The metric system provides weight measurements in grams, milligrams, and micrograms which serve the purpose of nutritional writing quite well. One ounce is equal to 28.35 grams. One milligram is one one-thousandth of a gram. One microgram is one one-thousandth of a milligram, a microscopic, infinitesimal amount. One microgram is approximately the amount of cobalamin, vitamin B_{12}, contained in one whole chicken egg.

The term 'pH' is used in several nutrient discussions. This is a common measure of acidity and alkalinity. It means 'potential hydrogen'. A pH of 7 is a neutral solution. A pH of 4.6 is quite acid, and a pH measuring of 8.2 is very alkaline. The pH of the food residues and the body fluids is a vitally important factor in health.

Finally, after the discussion of specific nutrients in the form of minerals, you will find references to biological transmutation. This is the ability of living organisms to change one basic element into another within the body. A careful consideration of the work of Louis C. Kervran should be sufficient to convince most readers that this transmutation of elements is not only possible for living organisms, but occurs routinely. How it occurs is still a complete mystery, and no nutritional work has yet taken this phenomenon into extensive consideration. In the standard study of inorganic chemistry, of course, transmutation is only possible at tremendous temperatures and pressures, as would be found in the sun. However, in nutrition we are dealing with biochemistry, and the rules seem to be more than a little different in this branch of study. Obviously, Kervran's discoveries have not yet been widely accepted, but his research is sound, and his conclusions are compelling. Perhaps in another fifty years or so the scientific community will reach the point of attempting to undertake more serious research on this biochemical phenomenon.

These are the basic avian nutritional concepts to keep in mind while reading the more detailed information on each individual nutrient. Once you have thoroughly digested all of the material in this volume, I can highly recommend many of the books in the bibliography for further, more detailed study of the science of nutrition.

"Any bird on a balanced, nutritious diet
will never overeat of any one item at any time."

CHAPTER 2

WATER

Water is seldom listed among the nutritional requirements of living things, but this substance is the most basic of all needs in nutrition. There are life forms that live without air or oxygen, but none can live without water. Though water is so often taken for granted in nutritional writing, it is the most essential nutrient and the first requirement for life. The turnover and exchange of water in the body exceeds that of any other nutrient. A 10% reduction in body content of any other nutrient usually will cause no noticeable effect, but a 10% reduction in water in the form of body fluids will cause symptoms of severe dehydration. A 20% reduction in body fluids is fatal.

Birds and other animals have three primary sources of water. First, the actual drinking of water is the main source. A number of factors may affect this source of water for cage birds. The growth of bacteria may make the water unpalatable, and birds will frequently will refuse to drink warm water. Cool, clean water is a necessity for avian nutrition. At times, outside water sources for birds, such as a continually dripping faucet, may harbor the growth of algae. These are tiny, green, one-celled plants that are harmless to the birds if eaten and are actually an excellent nutritional addition to the diet. Algae are nothing to be concerned about, since they will grow in any natural water source in profusion and supply a steady food supply to a variety of aquatic creatures.

The second water source is the food itself, since all foods contain a measurable percentage of their contents in the form of water. Vegetables, of course, have the highest percentage of water. The contents of tomatoes are about 94% water, and cucumbers are 96% water. Carrots and onions contain 88% water content, and bananas and sweet corn are relatively low in water content among the fruits and vegetables, with a 76% water content. Spinach greens are about 90% water, and kale has a water content of about 87%. The water content of oranges is 86%, and grapes are 82% water. Apples are approximately 85% water.

Nuts and grains contain far less water. Cereal grains range from 11% to 13% water, with a water content in millet of about 12%. The oily seeds and nuts contain the least water of any food items, usually a maximum of about 5% in such items as safflower seed, sunflower seed, and almonds. Walnuts, peanuts, and pecans contain even less water. If you've ever wondered why nuts make you thirsty, even when they're raw and unsalted, their low water content is the reason. It also follows that nuts are your best nutritional buy, since the water content is so small and the other nutritional contents are so high. As you might suspect, a whole egg, even hard boiled, averages 74% water, though some will test at about 65% water content.

The third source of water for the body is the internal metabolism. As proteins, fats and carbohydrates are metabolized, water is created as a by-product of this process of energy production. For example, about one pound of water will be formed within the body as one pound of fat is metabolized. Obviously, this is not a large amount in comparison to the body's needs, and this water source is minor in the life of most birds and animals. In some desert creatures, such as kangaroo rats, for example, this can be a very significant part of the body's needs for moisture. A chart of the water content of foods commonly used in bird feeding is included on page 33.

Budgerigars, the common grass parakeets so familiar as pets, can go for an incredible length of time without water. In proven tests, they have lived in perfect health for periods of 180 days – six months – without a drop of water. Their sole water sources were the small water content in their food and the by-products of their heat and energy production. The budgerigar has an extremely well developed internal system for water conservation, perfectly adapted for desert life. Testing has also shown that the skin of desert birds, such as the Zebra Finches, *Taeniopygia guttata*, becomes more leathery and impervious to the transfer of water during periods when liquid water is not available.

The body content of water may vary considerably at different times even within the same species. Chicks one week old may have a body water content of 85%, but this gradually decreases to 55% at maturity. The percentage of body water is closely related to the fat content of the body. The more fat stored within the body, the less will be the percentage of water content. This is why the normal variation from 50% to 75% water content in the human body can be so large. The average human body water content is 60%. In most birds, mammals, and humans, two-thirds of the body water is within the cells. The blood is 80% water, but this is less than 8% of the total water content of the body. The kidneys are very efficient in conserving water, and they will resorb enough water routinely to maintain blood volume at a normal level.

The water content of the birds' droppings varies a great deal, even within different strains of the same species. From 50% to 70% seems to be normal for chickens, and a similar amount can be expected in cage birds. Birds with very firm droppings, such as budgerigars, probably have less than 50% water content in their droppings. Under conditions of starvation, a bird can use up almost all of its glycogen or stored carbohydrate reserves, half of its protein and 40% of its total body weight and still live. However, the loss of only 20% of the water content of the body will kill the bird.

A bird will never voluntarily consume an excessive amount of water, since the body's needs are very closely controlled by factors that are not yet completely clear. The water consumed is absorbed very rapidly, and it is lost through the kidneys and through evaporation in breathing. Water performs a very important function for the body in the regulation of body temperature, since water evaporation removes excess heat. Whenever the body begins to overheat, the bird will begin to pant. This evaporates far more moisture and results in greater cooling. Humans accomplish the same cooling effect through sweating when the body becomes overheated. The evaporation of one quart of sweat will dissipate 580 calories of heat. The panting of birds and the higher water evaporation at higher temperatures greatly increase their need for water. The difference in temperature from 70° to 90° Fahrenheit may increase water consumption by 100%.

Water serves several other functions in the body. In its most important function, it acts as a solvent and carrier for body's nutrients, including the monosaccharides, the amino acids, phospholipids, vitamins, and minerals. These items will be covered in detail in the following sections. Water also carries the hormones and enzymes necessary for the proper functioning of every cell in the body. Water further serves as a lubricant, especially in the joints, and acts as a catalyst for many metabolic reactions.

Water carries a wide variety of substances in solution that are completely invisible, even when viewed under a microscope. These are dissolved minerals and compounds that the water picks up as it flows and exists in liquid form. Rainwater will pick up minerals and oxygen as it falls through the air. Unfortunately, minerals absorbed in this way are often the poisonous pollutants, such as lead, or toxic compounds, such as sulfuric acid. Ground water will absorb minerals wherever it flows, and this content is often a substantial source of minerals in the diet. Two minerals commonly found in water are chlorine from water treatment and inorganic iron from ground deposits. Both of these will destroy vitamin E on contact. Make every effort to exclude them from your birds' permanent water supply. Refer to the section on vitamin E for more information on this vitamin.

Water is also the carrier of the waste products of the cells. These include carbon dioxide, various nitrogen compounds from the breakdown of proteins, and other compounds that are poisonous or excess to the body's needs. These waste products are carried to the lungs and kidneys for excretion. Some also go to the liver where they are incorporated in the bile for excretion into the intestinal tract.

The most obvious symptom of a serious water deficiency in small birds is squinting. This characteristic seems to be specific for dehydration. The only other time you will notice this is if something is sprayed or placed directly into the bird's eyes. Squinting is a red flag of warning, and I cannot count the number of times birds have warned me of a problem with their water by this characteristic physical reaction. Normally, a bird without water for 24 hours or even less will begin squinting, and this symptom is obvious at a glance from several feet away. More severe dehydration and death are just a step away from the act of squinting.

Only once has squinting failed to develop in small birds within 24 hours of water deprivation in my experience. In an act of sheer stupidity, I moved several finches to a new cage with all food items, but neglected to give them any water. It was 48 hours before I discovered this error, yet the birds still were not squinting, and they showed no sign of dehydration. Of course, they were down at the water as soon as it was placed in the cage. They were thirsty, but clearly were not suffering from lack of water. I can only attribute this to the fact that the temperature was cool during this period and stayed at about 55° Fahrenheit (13° C.) This apparently enabled the finches to conserve their water reserves very efficiently. During a period of hot weather, such an extended period without water probably would have resulted in death.

The body contains far more water than any other substance. There is no substitute for water in the body's metabolism, and I cannot overstress the importance of a continuous water supply for the birds. If an emergency should occur that does away with almost all of your time for bird care temporarily, make sure that the birds have water along with some basic food item, such as one of the crumbled commercial foods for finches that they are used to eating. All else can wait in dire emergency. You can check a hundred cages for crumbles and water in five minutes, and a few days of limited feeding will not hurt healthy, adult birds in the least.

As a final comment on water, the classic symptom of the beginning of dehydration in the human body is a headache. When the body does not have enough moisture available to dissolve and carry away the toxins produced by the active brain chemistry, they build up rapidly, and the nerves are not lax in warning you of this lack of water for eliminating those toxins. Two 16 ounce glasses of water will cure any normal headache within 30 minutes.

THE WATER CONTENT OF THE FOODS
COMMONLY USED IN BIRD FEEDING

ITEM	PERCENTAGE OF WATER	PERCENTAGE OF FOOD VALUE
Apples	84.4	15.6
Barley	11.1	88.9
Buckwheat	11.0	89.0
Canary Seed	14.3	85.7
Corn, Feed (Average of varieties)	13.0	87.0
Corn, Sweet	72.7	27.3
Eggs	73.7	26.3
Flax Seed	7.1	92.9[4]
Fruit, General[1]	83.9	16.1
Game Bird Starter	11.0	89.0
Grapes	81.5	18.5
Greens, General[2]	88.6	11.4
Greens, Dandelion	85.6	14.4
Greens, Kale	87.5	12.5
Hemp Seed	8.8	91.2
Millet (Average of varieties)	10.5	89.5[4]
Milo (Average of varieties)	12.4	87.6
Monkey Chow	10.0	90.0
Niger	7.0	93.0[4]
Nuts, Shelled[3]	4.2	95.8
Oats	10.0	90.0
Oranges	86.0	14.0
Peanuts (Average of varieties)	13.2	86.8[4]
Poppy Seed	4.2	95.8
Pumpkin Seed	4.4	95.6
Rape Seed	7.3	92.7[4]
Rice	11.7	88.3
Safflower Seed	5.0	95.0[4]
Sesame Seed	5.4	94.6
Squash Seed	4.4	95.6
Sunflower Seed (shelled)	4.8	95.2
Wheat	10.5	89.5

[1] Average of peaches, pears, apples, cherries, oranges, grapes and blueberries
[2] Average of dandelion, kale, romaine, collards, and turnip greens
[3] Average of pecans, walnuts, almonds, hazelnuts, and Brazil nuts
[4] This figure includes waste in the form of the discarded shell

"The most obvious symptom of a serious water deficiency in small birds is squinting. Squinting is a red flag of warning that the birds are lacking water."

CHAPTER 3

PROTEINS

The modern world owes a Dutch chemist from Utrecht by the name of Gerrit Jan Mulder a humble note of thanks. In 1838 after many controlled experiments, he announced his conclusion that all living plants and animals contain a certain substance without which life is impossible. Though Mulder didn't know and couldn't discover what was in this substance, he was certain it was vital to life and named it protein, from a Greek word meaning first place. It took another hundred years for the first amino acid constituent of protein to be discovered and named.

Since that time, research has uncovered a great deal of information about proteins, and a summary of the known material will constitute this chapter. Hundreds of different types of proteins have been identified and named. As examples, the main protein in corn is zein, and the main one in milk is casein. Albumin is a protein in egg white, and hemoglobin is a vital protein component of the blood.

Protein is the raw material used by the body for building tissue. The muscles, toenails, beaks, feathers, and the bird's body organs are composed largely of protein. Protein is the second most plentiful substance in the body; only water is more abundant. Without protein, there can be no initial building of body tissue, nor can there be replacement of cells that wear out and die from use, damage, or disease. Proteins are composed of the most complex groupings of molecules known to science. Only living cells can make proteins; they do not casually form from inorganic chemical reactions, such as the sun's energy striking the earth or through the force of lightning.

The protein metabolism of all species of birds, mammals, and reptiles is very similar. The main differences are in the nature of the end products of protein metabolism. Nevertheless, as Paul Griminger has stated in Chapter 12 of *Avian Physiology* in reference to birds, "Information on wild species is extremely scanty."

The protein cycle begins with plants. Only plants can take up the necessary nitrogen and combine it with carbon, hydrogen, and oxygen to form proteins. Birds and animals, including insects, eat this plant material, extract the protein from it, and utilize it for their own bodies. This process is extremely complex, and much has yet to be learned about the make-up and utilization of proteins. When an organism dies, the proteins in its cells are broken down by bacterial and chemical action into their component parts, and the cycle is complete.

Each of these complex proteins is made up of substances called amino acids. Amino acids are the building blocks of proteins, and each type of protein contains different amino acids in differing quantities. A molecule of blood hemoglobin, for example, contains 574 amino acids in the globin portion of the molecule. The nitrogen of the amino group is unique to protein and constitutes an average of 16% of the amino acid molecules, which are the building blocks of all proteins. Nitrogen makes up a low point of 15% of the amino acids in milk, and a high point of 18% of the amino acids of nuts.

In the process of digestion, the digestive system breaks down the ingested proteins into their component single amino acids. These amino acids are then absorbed through the intestinal wall, molecule by molecule. They pass into the bloodstream and are absorbed by each cell, recombined, and used by each cell of the body in the necessary quantities to build the proteins that the cell needs for its life and functioning. Once absorbed, the cell utilizes the amino acids to form the proteins needed to build, repair, and replace its parts, or to divide for growth of the tissue of which it is a part.

Amino acids are divided into two major headings: the essential amino acids, and the non-essential amino acids. The term essential when applied to amino acids means that the body cannot make them in sufficient quantity from other materials on hand, and they must be consumed in the form of food and come from the diet. The non-essential amino acids can be synthesized by the body's organs by breaking down other food components and amino acids, or by combining them in the correct amounts. Keep in mind that all of the amino acids are necessary for the life of the body, but those termed 'essential' cannot be made in sufficient quantity within the cells of the body. In other words, it is essential to get them in the diet and the food supply. Frequent misunderstanding results from the use of the term 'essential' in this sense. Proteins which contain all of the essential amino acids in adequate quantities are referred to as complete proteins; those lacking one or more of the essential amino acids in sufficient quantity are referred to as incomplete proteins.

Extensive nutritional research has proven conclusively that all of the essential amino acids must be eaten within a few hours time in order for the body to use them for tissue building. The body can retain them chemically unchanged for only a few hours. If the amino acids in the body are not used, either because of incomplete supply or excess supply, they are filtered out of the blood by the liver. The liver strips away the nitrogen, converts it to uric acid, and the body then disposes of the nitrogen through the kidneys. The remaining components of the amino acid are utilized for energy or converted to fat and then stored as fat.

Within the plant kingdom, virtually all of the proteins are incomplete or at best unbalanced, as they are lacking one or more of the essential amino acids in sufficient quantity. Soybeans and nuts are the most complete protein foods in the plant kingdom. When several types of plant material are eaten, the protein content of one will complement that of the other. That is, one plant will supply the amino acids that the next one is lacking. Much as North Americans may chuckle over the Mexican diet of tortillas and frijoles, the corn and beans they represent are ideally complementary in their protein content. No one will ever suffer from a protein deficiency from eating an adequate quantity of corn and beans at one meal. Kwashiorkor, an abdominal bloating disease caused partially by lack of complete protein, is almost unknown in Mexico, but endemic in central Africa, where millet is the staple food with no other vegetative source to complement the incomplete protein found in millet. And yet, millet is one of the better sources of complete protein in the plant kingdom. A diet that is completely vegetarian with no animal-derived food from any source can still supply complete, balanced protein to the body, with a knowledgeable blend of foods from various vegetative sources.

Proteins from any animal source are mostly complete proteins, with gelatin being a notable exception. These animal proteins contain all of the essential amino acids in adequate quantities for utilization by the body for optimal health. For this reason, the use of animal protein is stressed in many works dealing with nutrition and the care and feeding of birds in captivity. Though gelatin is refined from animal products, the protein it contains is not complete.

While plant sources are normally low in the percentage of protein that they contain, animal sources are usually much higher in that percentage. Most grains, for example, contain from 11% to 13% protein, most of which is incomplete. Insects, by contrast, are an extremely good source of complete protein. Grasshoppers are 60% complete protein. The dry weight of an earthworm is about 72% pure, complete protein. With this in mind, it is easy to see why the nestlings of our wild birds thrive and grow so rapidly on a diet of insects and earthworms.

Though many of the available writings disagree for one reason or another, most of the current publications on the subject of nutrition list ten amino acids that are termed essential. The body cannot synthesize any of these essential amino acids at a rate sufficient to meet the needs for growth and maintenance. Alphabetically, their names are arginine, histidine, isoleucine, leucine, lysine, methionine, phenylalanine, threonine, tryptophan, and valine. Other works that disagree with this listing will usually list and include two additional amino acids, cystine and tyrosine.

Histidine and arginine apparently are not essential to all avian species, nor even to humans at all times. However, in young birds arginine cannot be formed sufficiently fast to fulfill all of the body's requirements, so it must be supplied in adequate quantity in the avian diet. The healthy body under ideal conditions can synthesize these two amino acids in adequate quantities when necessary. Histidine is an essential amino acid for human infants, however, and for this reason, it must be supplied in adequate quantities in the diet.

Glycine, usually considered as a non-essential amino acid, has been proven to be essential for the growth and development of baby chicks. For this reason, it will probably also be found to be an essential amino acid for many other avian species. With these facts in mind, it seems obvious that no hard and fast rules will apply as to which amino acids are essential to which species, and at which times. Nevertheless, most nutritional authorities consider the grouping of ten amino acids listed above as the definitive list of essential amino acids under most circumstances. These are then the amino acids that must be eaten in the food and taken together, in adequate quantity, at the same time, in order to perform the tasks that require protein in the body.

In any protein complex, the essential amino acid present in the smallest relative amount is called the limiting amino acid. Methionine is the limiting amino acid in soybeans. The limiting amino acid in wheat is lysine, and the limiting amino acid in corn is tryptophan, which it lacks in adequate quantities. Most of the seeds and other products from the plant kingdom will have one limiting amino acid that renders most of the protein content incomplete for that product when it is used as a food for birds. The proteins of the best quality that are found in the plant kingdom are found in soybeans, nuts, and sunflower seeds.

Some of the more important amino acids so far identified that are generally agreed to be non-essential are alanine, aspartic acid, cirrulline, cysteine, cystine, glutamic acid, glycine, hydroxyproline, hydroxyglumatic acid, norleucine, proline, serine, taurine, and tyrosine. Glycine, as one example, is the principal amino acid that is found in sugar cane. Though all of these amino acids are definitely necessary for nutritional purposes and protein building, the body can manufacture or synthesize each of them from one or more of the other amino acids. Any nutritional supplement that specifies these non-essential amino acids in its ingredients on the label is playing upon the nutritional ignorance of the aviculturist.

In reading on the subject of protein, you frequently will see references to the sulfur-containing amino acids. There are three primary sulfur-containing amino acids, and they are methionine, cysteine and cystine. Another one of less importance is taurine. While methionine is always included as one of the essential amino acids, cysteine, cystine and taurine are not on the listing of essential amino acids. Cysteine is, however, a primary protein component of the protein keratin, from which feathers are formed. Fully 20% of the amino acid content of the protein keratin is in the form of cysteine. These are the four amino acids that all contain the element sulfur as a mineral component of their molecular structure.

Collagen is the vital connective tissue that holds tissues of the body together. With poorly formed collagen, the cells literally come unglued and begin leaking blood and lymph, thus causing an internal or external bruise. One-third of the protein collagen is made up of the amino acid glycine. Proline and hydroxyproline make up another one-third of the amino acid content of collagen. This connective tissue can be boiled with water or acid to produce the common food item called gelatin. Lest we call the view of collagen as a glue too simplistic, what other glue do we have that will glue water together into a solid form, as gelatin does? Only cornstarch comes to mind.

There is also a great degree of importance attached to both the individual non-essential amino acids and to the individual essential amino acids in the body's metabolism, apart from their use as protein constituents. Tyrosine is one amino acid in particular where specific examples are known for its uses in the avian body. For example, tyrosine alone is used in the thyroid gland for the production of the hormone thyroxine. See the section on iodine for a complete discussion of this use. Also, the amino acid tyrosine is the foundation for the dark pigment melanin, so common in the brown and black coloring found in the feathers of birds and in the fur of animals.

The amino acids are joined together by what are called peptide linkages to form all proteins. In addition, water is necessary for the breakdown of protein in the digestive tract, and this is why water is then later a by-product of protein synthesis from the individual amino acids.

Glycine is the simplest of these amino acids, and most researchers consider myoglobin, an oxygen-carrying protein within the muscle cells, to be a simple protein. Yet, simple as it is, myoglobin is so complicated that only in 1961 was the complete composition and structure of myoglobin discovered. Myoglobin contains nineteen different amino acids in varying amounts to form a total of

150 amino acid units. The most complicated proteins, by contrast, can have thousands of amino acid units in their make-up.

Intestinal bacteria can change the amino acid histidine into histamine, which is a toxic compound. This histamine can be absorbed into the blood, giving characteristic allergy symptoms. Also, the breakdown of tissue protein in times of food scarcity forms histamine as a by-product. The liver can destroy histamine in the bloodstream by means of an enzyme called histaminase. Also, vitamins B_6, C, and pantothenic acid all have an antihistamine effect. Histamine is found in many soft tissues and in small amounts does seem to perform a useful function, particularly with respect to the functioning of the brain.

High temperatures used in drying some foods lower the protein value in them, since some of the essential amino acids are destroyed by high heat. For example, 90% of the tryptophan is lost in high heat drying of foods. For this reason, prolonged cooking or baking of foods at high temperatures is unwise either for foods meant for the birds or for foods meant for human consumption, quite apart from the loss of vitamins that occurs in such cooking.

The richest sources of complete protein for finches and other cage birds are, of course, the animal sources. No good source of animal protein is cheap, since any member of the animal kingdom must first consume a huge quantity of either plant or other animal material in order to incorporate sufficient protein into its own body. The members of the animal kingdom concentrate the protein from the plant kingdom and for this reason animals serve as good food sources of complete protein themselves.

Hard-boiled eggs always are one of the most reasonably priced complete protein foods obtainable for your birds. Eggs average about 13% high quality, complete protein. However, when the water content of the egg is subtracted from the calculation, the dry contents of the egg are over 60% high quality, complete protein. The author has always used mashed, hard-boiled eggs as a high-protein food for all species and families of birds. Eggs are cheap, highly nutritious, available anywhere, and they are easy to prepare. Also, eggs contain a nearly perfect balance of vitamins, minerals, and fats.

Once any bird learns that this is a food item, the bird will eat it regularly and willingly. In order to prepare this egg mixture, simply boil an egg for about ten minutes (a couple of minutes longer for extra large eggs). At high altitudes, a couple of extra minutes of boiling may be necessary to boil the eggs thoroughly. Cool the eggs in cold water, and then peel the shell off. You'll find that the shell peels off very easily, because the egg absorbs the water as it cools, and this additional water makes the egg much easier to shell. Once the shell is off, dry the egg gently in a paper towel to remove the excess moisture.

Once the egg is reasonably dry, mash it thoroughly with a fork to mix the white and the yolk uniformly. The resulting mix will be an appetizing, uniform, light yellow color. If the color is leaning towards olive, you have boiled the eggs too long. Longer boiling begins to tie up the free sulfur in the egg, which then forms these dirty green compounds, making the egg mix appear rather unappetizing. You can add a slightly heaping teaspoon of any commercial powdered vitamin-mineral supplement to the egg for even better results. I have always used and recommended Vionate® for this purpose, and it is still one of the most reasonably priced supplements that are available on the market for birds and animals.

Since this mixture still may be a little too damp, if you can find soy protein isolate, a slightly heaping teaspoon of that added to the mix and blended thoroughly will increase the protein content of the egg greatly and also will absorb much of the excess water. When mixed with these dry supplements, the egg will not spoil during the day unless it gets wet, even under very hot and humid conditions. Mashed, hard-boiled egg prepared in this manner will dry out and harden in the feeding dishes if the birds don't consume all of it. This characteristic of this particular egg mixture is invaluable to the aviculturist who must feed his charges only once a day. The addition of any oil, water, or high carbohydrate products will cause rapid and total spoilage of this mixture.

Most birds will not touch anything that is wet and mushy, and an egg mix that is too wet will be spoiled and rotten within a matter of hours. Any food that is this ideal for birds will also be an ideal food for the bacteria and other microorganisms that are constantly floating in the air and resting on all surfaces, just waiting for a place to grow and multiply. Also, remember that it is the white of the egg that is the primary protein, not the yolk! The yolk contains all of the other vital nutrients that a growing bird needs. Break the leftover eggshell into small pieces and feed it separately as an excellent and free calcium source for all of your birds. All of the birds in my experience will choose to eat these eggshell pieces over any other source of calcium and other minerals that is currently available on the market.

All finches and other birds in my experience will eat this egg mix daily and eagerly, once they become accustomed to it, and it will supply all of the complete protein necessary for raising any of the finches, doves, quail and small psittacines. If you don't need the entire egg for one feeding, it is safe to refrigerate the remainder for a few days. For longer periods, you can divide the finished mix into daily portions, wrap each portion in any clear freezer wrap, and freeze enough for each day's feeding in a separate package. Then you can thaw one of these each morning for use in your day's feeding. Freezing results in very little nutrient destruction, and this method works very well when a friend is caring for your birds during trips and vacations. Freezing does change the texture of the egg mix, however, so it is always better to feed the mix fresh if you can.

Live foods in the form of insects and worms have always figured prominently in the breeding of birds of all types in captivity, largely because they are such an excellent source of complete protein. Though most early breeders were not aware of the protein value of insects, they did recognize that all of these live foods figured prominently in the diets of wild birds of all kinds. For this reason, all of the early works on aviculture recommend insects and worms of various kinds as indispensable foods for birds bred in captivity.

Though many of the older source books on bird breeding state that live foods are indispensable for maintaining and breeding any of the exotic finches or softbills in captivity, many breeders succeed quite well by feeding only eggs, high-protein cereals, monkey biscuits, game-bird starter, and the commercial crumbled feeds now available commercially for most avian species. In my experience, the requirement for a good source of complete protein is the important factor for breeding these birds. Many breeders have raised the most delicate waxbills with no live food whatsoever by using mashed, hard-boiled egg or another source of adequate complete protein that is rich in the other vital nutrients.

However, live foods are always an excellent food for all of the finches, game birds, or soft-billed birds. Insects are probably the richest available source of complete protein, and the dried weight of many insects is over 70% protein. Many of our wild birds feed their young almost exclusively on insects, and I have never know a wild baby bird fed on insects to die in the nest for any reason except abandonment.

Insects, however, are sometimes very difficult to obtain, particularly in the winter. Several types of live foods are now available commercially, but they are usually quite expensive. Growing live foods in your home is always an alternative, but this takes a lot of space, a lot of effort and time, a strong stomach, and an understanding family. For most breeders, growing the live foods yourself is just not worth the trouble, and they end up feeding a high-protein substitute, such as the mashed, hard-boiled eggs; prepared commercial pellets and crumples for birds. Some breeders even feed monkey pellets, dog food and cat food to their birds regularly, all of which are excellent sources of complete protein.

Many finches and softbills, particularly the imported ones, will not feed any substitute to their young when they hatch, however. If no live foods are available, they will toss the newly hatched babies out of the nest and will abandon them, thus ending the breeding cycle. Fostering to a more domes-ticated and more dependable species is always a possibility to get your breeding strain started, but for various reasons, many breeders prefer not to do this. For those breeders who insist on offering their birds the natural insect foods, there are a variety of possibilities available. Each method for using insect foods has its advantages and disadvantages, and it is always better to give your birds a variety of these live foods for their own maintenance and for feeding their young when they begin to breed. With many of the imported birds, feeding this variety may be the only way of getting them to raise their own young without the use of foster parents.

The most common live food offered to all birds in captivity is undoubtedly the common mealworm, which has the scientific name *Tenebrio molitor*. In books on insects, you will probably see the adult beetle of this mealworm referred to as the Darkling Beetle. Mealworms are easy to raise, and most softbilled birds will accept them easily, even greedily. For the smallest insectivorous birds and the finches, these mealworms are really too large. Often the finches will just eat the head of the mealworms and will leave the rest of the body uneaten.

If the idea of growing worms in your home doesn't appeal to you, several companies specialize in raising them for the bird breeders and tropical fish hobbyists. You can buy these commercially in any quantity at a reasonable price. However, they are far too expensive to buy and too much trouble to raise for continuous feeding to the larger, more common birds, such as the Coturnix Quail, *Coturnix coturnix*, or the Ring-necked Pheasants, *Phasianus colchicus*. It is far more economical to reserve them for use with the rarer birds, especially the soft-billed birds that are by nature largely insectivorous.

Though many writings have stressed the danger of overfeeding mealworms, I wonder if these writers have ever really tried feeding them to the birds free choice, giving the birds all of the mealworms that they will eat. I have offered mealworms in the past in my own breeding to such birds as the Red-crested Cardinals, *Paroaria coronata*, free choice, and have never encountered any problem in doing so. Quite the contrary, I raised a number of young cardinals quite successfully. While feeding these youngsters, the parent birds consumed over a hundred mealworms every day. While I raised these cardinals, fertility, hatchability, and successful fledging were all 100%. Though they were in an outdoor aviary and were able to capture other native insects, their primary nestling food was the mealworm.

A close relative of the mealworm that I have used quite successfully is the Lesser Mealworm, *Alphitobius diaperinus*. In Europe, these are known as Buffalo Worms. Like the large mealworm, this little fellow is also the larval form of a black beetle. The Lesser Mealworm is only about one-half inch long when mature, and it is an excellent food for all of the exotic finches and other tiny insectivorous, soft-billed birds. While many small birds will refuse the regular mealworms, most of them will accept the Lesser Mealworm.

While breeding the Green Singing Finches, *Serinus mozambicus*, I fed the Lesser Mealworms in free choice quantities to the parent birds. Between the avid consumption by the parent birds, and the huge numbers of worms that they fed to a nest of young ones, it was not unusual for me to have to place several hundred Lesser Mealworms in each cage of Green Singing Finches with growing nestlings each day.

These Lesser Mealworms are found in North America, and any grain or grain by-product left out in the open will attract them sooner or later. The litter under the cages of a chicken farm or egg farm is an ideal place to look for them. They will breed much faster than the regular mealworms, and many more of them will fit into a container for breeding them. Be sure that the container is well covered, however, for the adult beetles can fly quite well, and they are sure to try to fly away to start a new colony. Lesser Mealworms are colored with alternating light and dark shades of brown striping. They are not the golden color shade of the large mealworms.

Don't neglect the earthworms as a potential food source for your softbills and other insectivorous birds. The smaller ones are easy to grow, and the smaller birds will prefer them when they are only about an inch long. Any good soil free of pesticides and rich in organic matter will have an abundance of earthworms in it, and you can keep a tubful of them indoors for the winter very easily, using them to compost organic refuse from the kitchen. Earthworms are an excellent live food for finches and soft-billed birds. Our native American robins, *Turdus migratorius*, raise their nestlings mainly on a diet of earthworms, so the earthworm's food value and protein content are obviously ideal for baby robins, as well as for many other insectivorous birds.

Though it is possible for earthworms to introduce small parasites and microorganisms from the soil to your birds, the danger of this is usually somewhat overstated, and I personally would not worry about it from earthworms grown in soil that has not previously been used for chickens, grazing of animals, or other farming activities. In order to be completely safe, keep small earthworms in a container with paper and some damp grain meal, and they will rapidly eat enough of this to clean the soil out of their digestive systems, and then will be perfectly safe to feed even to the smallest and most delicate finches. Since so many of these finches eat the white African termites as a regular diet and nestling food, the next possibility may be even more appealing to them as a food item.

There is another worm that is sometimes used in bird feeding and is used widely in feeding tropical fish. This worm is the whiteworm of the genus *Enchytraeus*, and it is also available commercially, mainly from aquarium suppliers. The whiteworm is a small, white worm, much like a miniature earthworm. The scientific name for the common whiteworm is *Enchytraeus albidus* in the family Enchytraeidae. They require fairly cool temperatures for their life cycle, and a refrigerator is usually the best place to keep and breed them. Many of the waxbills that are used to the mound termites of Africa will accept these whiteworms as a substitute live food for feeding their young.

Small crickets of the family Gryllidae are an ideal live food for all finches, especially if you can supply the birds with the small, immature ones. I have known breeders to raise the Pekin Robins, *Leiothrix lutea*, with adult crickets as their main nestling food. Any finch will accept the smaller crickets, and crickets are usually available commercially at any place in a fishing area that carries bait and tackle. The crickets raised commercially are a grayish-brown variety, since the black crickets native to the United States are much more difficult to breed for quantity sales.

Grasshoppers of the order Orthoptera are also an ideal live food for all finches, and the birds especially appreciate the young, immature grasshoppers with their tender legs. The availability of grasshoppers is seasonal, however, and you are more likely to be able to capture them in a field in the spring. I'm not aware of any individual or business that raises them commercially, so you will probably have to catch your own in the grass and fields in the area where you live.

Many avicultural books recommend ant eggs for finches, and these are also an excellent live food. Actually, these are not eggs at all, but the pupae that contain an immature, developing ant. They are available in some quantity through digging out the nest of any colony of large, native ants. Their easy availability was the primary factor that originally led early aviculturists to try them as a live food for finches.

British writers and bird breeders frequently recommend 'gentles' as live foods when raised and handled cleanly. Americans would refer to them as maggots, since they are the larvae of a fly. When they are left for a time in some type of fine bran or meal, they will be clean enough to feed to the finches. Though their reputation may be rather poor, they do make an excellent live food for all softbilled birds and insectivorous finches. Also, suppliers are now marketing them commercially as 'fly larvae' and they are available in quantity from several avicultural suppliers

The live food that is most likely to induce the delicate finches and other exotic species to breed is termites. Here in North America, they are an unparalleled pest in wood homes, but the termite species that abound in Africa are quite different. These African termite species build mounds that are so concrete-hard that they can wreck a tractor. These termite mounds provide food for many types of birds and animals, and even the human population comes out in force to partake of this bounty when the termites are swarming. Many of the waxbills and the other African species of insectivorous birds feed these termites as a primary nestling food for their nests of growing young. When these birds transferred to our aviaries don't find this abundant supply of termites available in our aviaries, they frequently throw their newly-hatched young out of the nest and abandon them.

Fruit flies of the genus *Drosophila* in the family Drosophilidae are another insect that is easy to culture. Any overripe fruit will draw them, and they will breed rapidly and in huge quantities. Many finches will wait avidly for these little delicacies to emerge from the fruit container, and they are a staple protein food for the hummingbirds kept in captivity. Though they are quite small, they make up for their size in the quantities in which they breed. There is now a commercial variety of fruit fly available that is wingless, so it can't fly. Though this is an advantage for breeding them in the home, these wingless fruit flies do not breed as prolifically as the regular fruit flies. Nevertheless, as they are wingless, the danger of them escaping is also far less. For the smaller and more insectivorous finches, as well as for all of the small softbilled birds and hummingbirds, fruit flies are an ideal high-protein food and they also contain the other vital nutrients that the birds need in constant and adequate amounts.

A valuable type of live food that is not often used is the larval stage of bees and wasps. In the warm summer months, their nests appear in abundance in any sheltered location. Each compartment contains a developing wasp, and using care not to get stung, you can harvest them at any size. Since these larval bees and wasps are white, many finches will accept them as substitutes for the termites that they are unable to find for their nestlings. Your neighbors are often very happy to have you remove these nests from their buildings, and you will gain a real nutritional bonanza for your small birds.

The small, juicy spiders that are so common around our homes and aviaries are also excellent live foods for your finches. I have noted the wild titmice and wrens going to extremes searching for these little delicacies around the house. If you can round up a few of them for your finches, the birds will stay in better health and condition. Certainly, you will never see one of these spiders that has managed to live long enough to spin a web in any aviary of finches!

Aphids of the family Aphidae are so common that we often overlook them as a potential live food for our small, insectivorous birds. These tiny creatures love to suck the juices from tender new plant growth, and you will often find them on the new growth of garden plants or weeds. Just cutting off the plant shoot with its hundreds of aphids and throwing it in for your softbills will give them a safe and nutritious change from the normal live foods that you may offer.

The greater interest in breeding finches and in maintaining and breeding the softbilled birds has spawned a host of new businesses that cater to the needs of these birds. A number of growers of insect foods for aviculturists now offer a considerable variety of live insect foods for birds. Some advertise insect foods that have not been available before, and waxworms are now being offered regularly. At least one active avicultural supplier is offering Grindal Worms,

Enchytraeus buchholtzi, which are similar to whiteworms, but thrive at warmer temperatures.

The commercial bug-killing lights are easily available, designed for night use around the home. They draw hundreds of nocturnal insects every night. You can place a collector under one of these lights to collect the insects that are killed when they come into the electric field of the light. If you can manage to collect them, every morning your birds will have a gourmet assortment of insects to add to their diet. All of the small finches and softbills will appreciate this addition to their normal selection of foods.

Insects are found everywhere, and many types can be found near our cages and aviaries. Robert Stroud, the 'Birdman of Alcatraz', relates in one of his books how his canary hen fed her young successfully on the insects that lived in the cage litter, when there was no other high-protein food available for them.

Any field has a wide variety of insect life, and a net passed through the grass will pick up an abundance of these insects that any finches will enjoy. The problem will be to manage to keep the insects from escaping from the net, or in trying to place them in a jar or other holding container. Still, if you are in an area where this is possible, the fields offer an excellent source of live insect food for your insectivorous birds.

Though I repeat that insects as such are not a requirement for keeping and breeding any of the delicate birds, with the imported birds, in particular, a variety of insect foods may be the only way to get them to raise their own young successfully. At any rate, insects are always a welcome and valuable addition to the diet of your exotic birds. Once you have built up a breeding strain of a species that will feed their young on a high-protein food that is easier for you to manage, you will no longer need to spend your time supplying live foods to your birds in order to be sure that their diets contain enough complete protein.

The dry dog foods are an ideal source of inexpensive, complete protein. Getting most birds to try this food after lightly soaking it or crumbling it may be a trick in itself. These birds are very stubborn about trying anything new, particularly when the food is damp. Softbills are usually far better subjects for the feeding of dog foods. Nevertheless, my lories were extremely fond of the crushed and crumbled dog food that they received each day. They would be down on this unusual food even before they headed for the dish containing the egg mix, which they also thoroughly enjoyed. This was by far the easiest and most complete diet for lories and lorikeets that I have ever encountered, and these birds stayed in beautiful health and condition on this unusual, but very nutritious food with its high content of complete protein.

When feeding dog foods or cat foods to birds, however, you must check the labels carefully to be certain that they contain vitamin D_3. Dogs and cats can make use of vitamin D_2 quite easily, but birds and the new world monkeys cannot. Supplementation for birds must be vitamin D_3, as this is the only form of the vitamin that they can use internally. The technical name for vitamin D_3 is cholecalciferol. See the section on vitamin D for a thorough discussion of this important nutrient.

From the plant kingdom, sunflower seeds supply about the highest protein content of any commonly fed plant material in aviculture, averaging about 26% in protein content. The sunflower seed protein is more nearly complete than that of most other plant material, also. Obviously, finches with their small beaks will not easily shell a sunflower seed, but shelled seed is always available from health food stores and nutritional centers. Many standard food chains now also carry this delicacy for human consumption. Be sure to get raw sunflower seed, not the toasted specialty item. And don't let the price scare you away, because pound for pound, sunflower seeds are one of your greatest nutritional values. The small birds require some time to get used to sunflower seeds, but once accustomed to them, they will eat them as readily as millet. Sunflower seed is far more nutritious than any of the cereal grains.

To introduce these nutritious sunflower seeds to small birds that are unfamiliar with them, chop a few of the shelled seeds into several smaller pieces. Most small finches and softbilled birds will try these little chunks and will find them much to their liking. If the birds refuse to touch these strange-looking chunks, you can take other foods away for a time and introduce them to this new food as I have recommended in the introduction to nutrients on page 15. Each day, make the chunks bigger, until you are offering a mix of a few seeds cut in half and a few left whole. The birds will rapidly get the idea that these large seeds are the same tasty item that they have been eating as small chunks, and they will then be quite happy to chip chunks off of the whole, shelled sunflower seed and eat them. All small birds in my experience have eaten shelled sunflower seeds daily, and larger birds such as pigeons, pheasants and ducks will choose the shelled sunflower seeds over all other seeds or pellets. In addition, there is no more nutritious seed that you can feed to your birds.

In offering shelled sunflower seed at the wild bird feeder, you will be rewarded by many soft-billed birds coming to the feeder. I have watched Red-headed Woodpeckers, *Melanerpes erythrocephalus*, sitting with newly-fledged young ones on the feeding station, stuffing them with the shelled sunflower seeds. All larger birds instinctively recognize these sunflower seeds as a nutritional bonanza and delicacy. The larger doves all consume them greedily, and the Green-winged or Emerald Doves, *Chalcophaps indica*, are particularly fond of the shelled sunflower seeds.

As an experiment, I have maintained non-breeding Society Finches on a diet of only shelled sunflower seed, white proso millet, and water for many months in perfect condition. This is strictly a maintenance diet for these finches, however, as it is very deficient in several nutrients, in particular, vitamins A, D, and B$_{12}$, and will allow no breeding whatsoever. Any eggs laid will fail to hatch with embryos dying in the shell. If one in a hundred does succeed in hatching out, the protein content of this simple maintenance diet is insufficient for successful rearing to healthy maturity. Restoration of the egg mixture previously described to this diet will result in 100% fertile clutches, hatches, and young fledged within one week of the return of the high-protein egg mix. This means that all hens laying one week after egg supplementation begins will lay fertile, hatchable clutches, and will raise all of their young to maturity.

Peanuts are rich in protein, with an average value of 25%. If fed to birds, peanuts should always be raw, never roasted, and particularly never roasted in oil and salted. As a protein source for the price, however, the peanuts are hard to beat. Most large food stores now carry shelled raw peanuts at a very reasonable price. You can also introduce peanuts to small birds in the way that I have recommended for sunflower seeds. With seeds that are this large, however, you may always have to break peanuts up into pieces for feeding birds as tiny as the tits and waxbills.

Any of the nuts are ideal sources of plant protein that is among the most complete of any found in the plant kingdom. The price per pound for shelled nuts is high, however, and economics will often prevent the average fancier from offering them to birds on a regular basis. Nevertheless, in referring to the chart of water content on page 33, you will find that the extremely low water content of nuts and the fact that there is no waste at all in shelled nuts will make them one of your very best nutritional buys.

The protein surprises of the plant world are pine nuts, also called pignolias, and soybeans. Pine nuts average 33% protein, while soybeans contain more than 35% well balanced protein. The pignolias are a nutritional specialty item, and you can expect to pay a relatively huge price per pound for them.

Soybeans are the basis for many of the prepared feeds and crumbles, as well as the other pet foods found on the market. Their high protein content blends well with the incomplete protein of the cereal grains so that an adequate amount of complete protein for all periods of life results from the blending of these feeds. Also, the soybeans are grown in huge quantities, so their price is always reasonable, and this makes the resulting blended feeds also quite reasonable in price.

At times, you may run into the term 'crude protein' as a percentage of the nutritional contents of an item. This term includes all parts of the food that can be considered as proteins, with a nitrogen base, regardless of whether they are digestible or not. In many cases, substantial portions of the listed crude protein content may be indigestible and constitute only bulk in the diet, and as far as research can now determine, bulk is not required in the nutrition of birds for the proper operation of the digestive system.

Protein deficiency is, unfortunately, the most common problem that you will encounter in the care and handling of small cage birds. Loss of weight, feather plucking, egg eating, poor feathering, and loss of young in the nest may all be the symptoms of a deficiency of complete protein in the diet. Without sufficient protein, the replacement of lost tissue is slow and may even stop completely. The bird will become listless, lose weight, and eventually will die.

Absorption of amino acids in the intestine of a chick is dependent upon the presence of vitamin B_6, also called pyridoxine. If that vitamin is lacking or deficient in the diet, the amino acids cannot be absorbed. Consequently, even though the diet may be rich in complete protein, it is completely unabsorbable, and the chick will die of protein deficiency. This would be quite unlikely to occur with natural whole foods, of course, as the same foods that are rich in complete protein are also usually rich in pyridoxine.

The body of a bird is predominantly protein. From one-fifth to one-quarter of the fat free body of a bird is protein. When you consider that much of the remainder is water, all of the minerals, vitamins and carbohydrates are but a small part of the total. In addition, up to one-third of the total protein of a bird's body may be in the form of keratin in the feathers. All muscles, organs, hormones, enzymes, and antibodies are formed from proteins. The importance of protein in cage bird nutrition cannot be over-emphasized.

Feather plucking is the most obvious warning symptom of a deficiency of protein. Feathers are almost pure protein, with traces of minerals. In cases of deficiency in the diet, the bird's only other source of protein is from destroying the feathers and body of its neighbors or itself. Most feather plucking in finches is usually started by protein deficiency. A diet of the standard finch seed mixes, grit, and minerals in the form of mineral blocks or cuttlebone is deficient in the essential amino acids lysine and tryptophan, not to mention the severe vitamin deficiencies it represents.

Loss of weight is an indication that the protein portions of the body are being used for energy to maintain body heat and energy. Muscle tissue is broken down first, since it is the least necessary for life. This breakdown may stem from several causes, chief among them the inability to digest food and extract the protein and other nutrients from it, possibly as the result of harmful disease microorganisms within the digestive tract. A deficiency of protein in the food will cause a gradual loss of weight, as the body robs one of its parts of protein to keep another going.

When protein and its constituent amino acids are broken down for energy by the bird's metabolism, the result is a large amount of excess nitrogen. This must be converted to uric acid for excretion by the kidneys. This necessary function causes a strain on the metabolic system and can easily lead to excess water consumption and a much higher water content of the droppings. In mild diarrhea of this type, a microorganism may not be directly responsible for the watery droppings.

Birds starved for complete protein can rarely be induced to breed. If they do breed, this so robs the hen of her meager protein resources that she may instinctively eat her own eggs as a source of replacement protein. Lest this be considered highly unusual, remember that it is one of nature's ways of maintaining population balances among the myriad species of life. If the protein content of the food supply were insufficient for two adult birds in the wild, it could not possibly be available for raising and supporting a nest of young ones. The breeding is thus terminated at an early stage by the female's egg eating. To do otherwise would only put an added burden on the hen when the young would be sure to die of protein deficiency anyway.

Protein requirements vary at different stages in the life of a bird. The requirement for a newly hatched bird for its first week of growth is very high. During the second, third, and fourth weeks, the young of small birds make their growth to a nearly full-sized body, mostly feathered, depending upon the species. This three week period is the most critical in terms of the protein requirement. If the diet is deficient for more than a couple of days during this period in either the quantity or quality of the protein consumed, the nestlings will be sure to die. You can prevent this only by assuring that the parent birds have available to them all of the high protein food they will consume. When the growing body is increasing in size so rapidly and the feathers are forming all over the body at the same time, the need for relatively huge quantities of protein is constant and crucial. A severe protein deficiency at this stage of the nestlings' development for only a few hours will mean the death of the growing nestlings.

After this period of maximum growth, the protein requirement gradually decreases. This will be noted in the decreasing amounts of the protein foods consumed. Though feathers are still growing and the body structure is still maturing, the bulk of the growth is completed at the end of the fourth week in most finches and other small birds. Many species develop more slowly than this, of course, as anyone who hand raises the psittacine species will attest. In the feather development, amino acids play a part in the color formation as well as the structure of the feathers. To repeat an example used before, melanin, the pigment responsible for dark browns and black coloring, is derived from the amino acid tyrosine.

Once the bird reaches maturity, the protein requirement is much lower, just enough to replace lost cells in the body and maintain the feather structure. You will note that mature finches when not breeding and not in a molt will consume very little high protein food, usually less than one-quarter teaspoon per day for each bird. By contrast, when feeding a nest of growing youngsters, a pair may clean up as much as three tablespoons of high protein food per day. A molt will again increase the amount of protein consumed, since the body requires larger amounts of protein for the formation of the feather structure.

When the hen is forming eggs, the protein requirement once again will increase. Eggs in themselves are rich in complete protein, since they must contain the full complement of protein necessary for the development of the embryo from one cell to a fully functioning baby bird in a period as short as eleven days in the Diamond Dove, *Geopelia cuneata*.

Though the individual amino acids cannot be retained in the body for long, once they have been incorporated into the body's protein complexes, they act secondarily as a food reserve. The proteins form an emergency reserve food supply that may be called upon from time to time in cases of simple protein deficiency or disease. As mentioned before, the body can break down the protein components of the muscles to provide the repair material for the vital organs or to provide energy when it is necessary to prevent death, as in cases of starvation. Once the emergency situation has passed, the body will replace the protein and will rebuild the depleted muscle tissue. Once this happens, the bird will regain its lost weight and once again will be in good health.

It seems impossible to get an excess of balanced protein in the diet. More protein than the body needs will never cause any problems, provided the vitamins and minerals necessary to break it down and utilize it are available and in sufficient supply. The liver breaks down any excess amino acids over the body's needs, so the body's cells can use them for energy.

Nevertheless, excessive intake of one or more of the essential amino acids in pure form can cause an amino acid imbalance or toxicity. This will result in less food intake and a decrease in growth. This will occur only in controlled nutritional experimentation, not with any natural, protein-rich food. In such nutritional testing, methionine has been shown to be the most toxic of the essential amino acids.

Utilization of the protein consumed may be adversely influenced by a number of factors. Disease has already been mentioned as a factor in the inability of a digestive system to digest the food and absorb the amino acids of the digested protein. The intestinal lining can also become coated with some substance that prevents the amino acids from passing through into the bloodstream. A variety of vitamin and mineral deficiencies will have a similar effect.

Any lack of essential vitamins and minerals may prevent the proper absorption and utilization of amino acids once they are made available by the digestive process. The vitamins and minerals are necessary at all levels of digestion, assimilation, and body-building. Vitamins and minerals make the creation of new tissue possible, while at the same time they may constitute vital and indispensable parts of that tissue. There are separate chapters later in this volume devoted to thorough discussions of all of the vitamins and minerals, though you can hardly discuss one aspect of nutrition without mentioning others, since all facets of the nutritive process are interrelated.

A bird in a cage is helpless in the face of your lack of knowledge of its protein needs. Protein is absolutely vital to its life. There is no substitute for that protein. It must be complete to be properly utilized, and it must be eaten in sufficient quantity. Neither the quantity nor the quality may be compromised without disastrous results. Adequate protein is one of those indispensable keys to keeping and breeding healthful birds. Never forget that protein deficiency is by far the most common nutritional deficiency encountered in the care and maintenance of birds in captivity.

"Adequate protein is one of those indispensable keys to keeping and breeding healthful birds. Never forget that protein deficiency is by far the most common nutritional deficiency encountered in the care and maintenance of birds in captivity."

CHAPTER 4

FATS

This chapter contains many terms that seem calculated to curl the hair of everyone who still has their hair. Yet, the explanations of a number of authorities are presented here in the most logical and concise forms I could manage. For one who has never delved into the subject of fats and their nutritional importance, the first reading probably will be somewhat incomprehensible, and certainly will not be totally assimilated. Once the contents of this chapter are thoroughly digested, however, no reference to fats that you encounter in the future will ever again be a mystery. We are indeed fortunate that enough material is available from the nutritional research over the years to give us a good idea of the functions of fats and their metabolism in both birds and people. Such an abundance of material is certainly not available with many of the other known nutrients.

Fats in the diet serve three primary purposes. First, they are a source of energy for the body's needs for heat production and for muscle action. Secondly, fats serve as carriers for the fat soluble vitamins, essential fatty acids and minerals. Third, they are the food storage mechanism for the body. In addition, fats remain in the digestive system longer than other food constituents and act to suppress the appetite, since they are digested rather slowly. For this reason, a snack of a food high in fat when you're hungry will do far more good than a candy bar would for the same purpose. Researchers have discovered that in maintaining chickens, a small amount of fat added to the diet will increase the efficiency of energy utilization and incorporation into the avian body. This will hold true even when the total energy value is the same for the two diets, one without fat, and one with fat added.

A dietary intake of food over and above the body's requirement for energy, growth, and rebuilding of cells will be stored as fat. This stored fat is a reserve source of body heat and energy for those times when the caloric value of the food is insufficient, as it is during a temporary fast. This stored fat also acts as a cushion for the body, and particularly for the vital organs. The kidneys are especially well protected by a fat cushion. Fat stored under the skin helps to protect muscles and nerves. It is also important in maintaining the body temperature and insulating the body from environmental changes.

Fats and oils may come from either animal or vegetable sources in the diet. The term 'fats' generally refers to those substances that are solid at room temperature, while the term 'oils' refers to those that are liquids at room temperature. One word, 'lipids', refers to both fats and oils together. The term 'lipids' will now be used frequently in the continuation of this discussion to refer to the fats and oils as a group.

Animal fats are predominantly solid at room temperature, while the sources from cold-blooded creatures and plants are predominantly liquid. Fish, for example contain mostly oils. Since they are cold blooded, fats would stiffen their body tissues, and could be deadly.

All of the whole fats and oils are made up of varying combinations of what are called 'fatty acids', which themselves may be in the form or either oils or fats. For example, more than one hundred different fatty acids have been identified in the butterfat of milk.

A slightly more technical way of presenting this distinction is with the terms saturated and unsaturated when applied to the fatty acids. Note the following diagram of stearic acid, found in most animal and vegetable lipids, a saturated fatty acid which is solid at room temperature:

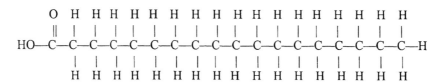

Diagram #1 – Stearic Acid

H = Hydrogen
C = Carbon
O = Oxygen

Such a saturated fatty acid contains all of the hydrogen atoms it can carry. Every available bond is solidly filled, so the compound is saturated and exists as a solid fat as a result. A saturated fat is solid at room temperature.

There are several ways generally used to write the formula for these chemical substances. The simplest formula lists only the atoms within the molecule, and the number of them that exists. For example, the simplest chemical formula for stearic acid would be $C_{18}H_{36}O_2$. This indicates that the compound contains 18 atoms of carbon, 36 atoms of hydrogen, and two atoms of oxygen, but it gives no hint of the way in which these atoms are distributed and organized.

The second simple method of writing the formula for stearic acid has the acid group or the carboxyl group (COOH) written separately. Though this is little improvement on the simplest formula, it does recognize that the molecule of this compound contains an acid group, also called a carboxyl group, and is explained more thoroughly below. For example, this simple formula for stearic acid is $C_{17}H_{35}COOH$. Note that when written in this manner, one carbon atom and one hydrogen atom are subtracted from the simplest formula and added as the COOH carboxyl group. In some references, you will see this formula written as $C_{17}H_{35}CO_2H$ to indicate the two atoms of oxygen. Still, none of these methods of writing the formula explains the order of the atoms within the fatty acid molecule.

There is also a more detailed and expanded method of writing the formula for a fatty acid that indicates the order in which the atoms occur in the substance and the number of atoms at each location on the molecule. Again, the example will be stearic acid, and the expanded chemical formula for stearic acid is written as $CH_3(CH2)_{16}COOH$. Note that this formula is written backwards from the atomic and molecular order outlined in the drawings. As already noted, when some of the simple formulas and these expanded formulas are written, the acid group or carboxyl group is written separately, and their atoms are not counted in the other parts of the formula.

Another way of naming these compounds is called systematic naming. In the systematic naming system, the stearic acid molecule would be described as an octadecanoic fatty acid to indicate the eighteen carbon atoms in its chain. The oleic acid molecule illustrated in the drawing on page 59 would be described as a 9-octadecanoic fatty acid to indicate that the open double bond is at the 9th carbon atom on the chain, counting from the acid group or carboxyl group.

In descriptions of the unsaturated fatty acids, you will run into two terms that need a little explanation in the systematic naming system. The words 'cis' and 'trans' are often used to clarify the chemical structure in any description of the unsaturated fatty acid molecules. These words describe the positions of the open double bonds along the carbon chain of the essential fatty acid. The word 'cis' means that the bonds are along the usual side of the molecule, as you will note in the diagrams of oleic acid and linoleic acid on pages 59 and 60. 'Trans' means that the open double bonds are on the other side of the molecule. Two examples of unsaturated fatty acids that have open double bonds on the opposite side of the molecule are vaccenic acid and eleostearic acid. When you write the systematic descriptions of the molecules of these two fatty acids, cis and trans will nearly always be used to specify that these molecules do not have the standard structure of a fatty acid molecule, but instead, they have open double bonds on both sides of the molecule.

When listed in large groups that include the chemically unusual fatty acids, oleic acid, described in diagram #4, may be more clearly described as a *cis*-9-octadecanoic acid, indicating that the open double bonds are on the usual side of the molecule, and not on the opposite side of the molecule, as is found in vaccenic acid and eleostearic acid.

In references on fats and the fatty acids, you may see any of these methods of describing the structure of a fatty acid used commonly. It is for this reason that all of these methods of naming and describing a fatty acid have been covered in this discussion.

As shown in the diagrams, the fatty acids are chains of carbon atoms which may or may not have hydrogen atoms attached. At one end of the chain, three hydrogen atoms are attached to the last carbon atom. This is referred to as a methyl group. The other end of the chain of carbon atoms is an acid group, also called a carboxyl group. This acid group consists of one carbon atom, one hydrogen atom, and two oxygen atoms. *This atomic structure is characteristic of all fatty acids.* Be certain to note, also, that in the standard written formula, the methyl group is written first, while in the diagrams of molecules, the methyl group is on the right side, written last. Since English is written from left to right, this can, does, and will create some confusion. In the Semitic languages (Arabic, Hebrew, etc.), for example, this problem does not exist, since those languages are written from right to left, as the molecules are drawn.

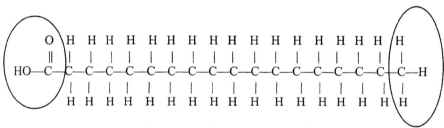

Diagram #2 – Stearic Acid
circling the acid or carboxyl group (left) and the methyl group (right)

The following drawing of the palmitic acid molecule, another saturated fatty acid, also points out these characteristics. Also, note that the palmitic acid molecule has sixteen carbon atoms in its chain, while the stearic acid molecule has eighteen carbon atoms in its carbon chain. Palmitic acid is found in most animal and vegetable fats and oils, and it is described as a hexadecanoic fatty acid to indicate the chain of sixteen carbon atoms. The simple formula for palmitic acid is written $C_{15}H_{31}COOH$ or $C_{16}H_{32}O_2$ and the expanded formula for this common fatty acid is $CH_3(CH_2)_{14}COOH$.

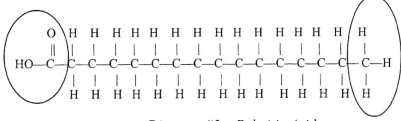

Diagram #3 – Palmitic Acid
Circling the methyl group on the right and the carboxyl group on the left

Unsaturated fatty acids may be monounsaturated or polyunsaturated. This means that one or more of the double bonds are open, and they are not attached to hydrogen atoms. This makes the resulting molecule more flexible, and therefore that fatty acid will be a liquid. Each of these double bond linkages will hold two additional atoms, either hydrogen atoms or the atoms of other elements. For example, two atoms of iodine can attach themselves to each empty double bond on the carbon chain.

The term 'monounsaturated' means that one of the possible double bond linkages is still open, leaving room for two additional atoms. The following illustration of oleic acid, a monounsaturated fatty acid, will illustrate this concept:

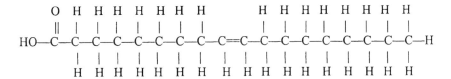

Diagram #4 – Oleic Acid

Oleic acid constitutes from 70% to 75% of the fatty acids in olive oil, 50% or more in peanut oil, and 40% of beef, lamb, and poultry fat. Oleic acid is a very common fatty acid, and it is found in most animal, marine, and vegetable oils. Most of the common monounsaturated fatty acids have the double bond linkage in the ninth position, as oleic acid shows, between the 9th and 10th carbon atoms, counting from the acid or carboxyl group. The simple chemical formula for oleic acid is $C_{17}H_{33}COOH$ or $C_{18}H_{34}O_2$. The expanded and more descriptive chemical formula for oleic acid is written $CH_3(CH_2)_7CH=CH(CH_2)_7COOH$. Remember this is backwards from the way the diagrams are laid out!

In naming these compounds by the systematic naming method, the oleic acid molecule would be described as a 9-octadecanoic fatty acid to indicate that the open double bond is at the 9th carbon atom on the chain. In large groups that include the chemically unusual fatty acids, oleic acid may be described as a *cis*-9-octadecanoic acid, indicating that the open double bond is on the usual side of the molecule, and not on the opposite side of the molecule, as is found in vaccenic acid and eleostearic acid.

Three of the fatty acids are essential, all of them polyunsaturated: linoleic acid, linolenic acid, and arachidonic acid. The term essential in this sense means that these fatty acids must be consumed as part of the diet, as the body cannot make them internally in adequate quantities. Of these, linoleic acid is the most important and always must come from the diet. The avian body is not able to synthesize it; neither the human nor the avian body is able to synthesize linoleic acid. The three essential fatty acids in their role as a vitamin will be covered in detail separately with the fat soluble vitamins, but their structures are illustrated here.

The designation 'polyunsaturated' indicates that two or more of the double bond linkages are open, leaving room for four, six or more additional atoms. The following drawing is a linoleic acid molecule, which is a polyunsaturated fatty acid and classified as a vitamin. It will illustrate this explanation and the general structure of a polyunsaturated fatty acid:

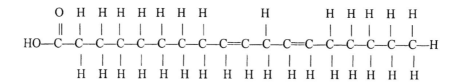

Diagram #5 – Linoleic Acid

Linoleic acid is chemically described with a systematic name as a 9, 12-octadecadienoic fatty acid, meaning that it has a chain of 18 carbon atoms with two double bond linkages at the 9th and 12th carbon atoms, counting from the carboxyl group. In large listings that include the unusual fatty acids, the linoleic acid systematic name may be expanded and written in a more detailed manner as *cis*-9, *cis*-12-octadecadienoic acid, to indicate that both of the open double bonds are on this one side of the molecule. The simple formula is written as either $C_{17}H_{31}COOH$ or $C_{18}H_{32}O_2$. The expanded formula for linoleic acid is $CH_3(CH_2)_4CH=CHCH_2CH=CH(CH_2)_7COOH$. In some references, you will also see this vitamin listed as 'linolic acid'. Linoleic acid is found in most vegetable oils. However, olive oil is a notable exception and contains no linoleic acid.

A second essential fatty acid is linolenic acid. (This often creates reader confusion, because linolenic acid is spelled with only one letter different than the previously discussed linoleic acid.) Linolenic acid has three double bond linkages that are open, and its name in the systematic naming system is written as a 9,12,15-octadecatrienoic acid. This means that linolenic acid has a chain of 18 carbon atoms, with open double bond linkages at the 9th, 12th and 15th carbon atoms, counting from the carboxyl group. When placed in a listing with the unusual fatty acids, the systematic name is written more clearly as a *cis*-9, *cis*-12, *cis*-15-octadecatrienoic acid, to indicate that all of the open double bonds are on the usual side of the molecule. Linolenic acid has the simple formula $C_{17}H_{29}COOH$ or $C_{18}H_{30}O_2$. The extended chemical formula used to describe the linolenic acid molecule is

$$CH_3CH_2CH=CHCH_2CH=CHCH_2CH=CH(CH_2)_7COOH$$

The following is a diagram of the linolenic acid molecule, which is found in most vegetable oils:

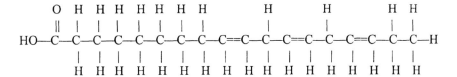

Diagram #6 – Linolenic Acid

Arachidonic acid is also a polyunsaturated fatty acid that is classified as essential in avian nutrition. The avian body cannot synthesize it in adequate quantities, and it must come from the diet. In the systematic naming system, arachidonic acid is called a 5,8,11,14-eicosatetraenoic acid. This means that the molecule consists of a chain of twenty carbon atoms with four open double hydrogen bonds at the 5th, 8th, 11th, and 14th carbon atoms, counting from the carboxyl group. In listings of the fatty acids, writers and scientists usually describe arachidonic acid in the systematic naming system as a *cis*-5, *cis*-8, *cis*-11, *cis*-14-eicosatetraenoic acid, to indicate that all of the open double bonds are on the usual side of the fatty acid molecule. The simple chemical formula for arachidonic acid is written as either $C_{19}H_{31}COOH$ or $C_{20}H_{32}O_2$. The extended chemical formula for arachidonic acid is written as follows:

$$CH_3(CH_2)_4CH=CHCH_2CH=CHCH_2CH=CHCH_2CH=CH(CH_2)_3COOH$$

The following is a diagram of the arachidonic acid molecule:

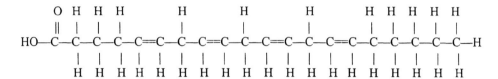

Diagram #7 – Arachidonic Acid

Fatty acids can be short-chain, with less than twelve carbon atoms, long-chain, with twelve to eighteen carbon atoms, or extra long-chain with twenty carbon atoms or more. Short-chain fatty acids occur mostly in milk fat and coconut oil. To further illustrate the complexity of fats, more than 100 different fatty acids have been identified in the butterfat of milk, as has been previously noted. The bulk of butterfat's contents are 29% palmitic acid, 11% stearic acid, and 25% oleic acid.

The shortest chain is butyric acid, found in the butterfat of milk. Butyric acid is a saturated fatty acid with a chain length of only four carbon atoms. The simple chemical formula for butyric acid can be written as C_3H_7COOH or $C_4H_8O_2$. The expanded formula for butyric acid is written $CH_3CH_2CH_2COOH$. The chemical formula for this polyunsaturated fatty acid can also be written $CH_3(CH_2)_2CO_2H$.

Saturated fatty acids can be any carbon chain length from four carbon atoms to eighteen or more. The most common ones are stearic acid with eighteen carbon atoms in the chain, palmitic acid with sixteen carbon atoms, myristic acid with fourteen carbon atoms, and lauric acid with twelve carbon atoms in their carbon chains.

Butyric acid, which contains only 4 carbon atoms in its carbon chain, has already been covered. Other saturated fatty acids that you are sure to encounter in the study of nutrition are caproic acid with six carbon atoms in its chain, caprylic acid with eight carbon atoms, capric acid with ten carbon atoms, arachidic acid with twenty carbon atoms, behenic acid with 22 carbon atoms, lignoceric acid with 24 carbon atoms in its chain, cerotic acid with 26 carbon atoms, montanic acid with 28 carbon atoms, and melissic acid with 30 carbon atoms in its chain. In order to make this coverage as complete as possible, a little information will follow on each of these saturated fatty acids. Stearic acid and palmitic acid have already been covered.

Myristic acid is a tetradecanoic fatty acid, and is one of the well-known saturated fatty acids. Myristic acid is found in most animal and vegetable fats and oils. The simple formulas for myristic acid are $C_{14}H_{28}O_2$ or $C_{13}H_{27}COOH$, while the extended formula is $CH_3(CH_2)_{12}COOH$. Myristic acid has fourteen carbon atoms in its chain.

Lauric acid is a saturated fatty acid with twelve carbon atoms in its chain. It is found in butter, coconut oil, palm nut oils, laurel oil and nutmeg oil. The simple chemical formula for lauric acid is $C_{11}H_{23}COOH$ or $C_{12}H_{24}O_2$. The expanded formula is $CH_3(CH_2)_{10}COOH$. Lauric acid is called a dodecanoic fatty acid to indicate that it has twelve carbon atoms in its structure. This form of naming is called systematic naming, as discussed on page 57 and 58 and will be used frequently to describe the structure of each of the fatty acid molecules.

Caproic acid is a short chain saturated fatty acid with only six carbon atoms in its chain. It is found in butter, coconut oil and palm nut oils. The simple chemical formula for caproic acid is $C_6H_{12}O_2$ or $C_5H_{11}COOH$, while the expanded formula is $CH_3(CH_2)_4COOH$. The systematic name for this saturated fatty acid is a hexanoic fatty acid.

Caprylic acid is an octanoic fatty acid, indicating that it has eight carbon atoms in its chain. Caprylic acid is a saturated fatty acid with the simple chemical formula $C_7H_{15}COOH$ or $C_8H_{16}O_2$ and the expanded chemical formula $CH_3(CH_2)_6COOH$. Caprylic acid is found in fats and oils together with caproic acid.

Capric acid is a decanoic fatty acid, which means that it has ten carbon atoms in the chain. Capric acid is found in butter, coconut oil, palm nut oils, laurel oil and nutmeg oil. The simple formula used for capric acid is $C_9H_{19}COOH$ or $C_{10}H_{20}O_2$, and its expanded formula is $CH_3(CH_2)_8COOH$.

Arachidic acid is an extra long-chain saturated fatty acid that is also called arachic acid and eicosanoic acid. It is an eicosanoic fatty acid, which indicates that it has twenty carbon atoms in the carbon chain. Arachidic acid is found in vegetables, peanut oil and other vegetable oils. The simple chemical formula for arachidic acid is $C_{20}H_{40}O_2$ or $C_{19}H_{39}COOH$. Its expanded chemical formula is $CH_3(CH_2)_{18}COOH$.

Behenic acid is another extra long-chain saturated fatty acid with 22 carbon atoms in its basic chain. The simple formula for behenic acid is $C_{21}H_{43}COOH$ or $C_{22}H_{44}O_2$, and the expanded formula for this molecule is $CH_3(CH_2)_{20}COOH$. Behenic acid is found only in oil of ben, extracted from the seeds of the Asiatic trees of the genus *Moringa*. Behenic acid is systematically named as a docosenoic fatty acid.

Lignoceric acid is an extra long-chain saturated fatty acid with a carbon chain that contains 24 carbon atoms. The simple formula for the lignoceric acid molecule is $C_{23}H_{47}COOH$ or $C_{24}H_{48}O_2$. The expanded formula used for this saturated fatty acid is $CH_3(CH_2)_{22}COOH$. Lignoceric acid is referred to as a tetracosanoic fatty acid in the systematic naming system.

Cerotic acid is another extra long-chain saturated fatty acid with 26 carbon atoms in its chain. Because of this, it is classified as a hexacosanoic fatty acid. The simple formula for cerotic acid is written $C_{25}H_{51}COOH$ or $C_{26}H_{52}O_2$, and the expanded chemical formula is $CH_3(CH_2)_{24}COOH$.

Montanic acid is a saturated extra long-chain fatty acid that has 28 carbon atoms in the carbon chain. It is called an octacosanoic fatty acid to describe this chain of 28 carbon atoms. The simple chemical formula for the montanic acid molecule is written as $C_{27}H_{55}COOH$ or $C_{28}H_{56}O_2$, and the expanded formula is $CH_3(CH_2)_{26}COOH$.

Melissic acid is an extra long-chain saturated fatty acid that is found in beeswax and in some other waxes. You may also see this compound called triacontanoic acid. Melissic acid's carbon chain contains 30 carbon atoms. The simple chemical formula for melissic acid is $C_{29}H_{59}COOH$ or $C_{30}H_{60}O_2$. The expanded chemical formula is written as $CH_3(CH_2)_{28}COOH$.

The unsaturated fatty acids also have a variety of carbon chain lengths and much greater variety in their structure, since each carbon chain can be either monounsaturated or polyunsaturated, with the long chains having up to six open double bonds. As previously mentioned, extra long-chain fatty acids occur mostly in fish oils. Oleic acid and linoleic acid are two of the unsaturated fatty acids that have already been discussed in an introductory way, but there are many other unsaturated fatty acids that you will encounter in the study of nutrition. In particular, the three fatty acids that are a dietary essential in nutrition will be covered in detail in the chapter on vitamins. Again, those are linoleic acid, linolenic acid, and arachidonic acid. A considerable number of other unsaturated fatty acids are commonly mentioned in discussions of the nutritional fats, and a short listing of them will follow.

Crotonic acid is a monounsaturated fatty acid with only four carbon atoms in its chain. It is classified as a 2-butenoic fatty acid. The simple formula for crotonic acid is C_3H_5COOH or $C_4H_6O_2$. The extended formula for crotonic acid is fairly simple, also: $CH_3CH=CHCOOH$.

Hypogeic acid is an unsaturated fatty acid that has 16 carbon atoms in its chain. It is found in peanuts and corn oil.

Palmitoleic acid is a monounsaturated fatty acid, and it also has 16 carbon atoms in its chain. Palmitoleic acid is found in cod liver oil. Palmitoleic acid is a 9-hexadecenoic or a *cis*-9-hexadecenoic fatty acid, and the simple chemical formula for palmitoleic acid is $C_{16}H_{30}O_2$ or $C_{15}H_{29}COOH$. The extended formula for this fatty acid is $CH_3(CH_2)_5CH=CH(CH_2)_7COOH$.

Physetoleic acid is another unsaturated fatty acid with 16 carbon atoms in its chain, and it is found in fish oils and other marine oils.

Rapic acid is an unsaturated fatty acid with 18 carbon atoms in its chain. Rapic acid is found in rapeseed, mustard seed and marine oils.

Ricinoleic acid is an unsaturated fatty acid with 18 carbon atoms in its carbon chain. It is unusual in that it also contains a hydroxyl group. The simple chemical formula for ricinoleic acid is $C_{17}H_{33}COOH$ or $C_{18}H_{34}O_2$. The expanded formula is $CH_3(CH_2)_5CH(OH)CH_2CH=CH(CH_2)_7COOH$. The systematic name is a 12-hydroxyl-*cis*-9-octadecenoic fatty acid.

Gadeloic acid is a monounsaturated fatty acid found in marine oils. Gadeloic acid has 20 carbon atoms in its chain. The simple formula for gadeloic acid is $C_{19}H_{37}COOH$ or $C_{20}H_{38}O_2$. The extended chemical formula for this fatty acid molecule is $CH_3(CH_2)_9CH=CH(CH_2)_7COOH$. Gadeloic acid is described as a 9-eicosenoic fatty acid, or in larger listings, it is listed as a *cis*-9-eicosenoic fatty acid.

Erucic acid is a monounsaturated fatty acid that is found in rapeseed, mustard seed, and marine oils. There are 22 atoms of carbon in the carbon chain of this fatty acid. The systematic name of this compound is written as a 13-docosenoic fatty acid, or in extensive listings as a *cis*-13-docosenoic fatty acid to indicate that the open double bond is on the usual side of the molecule. The simple formula for erucic acid is $C_{21}H_{41}COOH$ or $C_{22}H_{42}O_2$. The extended formula will be written $CH_3(CH_2)_7CH=CH(CH_2)_{11}COOH$.

Nervonic acid is another monounsaturated fatty acid. This fatty acid is described in the systematic naming system as a 15-tetracosenoic fatty acid, meaning that it has 24 carbon atoms on its chain, with the double bond linkage on the fifteenth carbon atom. The simple chemical formulas for nervonic acid are $C_{24}H_{46}O_2$ and $C_{23}H_{45}COOH$ The extended chemical formula for nervonic acid is $CH_3(CH_2)_7CH=CH(CH_2)_{13}COOH$.

Isovaleric acid is an unusual fatty acid with an odd number of carbon atoms; there are 5 carbon atoms in its carbon chain. Also, the isovaleric acid molecule contains two methyl groups, rather than the usual one. The simple chemical formula for isovaleric acid is $C_5H_{10}O_2$ or C_4H_9COOH. The extended chemical formula for isovaleric acid is $(CH_3)_2CHCH_2COOH$.

Clupanodonic acid is an extra long-chain polyunsaturated fatty acid with 22 carbon atoms in its carbon chain. Clupanodonic acid is found in fish oils and other marine oils. The systematic name describes this polyunsaturated fatty acid as a 4,7,10,13,16,19-docosahexaenoic acid. The simple chemical formula for clupanodonic acid is $C_{21}H_{31}COOH$ or $C_{22}H_{32}O_2$. Because of the 6 open double bonds, the extended formula is formidable:

$CH_3CH_2CH=CHCH_2CH=CHCH_2CH=CHCH_2CH=CHCH_2CH=CHCH_2CH=CH(CH_2)_2COOH$

Timnodonic acid is a non-essential polyunsaturated fatty acid with 20 carbon atoms in its chain.

With the exception of the essential unsaturated fatty acids, birds have no known requirement for dietary fat. Experimental hens were deprived of fat in the diet for 19 months. They showed no long-term difficulties, and at the end of this period, their eggs hatched normally.

When oxygen atoms attach themselves to the open linkages of the unsaturated fatty acid molecule, the fat becomes rancid. This is called oxidative rancidity, and the resulting compound is called a peroxide. All fats have a strong tendency to form peroxides, which are toxic in the body. Peroxides can destroy enzyme systems and break down red blood cells. In nature, natural antioxidants prevent this rancidity from happening. The most common and best antioxidant is vitamin E, which occurs naturally with the unsaturated fats. This oxygen-caused rancidity results in a large decrease in the energy value of the fats. Do not handle any fats in copper equipment, since copper is a catalyst for oxidative rancidity, and will cause any fats in copper containers to go rancid much faster than they would normally.

Fats can also turn rancid as a result of the actions of microorganisms. This process is called hydrolytic rancidity. Though it may affect the taste and odor of a fat, hydrolytic rancidity does not interfere with the fat's nutritional value.

The process of hydrogenation forces hydrogen through a lipid accompanied by a nickel catalyst to fill the open linkages in the unsaturated fatty acids. This alters the oils to a less unsaturated or a completely saturated state and prevents oxygen from attaching itself to these linkages. This makes the fatty acids more stable for storage, and they will not spoil as rapidly. In the case of linoleic acid, a polyunsaturated fatty acid, partial hydrogenation changes it to the monounsaturated oleic acid, which is not an avian dietary essential. The hydrogenation greatly increases the storage life of a fat product, since it takes the spaces where oxygen might otherwise attach itself to create rancidity. Nutritionally speaking, the hydrogenation process is an unconscionable disaster because of its destruction of linoleic acid, a vital fatty acid in nutrition.

Whether fat stored in the body is predominantly saturated and solid or predominantly unsaturated and more liquid is dependent upon its source. The body stores both types. Any fat made by the body from an excess of the carbohydrates in the diet through the process called lipogenesis will be solid and predominantly saturated, since the body is unable to form linoleic acid, the primary unsaturated fat in the body's metabolism. Also, birds are unable to form oleic acid, a monounsaturated fatty acid, for storage.

Fats stored from an excess fat intake in the diet will be softer, containing a portion of linoleic acid. Any human or bird deriving all of its excess calories from unsaturated fats will have very soft, flabby fat on the body. Though this may be a human social disaster, it is far superior from a nutritional point of view. The food value of fats in the diet depends on their absorption in the intestine. Also, fatty acids are not excreted in the urine, but must be excreted through the intestinal tract.

The body, whether bird, mammal, or fish, stores fat because it is the most efficient energy storage method in nature. Any given weight of fat furnishes 2.25 times as much energy when metabolized as the same weight of either protein or carbohydrate. Fats are the most concentrated dietary source of energy, yielding 9.4 calories per gram, compared with only 4.15 calories per gram for proteins and carbohydrates. Consequently, fat storage is over twice as efficient for energy storage in the body than are the other energy sources available. For this reason, when muscle tissue begins to be metabolized in a sick bird, you can be sure that all fat reserves not essential to life have already been utilized completely. Only the fats vital to the maintenance of life will remain. In starvation to death, the fat content of the body will not drop significantly below 4% of the total body weight.

The tissues of the body that store the fat are called adipose tissues. The adipose tissues contain the stored cellular fat in birds, animals and people. This fat is then available during times of food shortage or prolonged exercise as a ready reserve of energy for the body's cells.

Fat is stored in the marrow of animal bones, as well as in the adipose tissues in and around muscle tissue. In birds, little fat is stored in the bones, as they must be kept hollow for the sake of lightness and flight.

In the year 1814 the French chemist Michel-Eugène Chevreul (1786-1889) discovered that whole fats are composed of fatty acids and glycerol, also called glycerin. The suffix -ol indicates an alcohol in any chemical name. This noteworthy discovery has been the basis of all subsequent knowledge gained about the structure of fats. One, two or three fatty acids can attach themselves to the glycerol base. If only one fatty acid is attached, the compound is called a 'monoglyceride'. Two fatty acids attached to the glycerol forms a 'diglyceride'. If the maximum number of three fatty acids is attached, the resulting fat is a 'triglyceride'.

If a triglyceride has all three of its available positions filled with the same fatty acid, it is called a simple triglyceride. Only a few of the triglycerides occurring in nature are simple triglycerides. One example is tripalmitin, the glyceryl ester of palmitic acid. In tripalmitin, all three of the available positions are filled by palmitic acid.

Most of the triglycerides occurring in nature are mixed triglycerides. Mixed triglycerides may contain two different fatty acids or they may have the three positions filled by three different fatty acids, as illustrated in diagram #8.

Each mixed triglyceride that contains three different fatty acids can exist in three different forms, since any of the three fatty acids can be linked with the center carbon atom of the glycerol molecule. Any mixed triglyceride that contains only two types of fatty acids will have only two possible forms, as even though there are three available fatty acids, two of them are the same, and so there are only two possible types of fatty acid that can connect to the center carbon atom.

The following drawing will serve to illustrate the structure of a mixed triglyceride molecule:

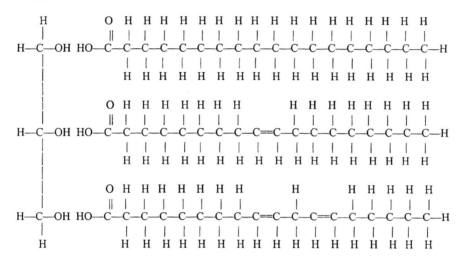

Diagram #8

A triglyceride molecule showing three attached fatty acids: stearic acid, oleic acid, and linoleic acid

Either saturated or unsaturated fatty acids can be attached to the glycerol in any combination. This will allow thousands of different kinds of fats and oils to be formed. The fatty acids are fairly heavy, and they make up from 94% to 96% of the weight of the triglyceride molecule.

Glycerol is the only part of the triglyceride molecule that can be converted to glucose for the direct energy needs of the cells. The fatty acids, whether saturated or unsaturated, must be radically transformed by the body's metabolic processes first.

In digestion, enzymes split off the fatty acids from the glycerol. These enzymes are called lipases. The outer positions will be stripped off first. The middle position will be taken away less rapidly and sometimes not at all. The resulting compound is called a monoglyceride. In birds, these resulting monoglycerides of the saturated fats will be absorbed by the intestines more easily than the free saturated fatty acids.

When glycerol joins with a fatty acid, the resulting compound technically is called an ester. Fats which are simple lipids are esters of glycerol and fatty acids. Any esters formed by the combination of any alcohol other than glycerol with fatty acids are called waxes.

The term 'compound lipids' refers to those fats with a glycerol base, two fatty acids, and the third available position having another chemical group, such as the B vitamin choline, linked with it through phosphoric acid. This combination forms lecithin, one of the most important and well-known compound lipids.

Phospholipids are complex fats linked chemically to phosphorus, and they are found in all plant and animal tissues. They are especially abundant in nervous tissue and may constitute up to 30% of the dry matter of the brain tissue. The triglycerides and phospholipids make up the vast majority of the circulating fats in the bloodstream.

Lipids that are circulating in the blood come from three sources. Intestinal absorption and synthesis, primarily in the liver, are the two primary sources. The third source is from the mobilization of fat deposits when caloric intake is insufficient for body needs. Of the portion absorbed into the bloodstream from the intestine, half of the fatty acids are linked into cholesterol and phospholipids. The rest will remain as glycerides or free fatty acids. Fats also may be attached to amino acids in the blood for easier transport through the bloodstream. These are known as lipoproteins.

The term cholesterol is familiar to everyone thanks to its notoriety in relation to heart and circulatory diseases. No discussion of fats would be complete without mention of it. A thorough, unbiased look at cholesterol indicates that it is definitely not the boogieman the news media would have us believe. Cholesterol is an essential constituent of blood, nerves, the brain, and other parts of the body. The body's own cells, especially in the liver, will manufacture cholesterol at the relatively high rate of two to three grams per day. This is more than four times as much as the average diet is likely to contain during the same period.

It should be obvious, then, that a low cholesterol diet may be little more than a fool's panacea. A really excessive intake of high cholesterol foods can, of course, increase the blood's cholesterol level, but nothing is going to stop the body's cells from manufacturing cholesterol. High dietary intake may suppress the normal body synthesis of cholesterol, but conversely, a low dietary intake will increase body synthesis of this substance.

A diet rich in polyunsaturated fats, particularly linoleic acid, and with adequate vitamins and minerals, is unlikely to cause any abnormal buildup of cholesterol deposits. Since all nutrients work together in the nutrition of man or birds, a deficiency of any will cause misappropriation of some others. This is what happens in the dangerous depositing of cholesterol in the circulatory system. It is definitely not normal for cholesterol to form in deposits of this type. Such abnormalities are virtually unknown in so-called primitive societies where refined food products are unknown. See the sections on chromium, vanadium and vitamin E for further information on circulatory and heart needs in nutrition.

Inadequate fat intake can cause excessive water retention, and this is why so many on low fat diets continually gain weight; the body is simply storing more water. On any low fat diet, deficiencies of the fat soluble vitamins are almost a certainty. The fats are the carriers of all of the fat soluble vitamins; water will not dissolve them. Also, without the presence of fat, the body cannot absorb the fat soluble vitamins A, D, E, K, or the essential fatty acids, even if they are present in the diet, as they may well be through vitamin supplementation. The importance of fats and the fatty acids in the diet of both birds and humans cannot be overemphasized. Low fat diets are not a panacea – they are dangerous to life and health. Fat free diets will result in death.

CHAPTER 5

CARBOHYDRATES

Carbohydrates are a third primary source of energy for birds, animals, and humans. In quantity consumed and energy value extracted, the carbohydrates usually rank first in the diets of most species of birds commonly maintained in aviculture. The carbohydrates function primarily in the diet as a source of energy in the avian body for heat and muscle work, but can also be stored to a certain extent.

Most carbohydrates are plant products, formed by photosynthesis, using sunlight in the presence of chlorophyll. Technically, the plants turn light energy into chemical energy by combining carbon, hydrogen and oxygen in a complex series of reactions. When metabolized, the carbohydrates yield carbon dioxide and water in the body as by-products. Molecular energy is the name we use to describe this subsequent conversion of the chemical energy that is stored in the molecules of food into kinetic energy for muscle action. The dry matter of most plants ranges from 60% to 90% carbohydrates.

As surprising as it may seem, there is no definite, known nutritional requirement for carbohydrates in the diet. Fats or protein can substitute, if perhaps less efficiently, for the known functions of carbohydrates in the metabolism. Nevertheless, it is fortunate that most species can digest and utilize carbohydrates easily, or the available food supply would be drastically reduced.

Carbohydrates are classed under several headings, depending upon their chemical structure. They range from very simple in their structure to incredibly complex. This structure determines whether the carbohydrate is digestible, absorbable, and capable of being utilized by the avian body. The characteristics and properties of these carbohydrates depend totally upon their molecular structure.

71

The food carbohydrates are classified as sugars and starches, and the sugars are the simplest of the carbohydrates in chemical structure. The sugars are subdivided into several categories, depending upon their structure, while the starches are composed of groupings of the various sugar molecules. As was true of the fatty acids in forming the fats, the numbers of combinations of starches possible through the structural joining of the various kinds of sugar molecules is astronomical.

The simplest of these sugars are called monosaccharides. These are the simplest carbohydrates. Monosaccharides contain from three to seven carbon atoms. By far the most important in nutrition is glucose, which will be covered in more detail later. It is found in fruits and in pure form in honey. This is why diluted honey can be such an instant pick-me-up for a sick bird after the cause of the sickness has been removed. Glucose needs no digestion; it is absorbed as is, circulates to the cells that need the energy, and is used almost instantly for energy without any chemical change being needed along the way.

Another important monosaccharide is fructose, and it is also called fruit sugar. As the name implies, this sugar is found primarily in fruits. Fructose is also known as levulose, and it is also found in vegetables and honey.

Galactose is one of the two simple sugars that make up each molecule of lactose, the compound sugar found in milk. The other simple sugar in lactose is glucose. In experimental chicken diets, over 10% of galactose content in the diet will produce toxicity in the form of a central nervous system disorder characterized by convulsions. Over 50% of the diet as galactose causes severe kidney damage, convulsive seizures, and death. These ill effects have occured only in nutritional testing, however, and they are certainly not possible on any normal diet.

Glucose, fructose, and galactose are the major forms of carbohydrate circulating in the bloodstreams of avian species. Though more than twenty monosaccharides have been identified by science, these three are the most important in the study of nutrition. All three are known in three separate forms, one with a straight carbon chain, one with a left facing molecule, and one with a right facing molecule.

One other monosaccharide is quite important in nutrition, and that is ribose. Ribose is found in corn and beets naturally and ribose alone forms the carbohydrate portion of both the DNA (deoxyribonucleic acid) molecule and the RNA (ribonucleic acid) molecule. Ribose is also a constituent of the vitamin riboflavin, also known as vitamin B_2.

The term disaccharide means two monosaccharides linked together to form a more complex sugar. The disaccharides are the simplest of the multiple sugars. Three of these disaccharides are important in the nutrition of birds, but the digestive system cannot absorb them until the enzymes have broken down the disaccharides into their component monosaccharides.

Sucrose is the most important of these disaccharides. It is formed by the combination of one glucose molecule and one fructose molecule. Sucrose is our common white sugar, extracted from sugar cane or sugar beets. In the process of digestion, an enzyme called sucrase or invertase splits these two joined molecules and releases the free monosaccharides glucose and fructose.

Maltose is the second important disaccharide. It is composed of two glucose molecules linked together. The enzyme maltase breaks these apart in the small intestine and thereby releases two molecules of glucose for each molecule of maltose.

Lactose is the third important disaccharide. Lactose is of great importance in human nutrition, since it is the sugar found in milk. One glucose molecule and one galactose molecule join to make one molecule of lactose. Lactose is the only common sugar that is of animal origin. The milk of cows is about 4.9% lactose, while the milk of humans is from 6% to 7% lactose. The digestion of lactose requires that the enzyme lactase be present to break the lactose molecule into its glucose and galactose constituents. Lactose is much less soluble than the other sugars, and it therefore is digested much more slowly in the intestinal tract.

For most birds, however, lactose has a very low energy value, because they lack the enzyme lactase to break it down or hydrolize it. Before giving any of your birds milk or milk products, test them for lactose tolerance. This means that you should give them a little of the product and then watch closely for any sign of diarrhea or other distress. Most avian species have not been tested for lactose tolerance, since no one has yet been willing to pay for the extensive testing that would be required for the over 9,000 living species of birds. Since milk is not a natural food for avian species, however, it is a safe bet that most species will not be able to digest milk products effectively because of their lactose content. Even within the same species, however, there may be strains in captivity that can tolerate lactose with no problem whatsoever, and other strains that will show definite symptoms of indigestion and diarrhea from any lactose-containing material that they consume.

Once past the infant stage, over half of the human race can no longer tolerate lactose in the diet. For the Caucasian peoples, over 90% can eat milk or milk products with no problem. This is why milk products can be so important in the nutrition of Americans and Europeans. With the native African peoples, this tolerance drops to about 50% of the population. Even half of black Americans cannot tolerate lactose, and milk products will upset their digestive systems and cause diarrhea, as the body tries to rid itself of this indigestible substance. Of the Asian peoples, 90% cannot tolerate lactose, because of the digestive upset it causes. This is why you find absolutely no milk products ever used in the justly famous and delicious Chinese cooking.

Once milk has been converted to other foods, such as cheese or yogurt, birds may be able to tolerate it. The bacteria in milk change the lactose into lactic acid, and this is what causes milk to go sour. The bacteria that transform milk into cheese and yogurt also often feed on the lactose in the milk, and leave these foods safe for the birds. However, the expense of such milk products is alone enough to limit their use as a food for birds when in the care of most aviculturists.

Many old books recommend milk sop, bread soaked in milk, as a food for cage birds. I do not, for the reasons already noted. Feeding this milk product can create far more problems with indigestion that it can solve through its nutritional value. Also, white bread is an extremely poor food for birds or people – Most of the vitamins and minerals have been removed in making the white flour (see the sections on the individual nutrients, both vitamins and minerals, for more information in this regard), and bread has a zero value of complete protein. Bread is a carbohydrate food only, and most cage birds are already forced to eat more carbohydrates than they need. Whole wheat bread is marginally better, but I still do not recommend any kind of bread as a food for birds.

The oligosaccharides are technically those multiple sugars that contain from three to six molecules of simple sugar. Most writings will omit this term and will use the word 'polysaccharide' to mean any complex sugar with three or more monosaccharide units.

The polysaccharides are those carbohydrates with over six monosaccharide molecules joined together. Starch is the only polysaccharide that can be used efficiently in metabolism where birds are concerned. Nutritionally, the starches are the most important group of carbohydrates. There can be more than a thousand simple monosaccharides, such as glucose, in a single polysaccharide carbohydrate chain. The resulting carbon chain formation can be straight or branched. Rice, wheat, corn, and millet contain about 70% starch. Even as much as 40% of the content of beans and other seeds is starch. Cereal grains are the most important source of starch in avian nutrition, but tubers, such as potatoes, are also important sources of the carbohydrates for our own human consumption. Agar and pectin are examples of common products that are polysaccharides.

The digestive process splits these complex carbohydrates into mono-saccharides through the action of the specific enzymes needed for each type of simple sugar in the carbohydrate chain. This splitting process is called hydrolysis. Hydrolysis occurs quite rapidly under the influence of enzymes, though the enzymes act only as catalysts. The enzymes speed up the reaction,

74

but are not altered in structure by so doing. The digestive tract can absorb only the resulting monosaccharides.

One of the organic acids formed during carbohydrate oxidation is required for complete oxidation of fats. Therefore, the body is not able to metabolize a fat completely without the presence of some carbohydrate in the diet. The products of incomplete fat oxidation are short-chain acids called ketones. An accumulation of ketones can cause the blood and urine to become acidic. Ketones are excreted as salts, so excretion may lead to severe sodium losses. This will reduce the blood's ability to carry carbon dioxide and can result in coma in severe cases. This usually occurs in humans during starvation or severe fast when the body is metabolizing stored fat, or also possibly in a diet that is very high in fat.

When the body has insufficient water available to carry away the excess ketones through the urine, the body will discharge these compounds into the lungs to be exhaled. This gives a characteristic and unpleasant ketone smell to the breath. Fortunately, just drinking more water can completely solve this human social problem. At least eight of the 16 ounce glasses of water daily is usually recommended, in addition to any other liquids or drinks in the daily diet.

Glucose is the most common monosaccharide, and it is by far the most important in the nutrition of birds and animals. Glucose is the blood sugar for all birds and animals, and the body controlls this function within very narrow limits. Glucose is the basic source of energy in all birds and animals. Glucose occurs in three structural forms, called the open-chain form and the ring forms. All three forms are equal in every respect, both nutritionally and metabolically. Glucose is highly soluble in water, is neither acidic nor alkaline, and the tissues utilize it directly. The body can convert glucose to other monosaccharides as needed in a reversible process.

Hydrolysis, the splitting of the starches and complex sugars into monosaccharides in the digestive system, results in the addition of water as they are broken down. Thus, one gram of starch after hydrolysis will yield more than one gram of absorbable monosaccharides. The liver can synthesize glucose from short-chain organic acids that form during the oxidation of carbohydrates and amino acids. Also, the liver can convert other carbohdrates into glucose. Pure glucose metabolism will yield less energy than will starch metabolism, because of the addition of the water in the digestion hydrolysis. The average energy content of both pure glucose and starch together is usually considered to be four calories per gram.

At the cell level, energy becomes available when glucose is broken down in the tissues. This occurs in a series of steps, with many intermediate reactions. This process is similar to a reversal of photosynthesis. All of these biochemical changes involve many enzymes and coenzymes. The incomplete breakdown of the glucose in the cells forms organic acids. Complete oxidation, by contrast, yields only carbon dioxide and water.

The energy released at each step in the breakdown of glucose forms high energy phosphates. Adenosine triphosphate is particularly important in this process. Adenosine triphosphate serves to soak up excess heat energy from the breakdown of glucose and fat. It might be called a storage tank for energy within the body.

The body can store carbohydrates within the body in the form of glycogen. Glycogen is a polysaccharide, similar to starch. For this reason, glycogen is sometimes called 'animal starch'. Glycogen is stored in the liver and in the muscles. During muscular exercise, lactic acid is formed from carbohydrate breakdown. It enters the blood and is carried to the liver, which can convert it back to glycogen.

The skeletal and smooth muscles use their glycogen reserves for energy on a continuous basis, but cardiac muscle does not. The heart muscle preserves its glycogen reserves and uses blood glucose primarily for the energy requirements of its work and maintenance. Surprisingly, in response to a 48 to 72 hour fast, avian heart muscle glycogen levels will double or even triple.

In times of fear or anger, the adrenal glands will release adrenalin, also called epinephrine. This hormone stimulates the rapid breakdown of glycogen in the liver. The consequent release of glucose raises the blood sugar level, allowing an almost immediate surge of extra energy for coping with the emergency triggering the emotion.

Insulin is a hormone produced by the pancreas which facilitates the entry of glucose into tissue cells. A lack of sufficient insulin causes a rise in the amount of glucose in the blood. Insulin also stimulates the formation of glycogen through direct absorption of the glucose by the cells, and also by stimulating certain enzymes, thus removing excess glucose from the blood.

Several noted authorities have stated that excess metabolizable energy, once absorbed, cannot be excreted by the animal body, but must be stored as fat. Another authority has called this into question by affirming that a large amount of galactose, one of the monosaccharides, will be absorbed rapidly, accumulate in the blood and tissues, and result in much of the galactose being excreted in the urine. I suspend judgment here; you may feel free to consult your family biochemist to resolve the contradiction.

The gross energy of a food is all the energy value that can be measured, including that which is indigestible to the birds. For example, cellulose, though it is a carbohydrate and an energy source, furnishes only bulk in the avian diet, since birds do not possess the enzyme cellulase in the digestive tract for breaking it down. Cellulose is completely unabsorbable. Nutritional authorities seem to agree that bulk is not a requirement in the avian diet, at least not in the diet of chickens. The insect skeletal material called chitin is also completely indigestible by chickens. Digestible energy is that value that can be broken down by digestion and absorbed. The term metabolizable energy refers to digestible energy corrected for losses such as in the excretion of nitrogen wastes. These two energy references are the most important where avian nutrition is concerned.

The best sources of carbohydrate content in the diet of seed-eating birds will be the cereal grains: wheat, millet, oats, canary seed, etc. For softbills, lories and similar feeders, fruit will be the best source. In preparing mixed foods from which birds cannot separate protein from carbohydrate, it is unwise in the extreme to dilute a high protein food with additional carbohydrate. Leave carbohydrates in their natural form or feed them separately. I strongly advise against mixing bread crumbs with hard boiled egg, for example, as a nestling food. Such a practice forces the birds to consume excess carbohydrate in order to get the protein content they crave, particularly while feeding young ones. This can and will cause obesity, as the birds are forced to eat an excess of carbohydrates in order to get the protein that they must have.

As previously mentioned, no bird will ever suffer from a carbohydrate deficiency. Carbohydrates in any form are simply not necessary in the nutrition of birds, though you can hardly keep from feeding some carbohydrate foods to your birds in any normal diet. Overloading cage birds with high carbohydrate foods, however, is a sure road to illness and death.

As a final note, a Rhode Island Red chicken requires energy in the amount of about 360 calories per day with its high rate of metabolism. Small birds, such as finches, consume a vastly greater proportion of calories with relation to their body weight. In translating this consumption to the calorie intake of a human adult, it is rather evident that the statement, "He eats like a bird," is hardly a compliment. Rather, it is in reality the grossest of gluttonous insults.

"In preparing mixed foods from which birds cannot separate protein from carbohydrate, it is unwise in the extreme to dilute a high protein food with additional carbohydrate. Leave carbohydrates in their natural form or feed them separately."

PART TWO

THE VITAMINS

"Your very best and most basic defense
against any disease and harmful microorganism
is the health of the birds.
The health of the birds is directly related
to the quality of their nutrition."

CHAPTER 6

INTRODUCTION TO VITAMINS

Casimir Funk coined the term 'vitamine' in 1912 to name those elusive substances containing nitrogen (amines) that were necessary for life (vita). He was a Polish biologist working at the Lister Institute in London at the time. Later, when researchers discovered more specific vitamins and found most to contain no nitrogen, the final 'e' was dropped from the word. The familiar spelling that we now use was the result.

Vitamins are defined as relatively complex organic substances that are essential in small amounts for the control of metabolic processes. In order to be classified as vitamins, they must be dietary essentials rather than products of synthesis within the body. They function as intact, free chemical compounds or as coenzymes in metabolic reactions in a variety of ways. The vitamins serve primarily as catalysts without which another chemical process in the body cannot occur. This is undoubtedly the most important function of most of the vitamins.

Vitamin C is one of the most versatile of the vitamins in its proven functions, but it is technically not a vitamin for birds, since they synthesize internally all that they require with a few exceptions noted in the section on this vitamin. As examples, vitamin C is vital to the formation of collagen, the material that holds individual cells and tissues together as functioning units. It also serves as a chelator that attaches itself to a mineral and transports it for use by the cells of the body. Vitamin C can also attach itself to poisons and carry them out of the body, including such toxic metals as cadmium. Since this compound is not a vitamin for most avian species, it will be referred to by its chemical name, ascorbic acid, in most further references to its use in the body.

Vitamins are classified into two groups. The first group consists of the fat soluble vitamins. These are found in fatty compounds and are carried by fats. They are not soluble in water and are usually found dissolved in fats. Vitamins A, D, E and K are all in the fat soluble group. The essential fatty acids also fall within the fat soluble vitamin group. These have been referred to as vitamin F in some writings in the United States, and they are known by this designation in Europe. The first edition of this book included these essential fatty acids in the chapter with the fats. However, since that time, I have become more convinced of the widespread deficiencies of the essential fatty acids in the diets of most cage birds, and now consider this to be one of the most likely of the dietary deficiencies that will be encountered in the care and breeding of birds in captivity. Therefore, the essential fatty acids are now discussed in a separate section in the chapter on the fat soluble vitamins.

The second group of vitamins is the water soluble vitamins. This group includes ascorbic acid and all of the B-complex vitamins. As the name implies, these vitamins are soluble in water and can be washed away easily with water. Cooking foods in water dissolves the water-soluble vitamins out of the food. The only thing the B-complex vitamins have in common is that they are all water soluble. Because of this, the old 'B' designations are gradually being dropped in favor of the chemical names of the individual vitamins. I have followed this modern practice in covering the individual vitamins in this volume. They are discussed in alphabetical order, organized by their chemical names. Though the formal names may cause a little short term confusion, over the many years of the future the new chemical method of naming the vitamins will be far more advantageous.

One may also note three other letter designations used for vitamins or compounds rather frequently in the past. The name 'vitamin P' is used in some references for the compounds that are usually known as the 'bioflavonoids'. The bioflavonoids are found in close contact with ascorbic acid in nature. All foods that contain vitamin C also contain bioflavonoids, so it is logical to assume that when consumed, they will also work together in the body's metabolism. Though most birds in captivity seem to be able to make their own ascorbic acid, they do not synthesize the bioflavonoids internally and may need to get them in the diet. The purpose these may serve in the body is still conjecture, but it certainly cannot do any harm to supply them in an avian diet. Fruits and peppers will be the best sources, but leafy greens should also supply enough of these compounds for the daily needs of the birds.

In some of the older references, you may see the term 'vitamin G' used for one of the B complex vitamins. This name was formerly in common usage for riboflavin, which has also been called vitamin B_2 in many older references, especially those that were written for the average, uninformed reader.

Another older vitamin designation you may encounter is 'vitamin H'. This is an older name for another of the B complex vitamins, now usually called biotin. A complete chart of all known historical vitamin designations is included in *Nutrition of the Chicken*, one of the volumes listed in the bibliography.

There are three other vitamin designations that the reader may encounter in further reading on the subject of nutrition. The compound referred to as vitamin M is apparently a part of the folacin group. As you read the material on any of the vitamins, you will note that many have several forms that are active in performing the functions of that vitamin in the body. The compound referred to as vitamin M is apparently one of those active forms of folacin.

Vitamin L is a nutritional factor that is necessary for lactation in the mammals. Vitamin L_1 is a compound derived from liver, and it may be related to anthranilic acid. Vitamin L_2 is a compound derived from yeast which is probably the compound now called adenosine. I do not recommend the use of these terms until research has proven conclusively that these compounds are not synthesized within the body. The true biological need for these compounds also must be determined.

The destruction of vitamins and other nutrients is a serious problem in food processing and cooking. The destruction of the amino acid tryptophan in high heat baking has already been noted in the section on the proteins and amino acids. Any amount of processing destroys some of the vitamins, removes minerals, and alters the chemical structure of fats and proteins. High heat accounts for most of this damage. These accumulated alterations of foods have resulted in widespread nutritional problems. This section will discuss a few of the specific deleterious effects of cooking and processing, and the sections on each individual vitamin will cover the available information on that particular nutrient.

The tryptophan-niacin relationship is an example of the far-reaching effects of any food processing. Though most of the components of protein are stable in heat, one of the essential amino acids is not. This amino acid is tryptophan, and it will be destroyed by heat. A longer period of exposure to heat and higher heat both accelerate this destruction, which renders all of the protein in the cooked food incomplete. Since incomplete protein can only serve as an energy source in the process of metabolism, the required body growth and repair will not occur until sufficient tryptophan appears in the diet to complement the remaining essential amino acids. Individual amino acids, of course, have some specific functions in the body apart from their combined role in tissue formation. Since the body can synthesize the niacin from an adequate supply of tryptophan, a niacin deficient diet that also lacks tryptophan is an invitation to several niacin deficiency symptoms. This is only one of the complex interrelationships found in the study of the individual nutrients.

In addition to this problem with niacin, four other vitamins in the B complex are destroyed or badly depleted by cooking. Thiamin (which is also spelled correctly as 'thiamine') is the most easily destroyed by the heat of cooking. Folacin is from 50% to 90% destroyed in cooking, and high heat will destroy it completely. Pyridoxine is also partly destroyed by cooking and completely destroyed by very high heat. Dry heat, such as that used in baking, will completely destroy pantothenic acid. All of the enzymes are known to be destroyed in heat of only 125° Fahrenheit, also, though the results of this are still unknown.

Cooking any food in water dissolves some of the water soluble vitamins into that water. At least twelve vitamins are affected in this way. If the cooking water is then incorporated into other foods, the vitamins can be salvaged in this way. Since most cooking water is discarded, the loss of vitamins in this manner is considerable.

Most food items that are cooked are first cut up or peeled in some manner. This opens the food item to another vitamin destructive process in the form of oxidation. Vitamin C is especially susceptible to this oxidative destruction. Though this vitamin is inconsequential in the nutrition of most cage birds, it is absolutely vital for the health of the human population. Oxidation will render biotin inactive, and thiamin is also very susceptible to oxidation damage. Vitamin A will be destroyed by oxidation, in addition. Much of this destruction occurs on contact with oxygen in the air. The longer these vitamin compounds are exposed to the air, the greater will be the destruction.

Light, acids, and alkalis are three other destructive influences on some of the vitamins. Riboflavin, for example, is particularly susceptible to destruction caused by exposure to light. Other vitamins are destroyed by exposure to either acid or alkaline solutions. The chart on the next page lists the destructive factors with a partial list of those vitamins affected by each destructive factor. It should be obvious from this that most vitamins are rather unstable compounds and great care must be taken to preserve them in the foods offered to your birds.

Many of the commercially available vitamin-mineral preparations for birds are prepared for mixing with the seed or drinking water. I cannot support either method of supplementation. Supplements in the drinking water are at least 75% wasted in splashing, bathing, and discarding when fouled by the birds. Powdered supplements mixed in the seed are probably at least 90% wasted in birds that shell their seed. For pigeons and the gallinaceous birds that would eat the seeds in their diet whole and unshelled, the waste will be reduced to perhaps 80%. Powdered supplements do not stick to the seed well. Most of the powder will sift down through the seed and will be lost in the bottom of the container.

Only by mixing a supplement completely with a soft food acceptable to the birds can you be assured that all of the birds will get the full benefit of the supplementation. This is the method of supplementation that I have always used for my own birds, and I have found it very effective with a minimum of waste. I estimate my supplement waste at less than 10% in soft food that is removed uneaten, and this is my own fault for giving the birds more food than they will consume during the day. My birds are always given all they will consume of this nutritious food, and for this reason a little excess supply is unavoidable. Nevertheless, this method still translates to an actual rate of consumption by the birds at over 90% of the supplement supplied. No other method of vitamin supplementation can equal this method.

PARTIAL OR TOTAL LOSS OF VITAMINS

DESTRUCTIVE FACTOR	LOSS OF WATER SOLUBLE VITAMINS	LOSS OF FAT SOLUBLE VITAMINS
Wet Heat	ascorbic acid, folacin pyridoxine, thiamine	stable
Dry Heat	ascorbic acid, folacin pantothenic acid, thiamine	E
Oxidation	ascorbic acid, biotin, pyridoxine, thiamine	A, D, E, K & essential fatty acids
Acids	pantothenic acid	K
Alkalis	biotin, cobalamin, pantothenic acid, pyridoxine, riboflavin, thiamin	E & K
Visible Light	folacin, riboflavin	K
Ultraviolet light	pyridoxine, riboflavin	A & E
Storage	ascorbic acid	Stable
Freezing	pyridoxine	Stable
Exposure to Trace minerals	ascorbic acid	A
Rancid Fats	all stable	D, E, K

As important as the vitamins are in nutrition, most act simply as catalysts for the completion of a biological reaction. Only a few are actually incorporated into the structure of the body, primarily the essential fatty acids and choline. Without the minerals, the vitamins are mostly useless. Nevertheless, they are vital to life and to the health of birds maintained in captivity. The specific functions of each vitamin are covered in the sections on each particular vitamin.

Never forget that no nutrient works totally alone in the avian or human body. All work in concert and in cooperation with other vitamins, minerals, and enzymes. A deficiency or total lack of one of these nutrients invariably will mean deficiencies or misappropriations of others. My only regret is that so little information and research specifically on birds is available to pass along to the readers of this volume.

The suspicion that vitamins may perform more esoteric functions than the strictly physical job of a catalyst is strengthened in viewing special photographs of the structure of vitamin crystals. Photographing them with magnification under polarized light reveals an unknown microscopic world. These micro-photographs reveal a pattern of structure and color that surpasses the appearance of any abstract art in beauty and design. The incredible, breathtaking beauty of the photograph of pantothenic acid, in particular, is proof of the unseen worlds that exist around us in the most delicate and perfect of microscopic structure. A number of these photographs of the vitamin crystals were published in *GEO* magazine, volume 2, in the July, 1980, issue.

CHAPTER 7

THE FAT SOLUBLE VITAMINS

VITAMIN A

Back in the year 1912, researchers concluded that a fat soluble substance was necessary for growth. It was named vitamin A. In 1919, the yellow pigments in vegetables were discovered to have the same effects, and by 1928, carotene was identified as a strong precursor of vitamin A. By 1930, the chemical structure of vitamin A had been identified, and the pure vitamin was almost colorless. This vitamin is measured in International Units or United States Pharmacopoeia Units at present. These two measurements are equal in potency. They represent the amount of vitamin A or the precursor that will cause a specific growth response in rats with depleted vitamin A reserves. The recent adoption of a new, different system to measure vitamin A potency is discussed later in this section.

Compounds with vitamin A activity come in several different forms. Vitamin A alcohol is called 'retinol', while vitamin A aldehyde bears the name 'retinal'. Vitamin A acid is known as 'retinoic acid'. Retinol can be oxidized to retinal in a reversible reaction. Retinoic acid is formed from retinal, and it cannot be converted back to that form of vitamin A.

With regard to vitamin A activity, retinal has 90% of the potency of retinol, and retinoic acid has about 60% of the potency of retinol. Retinol is stored in the liver combined with a lipoprotein, but the body cannot store retinoic acid. Preformed vitamin A in these three forms is found only in animal products – none of these forms of vitamin A occur in plant products of any kind.

Fortunately, vitamin A is stable under normal conditions of storage and food preparation. Heat, light, acid, and alkali will not break down the structure of vitamin A. However, it is unstable in the presence of oxygen and will suffer oxidation, especially under hot, humid conditions. Vitamin A also will oxidize in the presence of rancid fat. Also, exposure to ultraviolet light will destroy this vitamin, as will contact with trace minerals.

Research has identified ten vitamin A precursors or provitamins in plant material which are called 'carotenoids'. Carotenes are a part of the larger class of carotenoids, and for the sake of convenience, the simpler term carotene is usually used now to substitute for the names of the vitamin A precursors or provitamins. Any of the animals, humans, and all of the birds which consume these provitamin compounds in the form of the carotene pigments are able to form vitamin A from them.

The presence of the provitamins in fruits and vegetables and their potential vitamin A value is directly proportional to the depth of color of the green and yellow pigments in them. Many of the yellow and orange pigments are the provitamins. For example, lycopene is the carotene pigment found in tomatoes. Green pigment is not a precursor of vitamin A, but the green chlorophyll occurs everywhere with these yellow pigments and masks their yellow color. This accounts for the fact that so many tree leaves turn yellow or orange in the fall, after the chlorophyll has broken down. The leaves that show these colors in the autumn are good sources of the carotene pigments.

The carotenoids in their natural form participate in the production of lipochrome pigments, which give many of the colors to avian feathers. Any serious deficiency in carotenoids will lead to inadequate pigmentation or to color changes in developing feathers.

I need to stress at this point that not all yellow or orange pigments are vitamin A precursors. In animal products such as butter and eggs, for example, the depth of the yellow coloring is never an indication of vitamin A content in any way.

The vitamin A precursors, collectively referred to as carotene, are absorbed through the intestinal wall after digestion frees them from the plant cells. They are converted to one of the vitamin A compounds in the intestinal wall. This conversion is far from complete, however, since only about one-third of the absorbed carotene is converted to vitamin A. Some carotene enters the blood without conversion and is stored in the fat as carotene. In addition, some conversion of the carotene pigments to vitamin A also takes place in the liver and lungs.

Carotene is subject to destruction in the presence of unsaturated fatty acids, but antioxidants, such as vitamin E, will protect the carotene from this form of destruction. Carotene is also destroyed by high heat, such as that used in frying.

Exposure to oxygen, ultraviolet light, and even trace minerals will also destroy vitamin A.

Preformed vitamin A is found only in animal products after the animal has consumed carotene and converted it to vitamin A, or consumed pre-formed vitamin A in other animal food sources, such as insects and worms. Most of the preformed vitamin A in the food supply is combined with palmitic acid, one of the fatty acids, as vitamin A palmitate. During the digestive process, enzymes are able to split the palmitate to form free retinol for intestinal absorption. Any of the many factors which promote fat absorption also promote the absorption of vitamin A. Vitamin A also undergoes many changes in form from the point of absorption until it is finally utilized in the cell.

Unfortunately, mineral oil in the digestive tract will absorb both vitamin A and carotene and will carry them out of the body. Mineral oil should never be given to birds for any reason, particularly internally. Mineral oil is a petroleum by-product, and it is not suitable for nutritional purposes in any way. Should some condition call for an oil when dealing with cage birds, use safflower oil. Safflower oil is available commercially in most food stores. The cold-pressed type is the best type, and safflower oil is the very best nutritional oil available, as safflower oil has the highest percentage of the fatty acid and vitamin linoleic acid of any oil commercially available.

In research with chicks, investigators have noticed a variety of factors that will affect their requirement for vitamin A. Variations in the amount of vitamin A deposited within the egg will affect the later requirements of the hatched chick. Disease, stress, and genetic differences can all increase the requirement for this vitamin. Inadequate protein intake, variations in the potency of any supplement, and destruction in the feed through processing and oxidation will all affect the requirement for vitamin A.

When chicks in testing were fed dietary nitrite of only 0.4%, the result was depressed growth, lowered vitamin A levels, and enlargement of the thyroid gland. Nitrites are salts of nitrous acid, and they are used widely for preserving meats for human consumption.

Problems at the absorption level caused by destruction of vitamin A from disease or other factors, lack of bile salts for absorption, low absorption due to low fat levels in the diet, or damage to the intestinal wall will all affect the vitamin A requirement of chicks, and certainly this will also hold true for any of the birds that we maintain and raise in captivity.

Vitamin A serves a wide variety of functions in the cells of the body, serving numerous metabolic roles. All outer skin cells and mucous membranes depend upon this vitamin for their integrity. The eyes will not function without a constant, adequate supply of vitamin A. Reproduction depends on a sufficient supply of vitamin A, in addition to its use in the mucous membranes of the reproductive organs. This vitamin is also necessary for the stability of the cell membranes. Vitamin A seems to be necessary for the release of some enzymes, including one without which the body is unable to synthesize glycogen. Glycogen is the storage form of carbohydrate, in both the avian and human body. Refer to Chapter 5 for a complete discussion of carbohydrates and the storage of glycogen in the body.

The health and proper functioning of the mucous membranes in birds, animals and humans cannot be maintained without vitamin A. The surface cells, also called the epithelial cells, must have a sufficient supply of vitamin A or they will degenerate and die. This includes all mucous-secreting cells. The degeneration of these cells in a deficiency of vitamin A occurs with a dry layer of hard keratin forming. With this dry degeneration, the cell loses its ability to secrete mucus, and the hairlike cilia on the cell surface are also lost. These cilia are vital in their ability to catch, hold and gradually sweep away the dust, contaminants and microorganisms that are continually being taken into the body. Degeneration of these mucous cells and the loss of their cilia creates an open channel for invasion by harmful microorganisms.

Vitamin A is believed to be necessary for the formation of a carbohydrate found in the mucous. Once the cell ducts are clogged up by keratin, the outer layers of cells pile up, leaving a layer of hard, horny, keratinized cells in place of the normal, round, moist, ciliated mucous cells. This degeneration leaves the cells open to serious bacterial and viral infections that are usually the cause of eventual death in a severe vitamin A deficiency.

If the hardening of the mucous membranes occurs in the reproductive tract, the sperm are unable to travel to the egg after mating occurs, and the result may be a clutch of infertile eggs. Worse, when the hen attempts to lay the egg, she may become eggbound. A deficiency of vitamin A and the essential fatty acids in the diet of the birds is the basic cause of eggbinding. All other factors that have been noted or blamed for eggbinding are secondary. Eggbinding is the direct result of malnutrition, and if it continues to occur among your birds, you must add a food to your diet that the birds will consume regularly that is a rich source of these fat soluble vitamins. There is no substitute for vitamin A or the essential fatty acids in the avian diet. Birds must get these vitamins in their diets in order to remain in the peak of health and condition.

Normal growth depends upon a sufficient supply of vitamin A. Any bird or animal deprived of vitamin A will cease to grow when its stored vitamin A reserves are exhausted. This growth failure will appear before any other symptom of deficiency. Bones will fail to grow, while the nerve tissue, which does not require vitamin A for growth, continues to grow and expand. This will cause pressure on the nerves where they are protected by bones, with severe pain as an obvious result. When vitamin A is restored to the diet, the bone growth is again stimulated. In addition, for reasons that researchers have not yet been able to make clear, a deficiency of this vitamin may cause the formation of defective nervous tissue.

The human body is unable to make effective use of protein unless vitamin A is also present. This discovery was made while researchers were treating severe protein deficiency in the form of kwashiorkor. Protein alone did not aid in recovery, but vitamin A along with a minimal amount of protein enabled the protein to be absorbed and utilized in the body. This interaction of nutrients in nutrition, where one element reinforces and makes a second nutrient more effective, is called synergism.

The several forms of vitamin A within the body are specific in some uses for a specific function or reaction in the body. Retinoic acid, as an example, will perform all of the functions of vitamin A in the body except for vision and reproduction. This vitamin A acid cannot prevent night blindness, eventual complete blindness, nor reproductive failure. Specific requirements of this type have at the same time facilitated and made more difficult the unraveling of the mysteries of vitamin A functioning in the body.

Retinal, the aldehyde form of vitamin A, is the form required for use in the eye. The best understood function of vitamin A in the form of retinal is in the ability of the eye to adapt to darkness. In the retina of the eye, retinal combines with the protein opsin to form the compound called visual purple, or rhodopsin. This visual purple is the photoreceptor pigment in the rod cells of the retina. When light strikes the retina, it bleaches the visual purple to visual yellow, in the process separating the retinal from the opsin. This stimulates the optic nerve. During this process, some of the retinal is changed to retinol, which is reconverted to retinal.

A small amount of retinal is lost in these chemical changes and is replaced from the blood. The vitamin A content of the blood determines the speed of regeneration of the visual purple. This rhodopsin, allowing vision in dim light, regenerates in darkness. Vision in dim light is not possible until this cycle is complete. The speed of this adaptation in sight is directly related to the amount of vitamin A available. Vitamin A is also present in the cones of the retina, but they are not so sensitive to the amount of available vitamin A.

This vitamin plays a vital role in reproduction, also. Either the vitamin A alcohol, retinol, or the aldehyde form, retinal, must be present for normal reproduction. In pregnant female mammals, a deficiency of these will cause the resorption of the fetus. Also, the keratinization of the mucous cells of the reproductive tract is a common result of vitamin A deficiency.

When hens that are fed only retinoic acid begin laying, the rate of egg production, egg size, and all other factors are normal, but the eggs contain no vitamin A. Retinoic acid is not deposited in the egg by the hen's reproductive system. The eggs will be fertile, but after two or three days of incubation, the embryos will always die at the same stage of development from vitamin A deficiency. If the hen's diet is restored by a retinol supplement, hatchability is also restored immediately. Eggs can even be injected with retinol before incubation begins, and they will hatch normally. From this example of the use of vitamin A in avian reproduction, you can see how vitally important a steady supply of vitamin A is to all avian species and especially to those breeding birds in your care in cages and aviaries.

If retinoic acid alone is fed to growing chicks, growth will be normal, but the chicks gradually will become blind. Fortunately, however, this condition is not permanent in birds. Supplementation with retinol restores sight within two days, even after months of blindness.

Research has shown that the vitamin A intake of humans is below recommended levels more than is true for any other nutrient. A deficiency will show up only after the liver's reserves of vitamin A have been completely depleted. In such a deficiency, the skin will become dry and rough, especially on the shoulders, with an accompanying loss of appetite. Night blindness will appear, there will be hardening and opacity of the cornea of the eye, and the tear glands will stop secreting their fluid. Because of the damage to the mucous membranes, a deficiency will make the body highly susceptible to respiratory infections, and there will be adverse changes in both the reproductive tract and the gastrointestinal tract caused by cell keratinization. In juveniles, growth will cease, and the tooth enamel layer on new teeth will not form.

Hard work in hot weather will always raise the body's requirement for vitamin A. Also, in any protein deficiency, utilization of vitamin A will be depressed, since many proteins are involved in the body's utilization of this vitamin. A large number of enzymes that are also composed of protein are needed at many stages of vitamin A metabolism.

A number of deficiency symptoms appear in young chicks and will undoubtedly be very similar in all avian species. If the laying hen has been well supplied with vitamin A, a considerable amount is carried through her egg to the embryo, and the newly hatched chick can grow and develop normally for several weeks on this stored supply. Once any stored reserve is exhausted, however, growth will cease, and the chicks will appear drowsy, weak, uncoordinated, and emaciated. Ruffled feathers and anorexia or loss of appetite will also be evident in the chicks. If the deficiency is severe, there will be severe ataxia, or loss of muscular coordination, similar to that which occurs in severe vitamin E deficiency. The beaks, shanks, combs, and wattles of the chicks will also be very pale in color.

Adult chickens and other birds will exhibit much the same symptoms from vitamin A deficiency with a decrease in egg production, longer length of time between clutches, and reduced hatchability. They will also have a watery discharge from the eyes and nostrils, and the eyelids will stick together. The eyes fill with a white material and a severe deficiency eventually will destroy the eye. Vitamin A deficiency is also the major nutritional factor causing blood spots in eggs.

Time and again, you will read and hear of the dangers of an excessive intake of vitamin A. As far as I am concerned, this is a paranoia of fools. Though an excess intake of vitamin A to the point of toxicity is possible, it is rare in the extreme. It is impossible to get an excess of vitamin A on any normal, natural diet. Only in the naturally occurring vitamin A content of salt water fish liver and sea mammal liver is the vitamin A content sufficient to cause toxicity symptoms. Beef liver is a very rich source of this vitamin, and it will contain about 45,000 International Units in 100 grams, a small, average serving of about 3.5 ounces. Polar Bear liver, by contrast, is a notoriously rich source of vitamin A. An average serving of 100 grams contains 2,000,000 International Units of vitamin A, enough to cause serious toxicity symptoms. Nevertheless, even in any excess intake of vitamin A, recovery from all symptoms is rapid and complete as soon as the excess intake is stopped. You may feel certain that for every one person getting an excess of vitamin A in the world today, there are at least 10 million others with a very serious deficiency of this vitamin.

The commonest form of hypervitaminosis A, as a toxic excess of vitamin A is called, is in infants. Well-meaning mothers have been known to give their children a teaspoon of concentrated, synthetic vitamin A daily, when only one drop is recommended. The effect is cumulative, and over a period of months this will cause a variety of toxicity symptoms. Even so, it takes from six to fifteen months for such an excess to manifest itself as toxicity symptoms. Such symptoms may include nausea, diarrhea, scaly skin, weight loss, and skeletal pain. Toxic reactions can only be caused by the preformed vitamin A, and are never caused by the carotene.

An excess of vitamin A can be excreted both through the kidneys and the intestinal tract. When the consumption is above the body's ability to excrete the excess, toxicity symptoms will appear. In chicks this will take the form of weight loss, decreased food consumption, and sores around the mouth, nearby skin, and on the feet. The strength of the bones will be greatly decreased and bone abnormalities will become evident. The eyelids will be swollen and crusted to the point of being sealed. Death will result if the excess continues. Such ill effects will occur only under conditions of deliberate overdose under experimental conditions, certainly not on any normal avian diet.

The richest sources of preformed vitamin A are liver, the fish liver oils, and to a much lesser extent egg yolks. Eggs are the only animal source of vitamin A that are likely to be a part of the cage bird diet that is offered by the average aviculturist. Cod liver oil is an excellent source of vitamin A, but because of its tendency to become rancid, I do not recommend its use unless immediate consumption by the birds can be assured. Cod liver oil contains about 4,000 International Units of vitamin A per gram, but is a relatively poor source when compared with other processed fish and mammal liver oils. Tuna liver oil contains about 150,000 International Units per gram, while whale liver oil has an astonishing 400,000 International Units per gram.

Fruits and vegetables will contain no preformed vitamin A, only the precursors as the yellow and orange pigments, which are collectively called carotene. Carrots and dark green vegetables are good sources. Spinach is an especially good source of carotene, as is kale to a lesser extent. Some fruits will increase their carotene content with storage, and mangoes are a notable example of this characteristic.

A new system of measuring vitamin A potency has been adopted and will gradually replace the old designations of vitamin A in International Units. Now retinol equivalents, which are expressed in micrograms, are used to measure vitamin A activity. Dietary retinol is considered to be 100% utilized. Beta-carotene, the most active of the carotenoid precursors of vitamin A, yields about one-sixth the utilizable vitamin A activity of retinol. Therefore, one microgram of beta-carotene is equivalent to 0.167 micrograms of retinol.

The other provitamins are considered to yield only one-twelfth the activity per unit that retinol yields. When the provitamins are the source of vitamin A, the retinol equivalents may contain a sizable error factor. You may expect to see this new system of vitamin A measurement in common use much more widely in future years, and this new terminology eventually will completely replace the old International Unit measurement system.

In conclusion, adequate vitamin A should be on the mind of the bird breeder constantly. Fruits, vegetables and greens are appreciable sources of the provitamin for avian nutrition, but egg yolks will be the best for the preformed vitamin. Yellow corn fed raw, another good source of provitamin A, is relished by many birds, but white corn contains virtually no provitamin A. Even the best all vegetarian cage bird diet could benefit from vitamin A supplementation. As previously stated, a deficiency of vitamin A is probable in most common cage bird diets, and it is the second most likely deficiency to be noted. Only protein deficiency is more common. An excess in normal cage bird feeding is a virtual impossibility, while a deficiency is a probability. Unless you habitually feed your birds polar bear liver or whale liver oil, you can completely discount the possibility of vitamin A toxicity from any natural food. Use synthetic vitamin A with caution, of course, since most recorded cases of vitamin A toxicity were caused by overdose with the synthetic compound. Vitamin A is the second most likely deficiency to occur in birds maintained in captivity. Only the dietary deficiency of complete protein is more likely in the maintenance and breeding of birds in captivity.

VITAMIN D

It is fortunate for all of the birds and animals maintained in captivity that our knowledge of vitamin D in nutrition has progressed so far since its initial presumed existence in 1918. In that year, a British nutritionist by the name of Edward Mellanby (1884-1955) presented the first evidence for a fat soluble factor that would prevent and cure rickets. The relationship that is now accepted between sunshine and what we now call the sunshine vitamin, however, was not established until the late 1920's, and vitamin D was not isolated in its pure crystalline form until 1930. Other names given to this vitamin in the past have been the antirachitic factor and the rickets preventative.

There are a number of chemically distinct forms of vitamin D. The two primary forms are known in common terms as vitamin D_2 and vitamin D_3. The compound scientifically known as ergocalciferol comes from vegetable sources, and it is known as vitamin D_2. Ergocalciferol is also known by the name 'viosterol' in some writings. Cholecalciferol is more commonly called vitamin D_3, and this form of vitamin D comes only from animal sources.

Vitamin D is a necessary nutrient for all living creatures with a bony skeleton. This nutrient traditionally has been measured in terms of International Units, and one milligram contains 40,000 International Units. The designation of potency in vitamin D has changed recently, however. Future nutritional sources will list the intake of vitamin D as micrograms of cholecalciferol rather than as International Units.

I will stress several times in the subsequent discussion that only vitamin D_3 is biologically active in birds. Vitamin D_2 is useful and effective for most mammals, but is not a useful nutrient for birds. Birds must have vitamin D_3 to satisfy their biological requirement for this vitamin.

95

The deficiency disease caused by a severe vitamin D deficiency in humans is known as rickets. Similar symptoms occur in animals and birds and will be covered in detail later. Until the 1920's, rickets was an epidemic disease in England, particularly in the crowded industrial areas. In some areas as many as 80% of the children were suffering from rickets. This is a disease in which the bones are defectively formed due to the inadequate deposits of calcium and phosphorus in the bones. Bones in infants consequently remain soft and pliable and fail to harden normally.

When weight is placed on these bones, as when a child begins crawling and walking, the bones bend under the weight that they are structurally not able to support. When walking begins before the bones harden, bowed legs are the result. Also, the ends of the bones become enlarged as they flatten with the weight put on the poorly calcified ends. This causes such deformities as knock-knees. Rib deformity and beading can also result in a concave chest, which causes severe crowding of the chest cavity and its organs. In babies there is rapid enlargement of the head as the fontanels or soft spots fail to close. Growth is retarded, and teeth erupt late which are poorly formed and decay easily. These unfortunate symptoms of rickets are slowly reversible on a diet with adequate vitamin D intake.

Vitamin D is a fat soluble substance in the diet. If fat absorption is poor, the amount of vitamin D absorbed will also be poor. This vitamin is absorbed only in the presence of bile, and absorption seems to be complete for both major types of vitamin D in the human body. As vitamin D in the diet increases, magnesium absorption will also increase. Absorption in birds takes place primarily in the duodenum, the first section of the small intestine, and is facilitated by the presence of fat and bile salts.

Vitamin D can be formed by irradiation of precursors, or provitamins, with short wave ultraviolet light. The short wave ultraviolet light changes the molecular structure enough to form active vitamin D. This is possible either in natural sunlight or under intense artificial ultraviolet light. Ergocalciferol, the plant form of vitamin D, is formed by irradiation of the provitamin called ergosterol. The irradiation of 7-dehydrocholesterol, which is found only in animal tissues, forms cholecalciferol or vitamin D_3, the only form of the vitamin of value for the nutrition of birds. The discovery that the use of ultraviolet irradiation on chicks or the improvement of their diet will both prevent and cure rickets dates back to 1923.

The formation of vitamin D in the form of cholecalciferol on the skin is the same in birds, animals and humans. This vitamin D_3 precursor, or provitamin, 7-dehydrocholesterol, is synthesized within the body and travels to the skin surface via the hair or feather follicles or via the roots of the scales. When exposed to the short wave ultraviolet rays of the sun, this compound is converted into cholecalciferol, vitamin D_3, on the outer layers of the skin. The skin then resorbs the modified compound into the circulatory system for use within the body. This resorption takes some time, and a shower or bath immediately after a sun bath will wash away most of the newly formed vitamin D_3 before it can be absorbed.

Many types of artificial lights also emit ultraviolet rays, but few of them have the intensity that is necessary for the synthesis of vitamin D_3 on the skin. The presence of short wavelength ultraviolet rays alone is not enough; the intensity of the rays is also crucial. Natural sunlight, of course, has the intensity necessary. A sunlamp also has the necessary intensity, and exposing the birds to a sunlamp for less than an hour each day will allow the skin synthesis of enough vitamin D_3 to keep the birds in perfect health. However, the full spectrum lights do not emit the intensity necessary for the formation of vitamin D_3 on the skin. Even the commercial black lights, which emit a very high percentage of light in the ultraviolet range of the spectrum, do not have the intensity required for vitamin D_3 synthesis.

This sunlight-formed vitamin D_3 is of vital importance to birds and animals in captivity, since vitamin D occurs so irregularly in their diets. The skin of the legs and feet of a chicken will contain about eight times as much provitamin D as does the body skin, to assure the maximum possible skin synthesis of vitamin D_3. Contrary to older beliefs, the preen gland does not contain any appreciable amount of provitamin D that will be deposited on the feathers. From eleven to 45 minutes in the sun for a chick is sufficient to prevent rickets, and no further supplementation will aid growth. Research has shown that this sunlight irradiated 7-dehydrocholesterol is twice as active metabolically as the mixed vitamin D that is found in cod liver oil.

All authorities state that excess irradiation will form compounds that are toxic or antagonistic to vitamin D_3. I have been unable to discover exactly what constitutes 'over-irradiation' or excess irradiation, but presumably this is not a problem related to natural irradiation from sunlight.

This skin synthesis of vitamin D_3 is subject to a number of problems, primarily concerning the ability of ultraviolet light to reach the skin. The British problem with rickets, also common in the United States and other countries in the temperate zones, resulted from the lack of winter sunlight in the higher latitudes and more severe weather conditions throughout the year. Ultraviolet rays cannot penetrate fog, clouds, smog, smoke, window glass, window screening, clothing, or skin pigment. The presence of any of these factors reduces or eliminates completely the vitamin D available through irradiation. Children living in the deep mountain valleys of Switzerland in the Swiss Alps frequently showed symptoms of rickets, while the children in the higher elevations that received sunlight were immune.

Nature created darkly pigmented skin for human beings native to the tropics to cut down on the damaging ultraviolet light that reaches the skin. When this dark skin is moved to a northern temperate climate zone, the possibility of skin formation of vitamin D_3 by irradiation is drastically reduced. Black people are consequently far more likely to suffer from a vitamin D deficiency than are light-skinned people.

The intestinal absorption rate of calcium is greatly increased by adequate vitamin D in the dietary intake. Vitamin D is carried in the body attached to a blood protein. In some way it seems to cause an elevation in the calcium and phosphorus levels of the blood to a supersaturated point at which calcification will occur. The blood carries vitamin D to the liver, where it is converted into an active metabolic form. This must occur before it can induce the synthesis of the calcium-binding protein which is necessary for the intestinal absorption of calcium. Though both forms of vitamin D will perform this function in mammals, in birds only vitamin D_3 will act as the precursor of this essential hormone which promotes calcium absorption, bone formation, and eggshell formation in chickens and other birds. The fact that injected calcium was built into the bone tissue even in severe vitamin D deficiency proved conclusively that the usage of vitamin D in the body took place at a different location. This was proven later to be in the absorptive process, and research has proven that vitamin D is not involved in the actual transport of calcium.

Calcium uptake in the cells causes an increase in an enzyme that leads to release of phosphate into the bloodstream at the same time. Both calcium and phosphorus are then available simultaneously for bone and eggshell formation. The failure of bone calcification is more often caused by a lack of phosphate than by a lack of calcium. Vitamin D increases the rate of phosphate absorption and stimulates phosphate resorption from the kidneys. If this did not occur, all phosphorus would be lost in the urine.

The vitamin D requirement in birds depends on several factors: the sources of phosphorus in the diet, the amount of calcium in the diet, the ratio of calcium to phosphorus, and the extent of exposure to direct sunlight. The optimal dietary ratio for calcium and phosphorus has been proven to be two parts of calcium to one part of phosphorus. If these limits are any broader or narrower, the avian body's requirement for vitamin D will increase.

Vitamin D_3 is needed for normal egg production, the calcification of the eggshells, and hatchability. At one point in my early breeding efforts, after reading of the beneficial effects of vitamin D for calcium use in eggshell formation and in the avian body, I began supplementing my birds' diet with additional vitamin D in the form of a powder added to their egg mix daily. The result was nothing short of astounding. In a birdroom with about 80 pairs of finches, the next clutches laid increased in size by an average of 50%. In other words, the birds that had laid four eggs in each clutch began laying six; those laying five eggs per clutch had new clutches of seven or eight eggs, and those already laying six or seven eggs per clutch began laying 10 eggs in their next clutches. The additional vitamin D in the diet had made the hens' absorption and utilization of calcium so much easier that the size of each hen's clutch had increased dramatically.

A pair of Diamond Doves I had purchased at around the same time also showed the rapid effectiveness of adequate nutrition and the benefits of vitamin D_3 supplementation. Their condition when purchased indicated that they had been poorly nourished, but as soon as they settled down, and before they began eating the egg mix and crumbles that I supplied daily in the birds' diet, this pair went to nest, and the hen laid her clutch of two eggs. Both of these eggs were soft-shelled, indicating a very serious deficiency of vitamin D_3 in their diet. From the day I received them, the pair of doves had cleaned up about a half teaspoon of crushed eggshells each day, a huge amount of calcium for two birds this small, yet the hen had been able to absorb none of it. In order to get these doves to begin eating the good nutritional items that were in front of them and would prevent these problems, I removed all seed from the pair until I observed both of these Diamond Doves eating both the crumbles and the egg mix. A week later, the hen laid again, and this time both of her eggs were perfectly formed.

Any deficiency of vitamin D_3 in growing chicks will produce symptoms of rickets. Growth will be retarded with severe weakness in the legs. The beaks and claws will become soft and pliable. The chicks will take a few unsteady steps and squat to rest, swaying slightly as if they lacked complete equilibrium and sense of balance. Feathering will also be poor, and there will be abnormal blackening of the feathers in the breeds of chickens with colored feathers. Experimentation has proven that in any continuous and chronic deficiency, there will be a variety of skeletal disorders in growing chicks, including a downward curving spine and beading of the ribs.

Symptoms of vitamin D_3 deficiency will begin to appear from one to two months after the beginning of a deficient diet. First, there will be an increase in the number of thin shelled and soft-shelled eggs. Soon after that symptom, egg production will decrease and there will be a very noticeable reduction in hatchability. Hens may experience the loss of the use of their legs until an egg is laid, which will usually be soft-shelled. Then, leg use will return to normal. Hens will sit in a characteristic squat, resembling the posture of a penguin, and their beaks, claws, and bones will become soft and pliable.

Vitamin D is stored only in limited amounts, primarily in the liver. Though aquatic salt water species store sizable amounts of vitamin D in the liver, birds and other land animals do not. Though all liver is a good source of vitamin D, the liver of sea fish abounds in this vitamin. The richness of cod liver oil is well known, as it has about 10,000 International Units of vitamin D per 100 grams of cod liver oil. Comparatively, however, this is a relatively poor source, since swordfish liver oil may have one million International Units of cholecalciferol per 100 grams, and bluefin tuna liver oil can have as much as four million International Units of vitamin D_3 per 100 grams.

Fortunately, vitamin D is very stable to most nutritionally destructive forces. It is not destroyed by oxidation, as is vitamin A, though it will be destroyed by the formation of peroxides in the presence of rancidifying fats. Vitamin E, acting as a natural antioxidant, will prevent the destruction of cholecalciferol from oxidative reactions. In the body's metabolism, there is a definite antagonistic relationship between vitamin D and hydrocortisone, a hormone secreted by the adrenal glands.

A substantial percentage of the vitamin D content of chicken feeds is lost during storage. In general, in mixed poultry feeds, losses may range from zero to 50% in six months of storage. This destruction of vitamin D is accelerated in the presence of rancid fats.

A dietary intake of about 400 International Units per day is presumed to be an adequate intake for human beings, subject to the balance of calcium and phosphorus affecting that requirement, as already mentioned. Five times this amount is enough to cause retarded growth. At this rate of 2000 International Units per day, other toxicity symptoms may appear. Vitamin A will protect against any symptoms of toxicity even with this high intake, however.

An excess of vitamin D is technically called hypervitaminosis D. This condition will cause the resorption of calcium and other salts from the bones and abnormal deposits of calcium in the soft tissues of the body. Very high levels of intake in chicks will cause kidney damage due to the calcification of the kidney tubules. The symptoms of a gross intake of vitamin D with resulting vitamin D poisoning are nausea, loss of appetite, vomiting, cramps, diarrhea, and tingling in the fingers and toes. In comparing animals for sensitivity to large doses of vitamin D, cats seemed to be the most sensitive, and chickens the least sensitive. Dogs are intermediate.

Vitamin D intake in cage bird nutrition must be in the constant attention of the aviculturist. Since birds cannot utilize ergocalciferol from plant sources, only the cholecalciferol, vitamin D_3, synthesized on the skin or obtained from animal foods in the diet, will supply the need for this vitamin in the feeding and maintenance of your birds. If birds are maintained indoors exclusively, the first source of cholecalciferol will be lost completely. The needed ultraviolet light will not be present in normal incandescent or fluorescent bulbs, nor will it pass through window glass or screens. In this case, all vitamin D_3 must come from dietary sources.

Of the animal derived dietary sources, only eggs are commonly fed to cage birds. Presumably, insects would be a good source of vitamin D_3, but I can find no written confirmation of this as yet. Dairy products will contain vitamin D, but this is predominantly as ergocalciferol and of little value to the birds, apart from the problems with lactose content you are likely to encounter in feeding dairy products to your birds. Liver is always a good source, but is certainly not a common item in cage bird nutrition.

Cod liver oil mixed in the diet is favored by some, but it will turn rancid so rapidly with exposure to air that I do not recommend the use of cod liver oil in avian feeding unless immediate consumption can be assured. Nevertheless, if this oil can be provided in a readily consumed form, it is probably the best source of vitamin D_3 in an easily available form. If no alternative is available, I would recommend mixing cod liver oil in an item that will be consumed within fifteen minutes. Because of the danger of rancidity, I would not trust cod liver oil over a much longer period.

The only logical solution to the problem of vitamin D_3 deficiency is dietary supplementation with this vitamin, preferably as a dry, powdered addition to an already accepted soft food. Supplementation in this manner assures that the vitamin will be consumed and that waste will be held to a minimum. It also assures that no deficiency will develop and that rancidity or spoilage will not create a problem. Judging by my nutritional study and knowledge of cage birds and their feeding, a dietary deficiency of vitamin D_3 is the third most likely common deficiency that will be encountered in the maintenance and breeding of cage birds. Only protein deficiency and vitamin A deficiency are more likely.

VITAMIN E

Vitamin E was discovered as a fat soluble factor necessary for health by Herbert McLean Evans (1882-1971) and his co-workers in the year 1922. This vitamin was not isolated and identified until 1936 as a result of further research by Evans and his colleagues. The technical name for vitamin E and its close chemical relatives is 'tocopherols'. There are seven natural tocopherols which occur together, named after the first seven letters of the Greek alphabet: alpha, beta, gamma, delta, epsilon, zeta, and eta (α, β, γ, δ, ε, ζ, and η). The one which is by far the most biologically active is named alpha-tocopherol, and it alone receives the common designation vitamin E.

There is still wide disagreement over the activity of the other six related tocopherols, but all researchers agree that if they have any biological activity at all, it is minor in comparison to d-alpha-tocopherol, the nutritional necessity that we call vitamin E. Some researchers claim no activity at all for the remaining six tocopherols. Though these other tocopherols occurring in nature have no officially recognized equivalency to d-alpha-tocopherol, research has indicated that the relative potencies seem to be about 40% of the potency of alpha-tocopherol for beta-tocopherol, 10% for gamma-tocopherol, and only 1% for delta-tocopherol. The usage of the mixed tocopherols in early vitamin E testing would account for the early research failures in vitamin E supplementation.

Vitamin E has been synthesized since the late 1930's, but again there is wide disagreement as to the efficacy of the artificially produced vitamin. All researchers agree that the biological activity of the synthetic form is less, but how much less is in heated argument. Some authorities claim that the synthetic vitamin, called dl-alpha-tocopherol, has only one-fifth of the biological activity of the natural form. The 'l' after the 'd' in the name must be used to signify the synthetic form of this vitamin, and any vitamin E preparation will clearly state this difference, if you can understand the label.

Since vitamin E is a very unstable compound, it is customarily put into acetate form to improve its stability for storage and use. Fortunately, vitamin E is stable to acids and to heat, so cooking losses are minimal. Nevertheless, it is destroyed on exposure to oxygen, ultraviolet light, alkalis, chlorine, iron salts, and lead salts.

The measurement of the natural and synthetic forms of vitamin E is different. The natural form has been measured in International Units, while the synthetic form was measured in milligrams. One International Unit of d-alpha tocopherol equals one milligram of dl-alpha-tocopherol activity.

The future designation of measurement for d-alpha-tocopherol, the natural form of vitamin E, is still in doubt. Any designation of vitamin E activity in the near future likely will be stated in milligrams relative to the natural d-alpha-tocopherol. Farther in the future, you may see the biochemical designation RRR-alpha-tocopherol replace the term d-alpha-tocopherol for the natural vitamin, and the term all-rac-alpha-tocopherol replace the dl-alpha-tocopherol designation for the synthetic vitamin. These new terms have been adopted in biochemistry to more closely describe these substances, but they are not yet in general use in the labeling of vitamin E supplements.

Though vitamin E is found in small quantities in a wide variety of foods, any processing destroys part of it. As much as 86% of the vitamin E in whole wheat is removed in refining it to white flour. There are no truly rich natural sources of this nutrient. The most reliable sources are whole cereal grains, eggs, seeds, nuts, and deep green leafy vegetables. For herbivores, alfalfa is the most reliable source. Most of the vitamin E available for human or animal diet supplementation is distilled from oils that are to be used in the manufacture of paints and other chemical compounds. One ton of vegetable oil must be refined to produce only one cup of natural vitamin E, d-alpha-tocopherol. Because of the large amount of processing that is necessary, vitamin E is usually the most expensive vitamin supplement available. Since this is one of the fat soluble vitamins, it can be stored in the body for use in times of scarcity in the diet.

Vegetable oils have a respectable quantity of vitamin E, with the cold pressed oils considered richer than the oils extracted under heat. Normal wet cooking, such as boiling, will not destroy the vitamin E content in the cooked foods, fortunately, but dry heat is a vitamin E disaster. Though any exposure to air slowly destroys vitamin E, baking will destroy as much as 47% of the food content of this nutrient.

The needs of various species for vitamin E vary a great deal, as might be expected. Human needs are considerably larger than those of the mammals, as evidenced by the content of human milk. Human milk has over twice the vitamin E content of cow's milk. Significantly, in both cows and humans, the colostrum, milk produced by the mammary glands for the first few days after birth of the young, is ten time richer in vitamin E than is the milk produced later.

Surprisingly, no one has ever succeeded in producing a dietary deficiency of vitamin E in goats. Apparently the goat's body is easily able to synthesize all that is needed by the animal.

Digestion can be a major block to the body's utilization of vitamin E. Vitamin E is not well absorbed in the best of conditions. The best estimates indicate that less than half of the d-alpha-tocopherol ingested is absorbed. In the digestive tract it protects vitamins A and C from oxidation. In any problem with fat digestion, vitamin E and all of the other fat soluble vitamins are not freed for absorption. As an unfortunate result of any problem in fat digestion, these vitamins are then excreted along with the undigested fats.

A number of critical functions have been discovered for vitamin E over the years since its discovery. The acceptance of these functions by all authorities has been a long, slow process and is still not complete. It was only in 1959 that the Food and Drug Administration even admitted and stated that vitamin E is a necessary, vital nutrient. As was stated in the foreword, about fifty years are required for any new nutritional discovery to become finally accepted. Though this is a tragedy of unimaginable proportions, it is simply human nature in one of its less than spiritual manifestations.

It is most unfortunate that the first discovery of vitamin E function was in relation to sex and reproduction. This immediately got it labeled as a quack panacea in the eyes of numerous people who insist on equating sex with sin, and in the process did serious damage to further research on this vitamin and its metabolic functions. I can have only the greatest of pity for such puritanical ignorance. Fortunately, thorough research and sane examination of the effects of vitamin E have finally succeeded in overcoming this ingrained prejudice and in getting across the true value of this nutrient to most reasonable people.

The primary function of vitamin E is as an antioxidant and an oxygen conservator. The tocopherols are the main antioxidants present in all natural fats and oils. In this function, they prevent rancidity. Vitamin E, in particular, of all the tocopherols, unites with oxygen to prevent rancidity in fats. Through this function, it is able to improve the cell's functioning and prolong its life. Lest this be lost in passing, prolonging the life of the cells also means prolonging the life of the total organism. Vitamin E maintains the normal permeability of the cell membranes. Too little permeability causes interference with the cell's ability to feed itself. Too much permeability causes the cell to literally ooze its contents.

The oxygen conserving function of vitamin E has vast ramifications and effects throughout the body, since oxygen is used by every cell of the body in its metabolism. Muscle health is an especially important effect of vitamin E action. Since this vitamin conserves oxygen, this nutrient lowers the body's total need for oxygen. The result is a vast increase in muscular stamina and endurance. Rats in experimentation can swim twice as long before exhaustion occurs when they are under vitamin E supplementation, and their tolerance for high altitude oxygen deficiencies leaves them healthy and active when control specimens with no supplementation have died of oxygen deficiency. This information is obviously of greatest importance to athletes in the human realm.

Apparently this oxygen conserving function and prevention of destruction of fats by rancidity are the basis for vitamin E's action in healing. All wounds heal better and faster with ingested vitamin E and with its direct application to injured areas. It has proven itself a miraculous healing agent in the case of severe burns and scarring, but only if adequate nutrition has also supplied the remaining necessary nutrients for rebuilding the damaged tissues. A liberal application of vitamin E to an injured or burned area on the body twice a day, combined with additional internal supplementation, has on numerous reported occasions prevented the formation of scars even in the most severe burns and lacerations.

Even in black people, who have a tendency to form massive keloids, or scar tissue, vitamin E will completely prevent the formation of scar tissue in cases of severe burns or other injury. It seems quite likely that the members of our black population have a higher vitamin E requirement than either the Caucasians or Orientals.

Interior body scar tissue can be more disastrous than the cosmetic exterior scars. Research has proven that even in cirrhosis of the liver, massive internal scar tissue can be replaced with normal liver tissue with adequate nutrition and a high vitamin E intake. Even a goiter will not heal after iodine supplementation without adequate vitamin E to reduce and eliminate the goitrous internal scar tissue. Even long standing scars can be dissolved away and replaced by normal tissue with vitamin E application.

In my personal experience, I can give adequate nutrition and heavy vitamin E supplementation (1000 International Units daily) much of the credit for the healing of my left eye and the prevention of any serious scar tissue. In a serious carpentry accident in 1978, I had a 16-penny nail hit directly in the center of my left eye with devastating force. The cornea was lacerated completely across, the iris injured to the point where it will no longer contract, and the lens destroyed by the formation of an immediate trauma-caused cataract. An operation within six hours of the accident corrected all of the serious physical damage that it was possible to correct, including removal of the cataract. A long period of healing was required, obviously. My ophthalmologist, Dr. Joseph C. Yarbrough, Jr., of Anderson, South Carolina, remarked to me after the healing was substantially complete, "When you first came into my office, I wouldn't have given you a nickel's chance of ever again having any usable sight in that eye."

The final result? The cornea healed with no obvious scar. With a tinted contact lens to compensate for the loss of iris function and lens focus, the eye tests at 20/20 vision. Though a slight scar on the cornea is visible under magnification, it is not visible nor distorting in my field of vision in any way. Certainly, I owe a great deal to a very highly competent opthalmologist, Dr. Joseph C. Yarbrough, Jr. Secondly, I owe a great debt of thanks to the Almighty

Creative Forces that we call God and for the many prayers that aided my healing. But last, I owe this physical healing and once again perfect vision to superior nutrition and in particular to heavy vitamin E supplementation during the healing process.

Another major function of vitamin E is in its function as an anticoagulant which prevents untimely clotting of the blood. This is accomplished without the accompanying danger of hemorrhaging. Also, vitamin E seems to have some tendency to dissolve existing clots in the blood. Any deficiency of vitamin E will make the red blood cells abnormally susceptible to oxidation damage.

Without a doubt, vitamin E has achieved its greatest reputation in the treatment of circulatory diseases. All types of circulatory problems from atherosclerosis to phlebitis, varicose veins, and angina pectoris are aided immeasurably by regular vitamin E supplementation in adequate amounts. Research has proven conclusively that vitamin E supplementation in adequate amounts will completely cure angina pectoris.

As hens age, they tend to develop atherosclerosis like that of humans. This can be prevented or halted by the combination of vitamins A and E added to the diet, though either vitamin used alone is relatively ineffective. This is but a further illustration of the interaction of the nutrients used in the physical body.

Much of the older research on the effects of vitamin E was done with a lack of knowledge concerning the characteristics of vitamin E, and as a result, no value and no health improvements were shown. However, later research has indicated that the body has a physiological 'dam' that keeps lower amounts of vitamin E confined or inactive. A higher amount is necessary to break down or spill over this physiological dam and perform the resulting physical health improvements. Whereas 400 International Units of vitamin E supplementation may be virtually ineffective, 2400 units can give the greatest of benefits in the body. Since no toxicity has ever been observed for vitamin E, even with the supplementation of 3000 International Units daily over periods of years, no one need fear any ill effects from any excess over the body's true needs.

There is one major caution to observe, however. Supplementation for any individual with high blood pressure should begin at low levels under a doctor's guidance. The amount can be increased each week slowly, up to the optimal amount. An immediate, heavy, supplementary intake of this vitamin can further elevate blood pressure enough to cause a heart attack.

There are several other functions of vitamin E in the body that have been identified and proven. The body cannot utilize several of the amino acids without the presence of vitamin E. Also, vitamin E has been proven to prevent radiation damage to vitamin A and the fatty acids. Researchers also feel that vitamin E works closely with the vitamins of the B complex. Phospholipids seem to have a special affinity for vitamin E, and it prevents the formation of free radicals in the lipid cell membranes. In birds it is possible that vitamin E is involved in ascorbic acid synthesis, though this is not yet proven.

Vitamin E is essential to the production of the pituitary, adrenal, and sex hormones. In addition, this vitamin prevents these circulating hormones from being destroyed by oxidation as they circulate in the bloodstream. Vitamin E is more concentrated in the pituitary gland than in any other portion of the body.

Vitamin E is destroyed or rendered ineffective by a variety of common antagonists. Inorganic iron of the type found in iron rich water will destroy it, and inorganic chlorine, such as that used in water purification, will also destroy vitamin E on contact. Estrogen, the female hormone, will also destroy vitamin E, so those women taking 'The Pill' should exercise care that the two substances are not consumed together. Rancid fats in the diet will inactivate vitamin E, and finally, mineral oil dissolves this vitamin and does not readily release it.

Deficiencies of vitamin E cause a variety of problems in birds and animals. Several named diseases in a variety of animals are the direct result of vitamin E deficiency. Mink will die of 'yellow fat disease'. Lambs will succumb shortly after birth to 'stiff lamb disease'. Because of the likelihood of deficiency, vitamin E supplements are now added to the prepared feeds for chickens and turkeys.

Several different diseases in chickens have been thoroughly studied as symptoms of vitamin E deficiency. Before such diseases fully develop, hens' eggs will exhibit low hatchability, with embryos dying in the shell from the fourth day of incubation on, though egg production will not be affected. There will be a high mortality rate in any chicks that do hatch. Growing chicks will show a severe myopathy, or muscular disease, especially of the breast muscle at about four weeks of age, if the sulfur-containing amino acids are deficient along with vitamin E. In poults there will be sores and injuries in the muscle walls of the gizzard. In all species that have been tested, vitamin E deficiency results in lipid degeneration.

Nutritional muscular dystrophy is one specific disease that is caused by severe vitamin E deficiency. This involves degeneration of the skeletal muscles in chickens and other animals. Both selenium and vitamin E are intimately involved with the metabolism of the amino acid cysteine in the prevention of nutritional muscular dystrophy. In tests with guinea pigs, the damage to their muscles from muscular dystrophy is far greater when their diets are also lacking vitamin C. Guinea pigs are a true blessing to humanity, for they are the only mammal other than monkeys and one species of fruit-eating bat yet discovered that is incapable of synthesizing its own vitamin C. Consequently, it is forced to get this nutrient in its diet and serves as an excellent subject for the nutritional testing of vitamin C.

Nutritional encephalomalacia is a second named disease caused by vitamin E deficiency in chickens. In this disease an infected chick is characterized by sudden prostration with legs outstretched, spastic actions, and flexed toes. The head is retracted and often twisted sideways. Another name for this malady is 'crazy chick disease'. Encephalomalacia is a loss of muscular coordination resulting from hemorrhages and fluid accumulation within the cerebellum of the brain. The head may also curl under the breast. An autopsy will show lesions or injuries in the cerebellum and also sometimes in the cerebrum of the brain. This deficiency disease can also be characterized by fluid accumulation under the skin and in the heart and pericardium, the membrane enclosing the heart.

Exudative diathesis is a third named vitamin E deficiency disease that has been noted in chickens. It is an accumulation of fluid in all of the tissues caused by an abnormal increase in the permeability of the blood capillaries. Selenium, as well as vitamin E, is effective in treating this disease. Oral administration of 300 International Units of vitamin E per chick causes the total remission of this exudative diathesis in the chicks and maintains them for about one week in normal condition.

In pregnant rats, vitamin E deficiency interferes with placenta function and causes the death and dissolution of the fetuses. A deficiency in growing rats causes slackened growth with weight stabilizing or declining. Paralysis with dragging of the hindquarters is a symptom of severe deficiency in rats and other mammals.

Vitamin E deficiency in males can be more serious than in females. After 75 to 100 days of deficiency, male rats will become sterile, and this damage is permanent. Testicle degeneration will occur in all male animals as a result of severe vitamin E deficiency, with the same permanent damage to the male's fertility. This could very well be a cause for the frequent reports of infertile pairs of birds in aviculture. The vitamin E deficiency damage resulting in degeneration of the male sex glands is permanent and irreversible where fertility is concerned.

Vitamin E and selenium seem to be interdependent in all of their body functions. Vitamin E will reduce the selenium needs and requirements in at least two known ways. First, it maintains body selenium in an active form and prevents its loss from the body. Vitamin E also prevents the destruction of lipids within the cell membrane. This consequently reduces the amount of glutathione peroxidase, a selenium-containing enzyme, that is needed to destroy the peroxides formed within the cell. See the section on selenium for more detailed information concerning this nutrient interrelationship.

From the above discussion, representing only a limited summary of the information available on vitamin E, the importance of this tocopherol to the nutrition of birds is patently obvious. Vitamin E is one of the first nutrients that aviculturists should consider for diet supplementation in their birds. It is one of the most likely vitamins to be deficient in the average avian diet, if human and animal experience are any indication. Unlike the characteristics of most other deficiencies, a severe vitamin E deficiency in males will not be reversible by the restoration of adequate vitamin E in the diet. Never forget this fact, for it means that males that have suffered a severe vitamin E deficiency at any time in their lives subsequently will remain permanently sterile.

THE ESSENTIAL FATTY ACIDS

VITAMIN F

There are three of the fatty acids that are termed essential in the nutrition of birds and people. These are linoleic acid, linolenic acid, and arachidonic acid. Though all three are termed essential, linoleic acid is the only one the seems to be absolutely essential for birds. With an abundance of linoleic acid in the diet, the body is able to synthesize arachidonic acid from some of it. If quantities of linoleic acid are insufficient, this process cannot occur. In the presence of a variety of necessary vitamins and minerals, the body is also able to synthesize linolenic acid from an abundant supply of linoleic acid. Without linoleic acid, nothing will happen, and death will be the eventual result. Enough linoleic acid in the diet of chickens negates the need for any of the others. The essential fatty acids perform the functions of a vitamin in the body and are referred to in many writings as vitamin F. Especially in Europe, vitamin F is a common designation for the essential fatty acids.

As previously discussed in the chapter on fats, linoleic acid has two double bond linkages open and available. Linolenic acid has three available double bond linkages, and the arachidonic acid molecule has four available double bonds. Arachidonic acid forms one percent or less of most animal fats and less than one percent or none in the vegetable fats.

Vitamin E is very closely associated with these essential fatty acids in nature. Natural vegetable oils are rich in vitamin E, which serves the function of an antioxidant. This action prevents oxygen from forming peroxides and other toxic compounds by its oxidative actions on the fatty acids.

The outstanding function of the essential fatty acids is structural. They are required for the proper formation of the internal structure and cell membranes of every cell. The myelin nerve sheaths and connective tissues in the body also require essential fatty acids for their formation. They are critical for the health of the blood and arteries and vital for healthy nerves. Without the essential fatty acids, there would be no growth.

Linoleic acid, in particular, combines with other substances in the body in order to perform its functions. When combined with phosphorus, linoleic acid has its greatest biological activity. Such a combination occurs in the compound that we call lecithin.

Other dietary factors being equal, an increased intake of linoleic acid in the diet will lower blood cholesterol levels. It helps to protect against excessive water loss in an animal and has also been shown to be a protective factor against radiation damage. Linoleic acid is necessary for both growth and reproduction. A deficiency of linoleic acid in the diet of chickens will produce a striking reduction in the size of eggs laid.

It is significant that linolenic acid will reduce the adhesiveness of the blood platelets. This lessens the danger of a blood clot. Linoleic acid alone will not perform this function. This function is obviously one of the reasons for the continued classification of linolenic acid as essential.

For cage birds, the commonly fed oily seeds are excellent sources of the essential fatty acids, particularly of linoleic acid. Safflower is by far the best, if you can get the birds to eat it, since safflower oil ranges from 70% to 75% linoleic acid. Sunflower seeds are also an exceptionally good source, as are all walnuts. Flaxseed is probably the best source of linolenic acid.

In feeding canaries a variety of seeds free choice in equal amounts, the seeds I have offered are white proso millet, canary seed, rapeseed, flaxseed, and shelled sunflower seed. The flaxseed dish is invariably the first one emptied, with the sunflower a close second. Last emptied are the dishes of canary seed, millet, and rapeseed, in that order. Given a choice, all of the canaries will eat very little rape, preferring to get the oils in their diet from flaxseed and sunflower seed. Obviously, this gives the canaries a fairly high calorie diet which demands adequate space for exercise to forestall any serious increase in weight. Yet, the birds always can be trusted to choose a diet that is nutritionally balanced from a wide variety of offerings.

Human needs for linoleic acid are larger than the needs for most animals, as evidenced by the content of milk. Human milk will contain from two to four times as much linoleic acid as does the butterfat content of a cow's milk.

In experiments with rats, diets lacking in the essential fatty acids will cause numerous symptoms of deficiency. The rats show retarded growth, a higher metabolic rate, and changes in their skin and fur. Dryness and scruffiness in the skin and fur would be called dandruff in humans. Kidney disorders and kidney stones were common. With respect to reproduction, the problems were severe. Males were frequently sterile. In females, the litters were resorbed, labor was prolonged with hemorrhaging, and the resulting litters were underweight and sickly. Experiments with chickens have shown much the same symptoms and results.

A deficiency of the essential fatty acids together with the fat soluble vitamins, in particular vitamin A, is the cause of the common problem in cage birds known as eggbinding. In this condition, the tissues of the oviduct are neither elastic nor sufficiently lubricated to permit the passage of an egg. The

111

unfortunate result is an egg stuck in the oviduct. If the egg is not laid or forcefully removed, the immobile egg will inevitably cause the death of the hen. One case of eggbinding indicates a bird that probably is not eating all of the dietary offerings that you are providing. Several cases over a short period of time and a continuing problem indicate a major deficiency in these fat soluble vitamins in your diet, and the diet should be supplemented immediately to prevent any further recurrence of eggbinding.

It is vital to the lives of cage birds that their diets contain sufficient amounts of the essential fatty acids. Though cereal grains will have a good quantity of this vitamin in the germ of the seed, this represents only a tiny oil content for seeds of this type. No whole cereal grain is an adequate source of these unsaturated fatty acids. You must also have a choice of the fatty seeds available that the birds will accept and eat in order to be sure that they are getting a sufficient quantity of these essential fatty acids. As has been proven by experimentation, breeding is impossible without a sufficient quantity of the essential fatty acids in the diet.

VITAMIN K

If you have been under the assumption that vitamin K is only one vitamin, you are in for a big surprise. Actually, there are a considerable number of chemical compounds that perform the functions of vitamin K in the body. Researchers use the term vitamin K activity to describe the functions of these compounds. Carl Peter Henrick Dam discovered Vitamin K in Denmark in 1934 in his studies of blood coagulation. He named the compound vitamin K after the Danish spelling of 'Koagulation'.

All compounds with vitamin K activity belong to a chemical group called 'quinones'. This vitamin occurs in three distinct groups called K_1, K_2 and K_3. Any compound in the K_1 group is called a 'phylloquinone' or 'phytoquinone'. These occur naturally in the oily seeds and in green leafy plants. They were first isolated from alfalfa meal.

The compounds with vitamin K activity in the K_2 group are called the 'prenylmenaquinones'. This group of compounds is found in animal tissues and is produced by bacterial synthesis in the digestive tract.

A vitamin K compound in the K_3 group is called either a 'menadione' or a 'menaquinone'. All of the quinones in this group have been synthetically produced. Menaquinone is the simplest compound with vitamin K activity and is a yellow, crystalline powder.

Many of the synthetic forms of vitamin K are water soluble, while the naturally occurring forms are all fat soluble. All vitamin K compounds require the presence of some dietary fat for best absorption. Any deficiency is usually caused by a failure to absorb the available vitamin K in the digestive tract. Any lack of the bile acids will prevent the breakdown of fat in the digestive system and will prevent its subsequent absorption, along with the subsequent absorption of vitamin K.

I have encountered two conflicting philosophies with regard to the production of vitamin K by bacteria in the intestines of birds. The first states that the bacteria capable of manufacturing vitamin K are normally present in the intestines of animals and man. However, birds do not harbor these particular types of bacteria and for this reason, birds must get their vitamin K in their diets.

The second philosophy states synthesis of vitamin K by intestinal bacteria occurs in both birds and mammals. However, since most vitamin K absorption occurs in the upper intestinal tract and synthesis is in the lower tract, little of the vitamin available from this source will be absorbed. This leads to coprophagy, eating their own droppings, since the droppings are rich in vitamin K, as well as several of the B vitamins. Coprophagy is common in all cage birds.

Either of these philosophies may be true, or both of them may be true. Certainly, all birds are different, and some species may have to get their supply of vitamin K from the diet. Others, such as the gallinaceous birds, may harbor the bacteria needed to synthesize vitamin K, but as it cannot be absorbed in the lower intestinal tract where it is synthesized, the birds must resort to coprophagy to get this vitamin. Only time and a lot of very specialized research will be able to arrive at a definitive answer to these questions.

In testing done with rats, these animals obtain sufficient vitamin K from coprophagy to prevent any deficiency symptoms. However, if coprophagy is prevented, deficiency symptoms in the test animals will appear very shortly.

Vitamin K is essential to proper liver function, and the liver is the site of its metabolic activity. The natural, fat soluble forms of vitamin K are stored in the liver, primarily. In the liver, vitamin K is necessary for the formation of four blood proteins which are involved in blood clotting. Any deficiency will prevent the formation of these proteins and make the body susceptible to serious bleeding and greatly prolonged clotting time. After two or three weeks on a deficient diet, the blood of chicks will cease to clot properly. Bleeding and hemorrhages will be visible on the breast, legs, and wings, as well as internally. An affected bird can easily bleed to death from a bruise or small cut.

Vitamin K is also involved in the addition of phosphate to glucose. The added phosphate facilitates the conversion of glucose into glycogen, the storage form of carbohydrate, and its passage through the cell membranes.

Though the natural forms of vitamin K are non-toxic at very high dosage levels, the synthetic compound called menadione can cause the development of toxicity symptoms. Twelve milligrams daily is considered the safe upper limit of intake for human beings, but 10 milligrams at one time will be toxic to newborn babies. In addition, a high vitamin K intake in the diet of hens has been proven to increase blood spotting in their eggs.

The highest natural sources of vitamin K are the dark green, leafy vegetables. Alfalfa is especially rich in this vitamin. Fruits and seeds for avian consumption, particularly the oily seeds, contain some vitamin K, as well. Humans apparently have a lower requirement for vitamin K than the animals, since human milk contains only one quarter the amount of vitamin K activity that is contained in cow's milk.

Vitamin K is stable to heat, but a variety of influences are capable of destroying it. Mineral oil will absorb it and cause its excretion. Light, acids, alkalis, and oxidizing agents will all destroy vitamin K. Radiation and x-rays are very destructive of vitamin K, and it is also destroyed in the presence of rancid fats.

The small amounts needed in the body of a bird should be supplied in adequate quantities in any dark greens and oily seeds in the diet. Birds that are maintained on a diet of raw, unprocessed foods should need no supplementation with vitamin K.

"Supplements in the drinking water are at least 75% wasted in splashing, bathing, and discarding when fouled by the birds. Powdered supplements mixed in the seed are probably at least 90% wasted in birds that shell their seed."

CHAPTER 8

THE WATER SOLUBLE VITAMINS

ASCORBIC ACID

The terms ascorbic acid and vitamin C are generally interchangeable in any discussion of nutrition. Ascorbic acid is the scientific term for this nutrient, while vitamin C is the name applied by most writers aimed at the general public. Also, for most birds, ascorbic acid cannot be classified as a vitamin, since a vitamin by definition is an essential chemical nutrient extracted from the diet. For almost all birds commonly maintained in aviculture, ascorbic acid is not a vitamin, since the birds manufacture their own supply in either the liver or the kidneys, depending upon the species. Only man, the primates, guinea pigs, one species of fruit-eating bat, and the birds mentioned in the subsequent discussion are unable to synthesize their own ascorbic acid internally.

Nevertheless, ascorbic acid fulfills the same functions in the avian body as it does in the human body. It is vital to life. It is a potent killer of viruses and acts as a detoxifier in the blood. Ascorbic acid seems to react with any foreign substance in the blood, attaching itself to the molecule and carrying it out of the body.

Ascorbic acid is vital to the formation of the collagen which holds the cells together. Collagen acts as a glue to bind the cells to each other. When animal

117

tissue is boiled down to extract the collagen, the resulting compound is called gelatin. Any weakness in this collagen will result in cell separation and escape of blood from the capillaries and fluids from the cells. In humans, this means that bruising occurs very easily.

In the less advanced species of birds, such as the pigeons, gallinaceous birds, and even the psittacines, the kidneys are the source of ascorbic acid production in the body. In the more advanced species of birds, most of the passerine birds, in particular, the source of ascorbic acid is the liver. Most species have not yet been tested specifically to see which organ is the seat of ascorbic acid synthesis. Research that was completed by two Indian scientists, C. Ray Chaudhuri and I. B. Chatterjee, indicates sixteen species that are unable to manufacture their own vitamin C and must obtain it from their diet, based upon studies of their enzyme metabolism. This would mean that ascorbic acid is a true vitamin for these species. The most well known of these 16 avian species in aviculture is the Red-vented Bulbul, *Pycnonotus cafer*, of the family Pycnonotidae, which was the only known subject of an actual feeding trial on birds with relation to vitamin C. The bulbuls did develop the symptoms of scurvy on a deficient diet. These symptoms of scurvy were cured by vitamin C supplementation.

In periods of stress, the need for ascorbic acid skyrockets, probably beyond the avian body's ability to synthesize it. In humans, under severe stress, the limited vitamin C storage in the adrenal glands is depleted in a matter of seconds. At times of severe stress, therefore, an addition of ascorbic acid to the avian diet could be of value. In normal maintenance and breeding of avicultural species, however, supplementation with vitamin C is a useless waste. The inclusion of vitamin C in many supplements for avian consumption is a condescension to the nutritional ignorance of the aviculturist, not a necessity for the birds.

Chicken eggs contain no vitamin C until their incubation begins. As soon as the chick embryo begins developing, ascorbic acid is detectable in the egg, synthesized by the embryo. Nevertheless, research has proven that the cost of production of eggs in commercial egg farms is less when vitamin C is given to the hens. The vitamin C seems to aid the hens to develop stronger shells on their eggs, and because of this, the breakage in handling is less.

Vitamin C is the most easily destroyed of all the vitamins. The greatest destruction occurs as a result of exposure to oxygen with the resulting oxidation of the vitamin C. Storage and exposure to trace minerals are also very destructive of vitamin C. Cooking destroys much of the vitamin C in foods, also, since it is unstable in heat. Fortunately, freezing does not damage the vitamin C content of foods.

While your birds are safe from the effects of scurvy, or acute vitamin C deficiency symptoms, you are not. Human beings cannot synthesize their own ascorbic acid. A study by the United States Department of Agriculture indicated that half of the students in the United States were not getting even the daily amount of vitamin C recommended by the U. S. Food and Drug Administration. Many researchers feel that even these recommended amounts are far too low for optimal health.

Bruises are a common symptom of vitamin C deficiency in humans. Vitamin C is a vital ingredient in the formation of collagen, a component of all cell walls and connective tissue. With insufficient vitamin C, collagen is poorly formed and separates with the slightest pressure. This separation permits blood to escape from the capillaries into the tissues, thus causing a bruise. If you bruise easily, you have a severe vitamin C deficiency, technically called sub-clinical scurvy.

The human race suffers from the problem that Irwin Stone has named hypoascorbemia, which is the genetic inability to synthesize ascorbic acid. A vital enzyme link in the transformation of glucose into ascorbic acid is missing in humans and the other species previously mentioned.

A staggering amount of needless suffering occurs each day in the human sphere simply because of lack of knowledge on the subject of vitamin C and other facets of nutrition. Nevertheless, anyone who expects immediate results with increased vitamin C intake or supplementation is doomed to failure and disappointment. The building of all of these defective cells in the body has taken years, and rebuilding them all with an adequate supply of vitamin C will not occur in a few days, or even months. Years are required to correct the damage of the past years of inadequate nutrition. With a sensible diet and a minimum of refined food products, the human body will rebuild its deficient tissues over a period of years. Impatience over the long term has been the fatal flaw in most research to date on the usefulness of vitamin C supplementation in the diet. For your further reading and information, I highly recommend the book by Irwin Stone, *The Healing Factor.*

BIOTIN

Biotin was recognized as a dietary essential first in 1924, but its actual structure was not understood fully until much later, and it was not synthesized until 1943. This is one of the sulfur-containing vitamins. There are at least five known forms of biotin, and it occurs naturally in both free and bound forms. The biotin found in animal sources is bound to a protein and is fat soluble. The biotin occurring in plant sources is free biotin, and it is water soluble. Biotin is classified as a water soluble vitamin.

Biotin participates in many biological reactions in the human and avian body. The requirement is extremely small, measured in micrograms, but for its necessary functions, it is vital. Biotin found within the cells occurs bound to a protein, where it functions as an enzyme. It is involved in both the synthesis and oxidation of fatty acids and in the oxidation of carbohydrates. Biotin is necessary for the removal of the amino groups from several amino acids before they can be broken down for energy. It is also necessary in the synthesis of nicotinic acid and for the synthesis of at least one of the digestive enzymes. The best established role of biotin in nutrition is in the addition or removal of carbon dioxide in various metabolic reactions.

Though much remains to be learned about this vitamin, it does not appear that humans need a dietary source, and deficiency is unlikely to occur in humans. Human milk has only one-tenth of the biotin found in cow's milk. Intestinal microbial synthesis provides a large quantity of biotin for both humans and mammals. Because of this, it is difficult even to induce a deficiency state in mammals. Coprophagy can be a sizable source of biotin in some mammals, again as a by-product of the microbial action. Any possible deficiency in humans would be signaled by changes in the skin with scaliness and hardening in the region of the eye. Loss of hair and muscular atrophy will follow the skin manifestations. Nausea, loss of appetite, and muscle pains are also symptoms of severe biotin deficiency. These human symptoms are very similar to those of thiamin deficiency. Any excess of biotin is excreted in the urine. At times, urinary excretion in humans can be greater than dietary intake. This again indicates a sizable biotin source from intestinal microbial synthesis.

Chickens, by contrast, do not seem to have the advantage of microbial synthesis as a source of biotin, and a diet low in biotin will produce definite symptoms of deficiency. In chicks, skin inflammation is a symptom, and the bottoms of the feet become rough and callused with deep fissures which may bleed. The toes can die completely and slough off. The tops of the feet and legs show only dry scaliness. Also, sores appear in the corner of the mouth and spread to the whole area around the beak. Eventually, the eyelids become swollen and stick together. In breeding hens, a deficiency will cause a reduction in the hatchability of the eggs, but no decrease in the egg production. These deficiency symptoms in chickens are very similar to those of pantothenic acid deficiency.

Dietary sources of biotin are found in both plant and animal products. Liver, kidney, milk, and egg yolk, are the richest known animal sources, with cauliflower, green leafy plants, peanuts, yeast, legumes and nuts the richest plant sources. Grains, meat and fish are poor sources of biotin in the diet and should not be relied upon for the dietary content. Research has determined that much of the biotin in natural food sources is biologically unavailable.

Biotin is stable in ordinary conditions, but some will be lost in cooking, since biotin is water soluble. Though biotin is stable to heat, both alkalis and oxidation will render it inactive. Oxidative rancidity is especially destructive to biotin, but the presence of vitamin E at the same time will prevent most of this destruction.

Symptoms of biotin deficiency can occur either in diets low in biotin or in diets high in raw egg white. Raw egg whites contain a protein called avidin, which binds biotin and makes it nutritionally unavailable. For this reason, raw egg whites are used frequently to induce a biotin deficiency for experimental purposes. Avidin will bind biotin into a protein too large for absorption, and the body is unable to break up this protein. However, since it only takes 27 raw egg whites daily to cause a deficiency of biotin in humans, there seems little likelihood of a deficiency developing from this cause in any normal and rational diet. Also, moist heat denatures the avidin, changing it into a form that can no longer bind biotin. Thus, any amount of cooking renders the avidin in egg whites completely harmless for human or avian nutrition.

For nutritional purposes in cage bird maintenance, biotin deserves a little closer attention. Without the microbial synthesis, birds are much more likely than animals to develop a biotin deficiency. Particularly for seed-eating birds, grains are a poor source of biotin. The diet must include eggs, greens, peanuts, nuts, sunflower seeds, or another high quality biotin source in order to provide biotin in sufficient quantities. Since so little biotin is needed in the avian diet, there is little likelihood of a deficiency developing in finches or other cage birds that are maintained on a varied diet.

CHOLINE

Choline is a vitally important compound in the body's functioning and metabolism. Under most conditions, humans and animals appear to synthesize biotin in adequate quantities internally. Rats, for example, synthesize their own supply of choline in the liver. For this reason, it is technically not a vitamin for many species, including humans. However, in guinea pigs, young chickens, and turkeys, choline is not synthesized in adequate quantities in the body, and choline is definitely a vitamin for these species, especially while growing. It seems probable that this will be true for all species of birds, but only further extensive research can reveal the actual dietary requirement for choline in other birds that we maintain and breed in captivity. This section has been written on the assumption that choline will be proven as essential to other birds as it is to chickens and turkeys.

Pure choline is a strongly alkaline liquid, first isolated by Adolph Strecker (1822-1876) in 1862. Additional research showed it to be the active ingredient in lecithin in 1932. Though choline is present in relatively large amounts in all foods that contain fat, it is water soluble and is generally classified as part of the B complex of water soluble vitamins. Fruits and vegetables contain virtually no choline, with the exception of legumes, such as beans and peas. Liver, meats and nuts are good sources, and there is some choline in the cereal grains. Eggs contain a large amount of choline, and the egg yolk, in particular, is an excellent food source of this vitamin. One large egg will contain about 170 milligrams of choline. For cage bird nutrition, the fatty seeds, eggs, and nuts are probably the best dietary sources.

Choline functions in the body in three primary areas. First, it forms a compound that is necessary for transmitting nerve impulses from one nerve ending to the next. The second primary function is structural in nature. Choline forms an actual part of fat and nerve tissue, and it is an essential part of the fatty compound called lecithin. Unlike other vitamins, so far as is known, choline does not catalyze any reactions or act as a part of any coenzyme in the body.

123

The third function of choline is in relation to the methyl groups that are a part of the choline molecule. These are loosely bound units consisting of one carbon atom and three hydrogen atoms, as you have noted in the structure of the fatty acid molecules. The effectiveness of choline is due to the three available methyl groups in each molecule of this vitamin which are detached for a wide range of uses in the body. In order to act as a methyl donor, choline must first be oxidized in the body into a compound called betaine. In this manner, choline plays a vital role in the formation of phospholipids. These methyl groups are necessary to mobilize fat from the liver to be transported in the bloodstream to each of the body's cells. In this way, choline prevents the accumulation of fat in the liver. An addition of choline to the diet will prevent the development of a fatty liver. Choline also exerts a protective action in cirrhosis of the liver in alcoholics. A folacin deficiency will exaggerate a choline deficiency, because methyl transfer in the body's metabolism is affected.

These important methyl groups can also come from other sources, such as the amino acid methionine, or they can be synthesized in the body in the presence of adequate folacin or cobalamin. For this reason, the choline requirement depends largely upon the amount of folacin and cobalamin in the diet. Because of this methyl donor function, the level of methionine in the diet is important in relation to the need for choline, and vice versa. However, in chicks methionine cannot serve this function, and this is probably also true in other avian species.

As previously mentioned, choline is a dietary requirement for growth in chickens and turkeys. A deficiency of this vitamin will result in perosis in chicks. This disease shows its first symptoms as pinpoint hemorrhages and slight puffiness around the hock joint. The leg bones then twist out of alignment, and the leg is unable to support the weight of the bird. The amount of choline necessary to prevent perosis is greater than that required for normal growth. Also, any folacin or cobalamin deficiency will cause a large increase in the choline requirement, as was previously mentioned. In chickens, the perosis caused by deficiency can be cured by adding either folacin, manganese, or choline to the diet. A deficiency in chicks is probably caused by their inability to synthesize choline in adequate quantities.

The chick's ability to synthesize choline increases with age. Choline supplementation in the diet during this growth period will further require supplementation in the diet at maturity for maximum egg production and for keeping liver fat at a low level.

Even with lower egg production, however, the choline content of the eggs of chickens is not affected. Laying hens can synthesize sizable amounts of choline, so the choline content of the eggs produced will not be reduced, even in a deficient diet.

A number of other facts about choline may be of interest. First of all, a deficiency in animals will show up first as spots of hemorrhage in the kidneys. Hormones in the body also have an effect on the choline requirements, and one hormone seems to spare the choline requirement in the body. Because of the presence of female hormones, female rats are much less susceptible to an induced choline deficiency than are male rats.

Choline supplementation in the average cage bird diet should not be necessary. Three items that are commonly offered to cage birds are hard-boiled eggs, peanuts, and sunflower seeds. All of these are rich in choline. Any fatty item offered in the diet should have enough choline content to prevent any possible deficiency in birds in captivity. This is not a nutrient about which the breeder needs to be overly concerned. Deficiency in any average diet for any birds maintained and bred in our cages and aviaries is very unlikely.

COBALAMIN

The year 1926 marked a major advance in nutritional knowledge with the discovery that large amounts of raw liver would completely cure an invariably fatal disease, pernicious anemia. Three-quarters of a pound of raw liver each day was required to effect this cure. Fortunately in 1948, vitamin B_{12} was isolated from liver as small, red crystals which proved to be the curative factor. Since these crystals contained four percent cobalt, the compound was given the name 'cobalamin'. Several similar chemical compounds exhibit vitamin B_{12} activity with cyanocobalamin being the most active. This form of cobalamin has a cyanide group attached to the basic structure of the cobalamin molecule. The cyanide group was used in the original isolation of this vitamin, and it does not occur in the vitamin as it exists naturally in food items. There is no apparent nutritional difference, according to some reports, between the biological activity of cobalamin and cyanocobalamin. Cobalamin is also water soluble, and the cobalamin crystals will absorb water vapor on exposure to the air.

The best source of cobalamin is liver, which contains about one part per million of this vitamin. Oysters are a good source, and it is also found in kidney, meat, eggs and milk. Only those and other animal foods are dependable sources of cobalamin. One ton of liver must be processed to get only 20 milligrams of cobalamin. So little cobalamin is needed for human health that intake is virtually always adequate for anyone who is not a strict vegetarian.

Plant material is virtually devoid of cobalamin. The tiny amounts that are found in some plants, such as comfrey and alfalfa, have been absorbed from the soil after bacteria have synthesized and excreted the cobalamin in that soil. The respectable amounts of this vitamin found in some varieties of seaweed also seem to be concentrated there after synthesis by bacteria associating with the seaweed.

This vitamin is now freely available commercially as a by-product of the antibiotic producing *Streptomyces* bacteria. Synthesis in the digestive tract by bacterial action is also possible if sufficient cobalt is available in the diet. Microorganisms in the human digestive tract can synthesize cobalamin, but the site of this synthesis is too far down in the colon to permit absorption. Many varieties of bacteria and actinomycetes have the ability to synthesize cobalamin.

Any deficiency of cobalamin is usually an absorption problem rather than a dietary deficiency. The cobalamin molecule is complicated and the digestive system cannot absorb it without the presence of an intrinsic factor. This factor is a secretion of the cells in the stomach wall, a glycoprotein, and it is found in normal gastric juice. It is apparently different in every species. As this factor mixes with food, it releases cobalamin from the protein complexes in which it occurs. Without the presence of this intrinsic factor, cobalamin will not be absorbed. The only exception to this is in the administration of massive doses, 1000 times the normal amount given. Some of this massive concentration of cobalamin will pass through the intestinal wall by diffusion. Injection is the best method for immediate supplementation of cobalamin, since this form of administration bypasses the need for the intrinsic factor.

Absorption and subsequent utilization of cobalamin are also affected by other factors. A pyridoxine deficiency in the diet will lower the efficiency of the absorption of cobalamin, and any lack of iron will do the same. Also, in hypothyroidism, which is low thyroid gland activity, absorption efficiency will be lowered. Once absorbed, cobalamin is bound to a protein in the bloodstream and circulates to the body's tissues in this form. These blood proteins are called transcobalamines. If absorption is in excess of the blood's capacity to bind it, cobalamin is excreted in the urine. Any limitation of this binding capacity in the bloodstream can also cause a deficiency as the body cells are deprived of the vitamin's usefulness.

Cobalamin is necessary for normal growth, the maintenance of healthy nervous tissue, and for normal red blood cell formation. It is necessary for normal carbohydrate metabolism and also appears to function in both fat and protein metabolism. Cobalamin is essential for the formation of the single carbon units called methyl groups which are incorporated into many of the compounds used by and made a part of the body. Cobalamin has the ability to promote nitrogen retention in the body and thus raises the biological value of protein in the food. Cobalamin has also been effective in the treatment of hepatitis. A complex interrelationship exists between cobalamin and folacin, and also between cobalamin and many of the other nutrients that are required for the health of the body.

Fortunately, cobalamin is stored to a considerable degree in the liver in an enzyme form. Liver uptake is facilitated by the presence of ascorbic acid, and the cobalamin is stored at the rate of one to two micrograms per gram of liver tissue. The average storage amount in humans is around 2,000 micrograms, or two milligrams, which amounts to about a six year supply. Body stores may be as high as 11,000 micrograms, which is 11 milligrams of cobalamin, an amount that would be sufficient to last a normal human for an incredible 33 years. No other nutrient required in the body's metabolism is stored to this extent.

A number of other interesting facts are now available regarding the vitamin cobalamin. This vitamin is more stable than many other vitamin compounds, but alkalis destroy it. Acids, and oxidation have little effect on cobalamin. About 70% of the cobalamin in foods will be retained in cooking, and it seems to be completely non-toxic. Injected doses as high as 1600 milligrams per kilogram of body weight have proven to be completely harmless. The use of the antibiotics Aureomycin and penicillin have stimulated the growth of animals, apparently because they inhibit the growth of the organisms that destroy cobalamin.

With particular reference to cage birds, any deficiency of cobalamin will reduce the rate of growth in nestlings and will also cause embryos to die in the shell, thus decreasing the hatchability of the eggs, based upon research with chickens. A severe deficiency will result in death. Aviculturists need to pay particular attention to the supply of this vitamin in the avian diets, since cobalamin does not occur in any common plant sources routinely and in sufficient quantity. A source of animal food such as egg or insects must be provided to fulfill the birds' cobalamin requirement. Alternately, a cobalamin supplement must be mixed with another commonly fed item to insure against any dietary deficiency of this vitamin.

Through coprophagy, birds may get the benefit of bacterial synthesis of this vitamin in the droppings, but this has not been definitely proven, and cannot be counted upon to give the birds the vitamin B_{12} that they must have for their full health and breeding.

Most commercial supplements and crumbled feeds have cobalamin added, since its necessity in nutrition is now universally recognized. Considering the few micrograms required even for a large number of finches, no aviculturist can afford to take a chance on a cobalamin deficiency. Since five micrograms is presumed to be a very adequate daily supplement for human beings, one microgram, the approximate amount present in one chicken egg, should be sufficient to prevent any deficiency in a large number of finches or other small birds, when fed on a daily basis.

FOLACIN

The vitamin that we now call folacin has gone through a number of other temporary names and name changes in the past. The most well known of these is 'folic acid', and this term is still widely used to identify this vitamin. Other common names given to this compound, before exact identification was made, are vitamin M, Factor U, and Factor R. Folacin was discovered during the search for the anti-pernicious anemia factor in liver. This vitamin exists in nature in both free and bound forms. It has been proven to be a dietary essential for chickens, monkeys, humans, and guinea pigs. Rats do not appear to need this vitamin, apparently producing their own supply through intestinal microbial synthesis. Neither is it a dietary essential for dogs and rabbits. Folacin was isolated and synthesized in 1945.

Folacin is absorbed primarily in the upper part of the small intestine by both active transport and diffusion. The presence of ascorbic acid also assists the absorption of folacin. A high percentage of the folacin in liver, yeast and eggs is absorbed, but as little as 10% of the folacin in other foods may be available. The liver is able to store reserves of folacin that are adequate for four or five months.

Substances with folic acid activity, called 'folates', are synthesized by plants, in animal tissues, and by intestinal microorganisms. The term folate refers to all of the substances that give rise to folacin in the body. The term folacin is now used to describe only the form from which the active coenzymes are directly derived. Folates occur in foods as a combination of pterin and para-aminobenzoic acid, commonly called PABA. For some time, researchers felt that PABA was a vitamin in its own right, but further research revealed it to be a part of the folate molecule. Folate must go through several changes in the presence of various enzymes and coenzymes to form the citrovorum factor, also called folinic acid. This is considered to be the biologically active form of this vitamin, and it is in the form of folinic acid that the liver stores folacin.

Para-aminobenzoic acid alone has been found to be an ideal dressing for burns and sunburns, rivaling vitamin E in its positive effects. Arsenic and sulfa compounds will destroy PABA, and it has been a prescription item because of its antagonism to sulfa compounds. Another effective use for PABA is in

129

treatment of the condition called vitiligo, characterized by spots of white appearing on the skin, totally lacking in pigment. A high intake of PABA over a period of time seems to be effective in restoring normal pigmentation to affected areas of skin.

Animals appear to differ greatly in their requirements for folacin. This seems to be primarily due to the animal's ability to utilize intestinal microbial synthesis as a source of folacin. The requirement is small, and humans require less than one milligram per day. Yet, one authority has stated that further research may reveal that folacin deficiency is the most common vitamin deficiency in the United States. In one test, 20% of pregnant women were shown to be deficient in folacin to the point of symptoms of blood poisoning. The need for folacin always increases in pregnancy and in any iron deficiency.

Folacin acts as an intermediary in a variety of biological functions. It aids in the transfer of single carbon units, such as methyl groups, from one substance to another. Folacin is active in the synthesis of parts of the nucleic acid molecules DNA and RNA. Because of this important function, folacin is very important in rapid cell division and normal growth. It is also involved in normal blood formation and is used in the synthesis of choline, another of the B complex vitamins. One unfortunate action of folacin is to mask the symptoms of pernicious anemia, a disease which is caused by a cobalamin deficiency, until irreparable damage has been done in the body.

The dietary sources of folacin and the destructive influences on it must both be considered when trying to assure an adequate dietary intake for cage birds. Of the items commonly offered in avian diets, only peanuts, walnuts, and wheat are excellent sources. Liver, brewer's yeast, asparagus, mushrooms, broccoli, lemons, and bananas are very good sources. A varied diet of whole foods should contain a sufficient supply of folacin to prevent any deficiency from developing. Processing and cooking losses are disastrous where folacin is concerned, and the losses will range from 50% to 90% of the folacin content in processed and cooked foods. Exposure to light will destroy folacin, and high heat also will destroy this vitamin.

As previously mentioned, folacin deficiency may be more widespread than is generally realized. A folacin deficiency may result from inadequate intake, poor absorption of the vitamin, excessive demands, or possibly from metabolic derangements. Alcohol is a particularly destructive influence on the human body's folacin supply. Studies have shown that fully 90% of alcoholics also suffer from a folacin deficiency. A dietary deficiency of folacin will cause the formation of abnormally large red blood cells and reduced production of white blood cells. Two named forms of anemia caused by such blood abnormalities resulting from folacin deficiency are macrocytic anemia and megaloblastic anemia. Rheumatoid arthritis may be in large part a human symptom of folacin deficiency, and lack of this vitamin is suspected of causing such birth defects as harelip and cleft palate. Almost all of the deficiency symptoms can be attributed to a failure to metabolize single carbon units in the body.

Symptoms of a deficiency in chicks include macrocytic anemia, poor growth, very poor feathering, anemic appearance, and perosis. Folacin is required for the production of feather pigmentation in several of the dark colored chicken breeds. A deficiency in the breeding diet will cause a large increase in embryonic mortality. Embryos will die within the shell soon after pipping the air cell. Presumably the same symptoms will occur in any birds kept in captivity, though research is not yet available regarding specific symptoms of folacin deficiency in the commonly kept cage birds.

GLUCOSE TOLERANCE
FACTOR

The Glucose Tolerance Factor is one of the more recent discoveries in the field of nutrition. Though it is classified as an essential trace element at present, in all probability it will be reclassified as a vitamin at some point in the future. The trace mineral that is the basis of the GTF molecule is chromium. Only the trivalent chromium is useful in the nutrition of humans, birds, and animals, as other forms of chromium can be toxic.

This discovery of Trivalent Chromium, also known as CrIII or Cr+++ in 1957 was accidental, as are most major discoveries. K. Schwarz and Walter Mertz were engaged in experimentation with their laboratory animals when the tests began producing completely unexpected results. Chronic and expected deficiency symptoms disappeared overnight for no apparent reason. Careful investigation revealed that a new laboratory assistant, more experienced than the former, was disinfecting all washed glassware with chromic acid. Even subsequent thorough rinsing left enough residue on the glassware to supply the laboratory rats with the trace amounts of chromium necessary for Glucose Tolerance Factor synthesis.

The GTF molecule consists of chromium bound in an organic form. Trivalent chromium is the center of the GTF molecule. The molecule also contains two niacin molecules and three amino acids – glutamic acid, glycine, and cysteine. In structure, this molecule resembles a hormone.

The Glucose Tolerance Factor has been crystallized from brewer's yeast. Unlike cobalamin, GTF is well absorbed in the digestive tract. The body cannot easily synthesize it, but intestinal bacteria may be able to do so with an abundance of chromium in the diet. This factor is apparently completely non-toxic, either by mouth or intravenously.

GTF is released into the blood in response to insulin. The blood carries it to the tissues where insulin is working, and it becomes involved in sugar utilization at that point. GTF works closely with insulin to maintain the delicate balance needed between the two extremes of blood sugar content: hypoglycemia (low blood sugar) and hyperglycemia (high blood sugar).

Research conducted since *Nutrition of Finches and Other Cage Birds* was originally published has proven conclusively that adequate trivalent chromium in the diet is a major factor in the prevention of cardiovascular disease. In testing of persons with heart disease and those without, the chromium levels were uniformly low in those experiencing heart disease, and much higher in the people who were free of heart disease. There can now be no doubt at this stage of research that the chromium levels in the average North American diet are disastrously low. Wild animals in North America have chromium levels that are ten times as high as the chromium levels of the people. The preponderance of refined foods in these North American diets has caused a disastrous decrease in the overall chromium levels in the diets. In the refining of wheat into white flour, for example, 83% of the chromium content is removed. The refining of cane and beet sugar into white sugar is even worse, and this refining removes 92% of the chromium content.

There is no reason to believe that the functions of GTF in the avian body will differ significantly from the functions in rats and humans. A diet with sufficient chromium content should ensure that no deficiency of the Glucose Tolerance Factor will occur in cage birds. Refer to the section on chromium for further information with respect to chromium in the diet and its nutritional and metabolic functions.

INOSITOL

The study of this vitamin presents an unusual grouping of facts, plus many uncertainties. Though inositol is classified as a B complex vitamin and was discovered in 1928, very little information exists about this vitamin. It is one of nine separate compounds containing six carbon atoms, all of which are very closely related to glucose chemically. Of these 9 compounds, only nyoinositol is biologically active, and in all writings the name is shortened to 'inositol'.

Most surveys of the known material on inositol will state that the biological significance of this vitamin in human nutrition is unknown. Yet, research has proven that human cells fail to grow without inositol present. It is essential for the growth of liver and bone marrow cells. A number of other roles have been suggested for inositol, but are not yet clearly proven. Perhaps the contradiction becomes more understandable when we discover that the body synthesis occurs within the individual cells, not through the action of intestinal bacteria. If this internal synthesis can be finally proven beyond question, researchers will not classify inositol as a vitamin in human nutrition, as only those compounds which are dietary essentials can fall within the category of vitamins.

Together with choline, inositol performs the function of preventing the accumulation of excess fat in the livers of experimental animals. Inositol seems to work in the body very closely with folacin, pantothenic acid, pyridoxine, and choline. Inositol also seems to stimulate the synthesis of biotin in the intestine of animals.

Though this compound may not be a vitamin for humans, birds and animals have been proven to have a more positive need for inositol. It is definitely a vitamin for mice, and severe deficiency symptoms appear when it is removed from their diet. In an inositol deficiency, mice will develop an abnormality called spectacled eye, and loss of fur, failure of lactation, and growth failure will also appear. Inositol promotes the growth of yeast, and chickens also seem to require inositol for normal health and development. The deficiency symptoms that are reported in chicks are similar to the encephalomalacia and exudative diathesis that is found in chicks suffering from a severe deficiency of vitamin E.

134

Inositol is present in nearly all plant and animal tissues in fairly high concentrations, certainly higher than those in which vitamins normally occur. It actually appears to be a structural component of cells and seems to participate in one step of the formation of nucleic acids, which are in turn used to synthesize RNA, ribonucleic acid. Inositol has the added effect of mobilizing fat from the liver, even when the diet contains a good supply of choline and other methyl donors. See the section on choline for a more complete explanation of methyl donors, and the chapter on fats for diagrams of the methyl groups.

Inositol occurs mainly as a phospholipid in the cells of animals in a form sometimes called 'liposito1'. Some fish and sharks may store carbohydrate as inositol rather than as glycogen in the manner of all birds and land animals. There are large amounts of inositol in the brain, the spinal cord nerves, and in their fluids, indicating that the nervous system depends heavily on this substance for its proper functioning.

The wide occurrence of inositol in natural food items would make any deficiency very unlikely. Fruits, meat, nuts, vegetables, grains, and yeast are all good food sources of inositol. In the grains, inositol is present in the form of a compound called phytic acid. In this form, it occurs as a complex, water soluble compound which will bind calcium, iron and zinc in an insoluble complex, unavailable for absorption and use in the body. Sprouted seed may be a better source of inositol than whole grain seeds, since inositol seems to be freed from the phytic acid complex in the germination process. However, as any shortage of inositol on a varied diet is highly unlikely, the aviculturist need have no concern about a deficiency of inositol in any normal avian diet.

LIPOIC ACID

Lipoic is one of the more recent discoveries in the field of nutrition, and it is recognized by most modern sources as a vitamin. Lipoic acid is a sulfur-containing fatty acid which also goes by the name of thioctic acid. It is classified as a water soluble vitamin. Lipoic acid has been identified in five distinct forms. Three of these forms are fat soluble, but all three can be reversibly oxidized to the water soluble beta-lipoic acid.

Researchers have found lipoic acid to be an essential nutrient for several microorganisms. Any possible requirement for birds or higher animals is not yet known. Where investigated, lipoic acid is an essential component of the chemistry of metabolism in very small amounts. No deficiency has yet been induced in experimental animals and any required amount is now assumed to be provided by synthesis within the body.

Lipoic acid occurs in a wide variety of natural foods, and it has been isolated from liver and yeast. In its active form, lipoic acid is bound to a protein. Any possible requirement for lipoic acid in the nutrition of birds is unknown at this time, but adequate amounts should be supplied in any varied diet for cage birds.

NIACIN

This vitamin occurs in two primary forms in foods. Nicotinic acid is the form of niacin that is present in plants, and nicotinamide is the metabolic form of niacin occurring in animals. Either of these compounds will perform the functions of niacin in the body, but apparently nicotinic acid is not converted to nicotinamide in the body. Niacin is soluble in water, so it is classified as one of the water soluble vitamins.

Nicotinic acid was prepared as far back as 1867 in Germany, and it was easily available in this form long before its importance as a vitamin in nutrition was recognized. The term 'niacin' is now used in all nutritional references to describe this vitamin in preference to the old designation of vitamin B_3.

The white crystalline substance of nicotinic acid was first isolated from yeast and rice bran in 1912, but again, its nutritional importance was not discovered at this time. In 1936, nicotinamide was isolated and the nutritional importance of niacin was fully recognized. The name 'niacinamide' to describe this form of the vitamin replaces the name 'nicotinamide' many times in nutritional references, but both names refer to the same substance.

The disease which resulted in the push to find and identify niacin is called by its Italian name, 'pellagra', in the English-speaking countries. In Spain, it is called 'mal de la rosa'. When this disease strikes dogs, it is called 'black tongue disease'. The symptoms in order of their occurrence are called the four 'D's': dermatitis, diarrhea, depression or dementia, and death. Though pellagra was first described in the 18th century, only in 1917 did Joseph Goldberger (1874-1929) associate it with the absence of a dietary factor. Goldberger was able to cause pellagra by diet restriction.

The disease first causes a characteristic type of skin inflammation which occurs almost totally on areas exposed to sunlight in a very symmetrical pattern on both sides of the body. There will also be inflammation and redness of the tongue and lips with cracks at the corners of the mouth and inflammation of the mucous membranes, including the mucous linings of the gastrointestinal tract.

This gastrointestinal disturbance and inflammation is the cause of the diarrhea that is the next stage of this disease.

Next, the symptoms of mental depression will be evident, including un-reasoning paranoia. The severest mental symptoms directly precede death from niacin deficiency. Dr. R. Glen Green of Canada has noted peculiar visual effects in persons suffering from niacin deficiency. Printed words seem to wiggle around, faces change in size, everything looks foggy, the world seems unstable and moving, and buildings seem to be falling on you. These are apparently the first noticeable symptoms in humans of a niacin deficiency.

Niacin is required by all cells in the body. It is readily absorbed in the digestive tract and can be stored in the body to a limited extent. Niacin in the form of nicotinic acid is frequently bound in an unabsorbable form. This lack of availability greatly affects the dietary requirement for this vitamin. Only treatment with an alkaline solution will release this bound niacin for absorption. Diets rich in corn are frequently pellagra-producing diets, since the nicotinic acid found in corn is not absorbable. Nevertheless, in Central America, where corn may constitute 80% of the diet, no niacin deficiency is known. This is because of the alkali treatment used in the preparation of tortillas and other corn products in that area.

Another strong factor affecting the body's requirement for niacin is the ability of the cells to synthesize niacin from the amino acid tryptophan. This means that the body's niacin requirement is partly dependent upon the amount of tryptophan in the diet. Pyridoxine, thiamin, riboflavin, and possibly biotin must be present for this synthesis to take place, and there are wide differences in the ability of various animals to effect this synthesis. Cats, for example, are unable to do it at all. The body cells in the species with this ability to synthesize niacin can convert tryptophan at a ratio of sixty milligrams of tryptophan to one milligram of niacin.

Niacin is also a part of two important enzymes in the body that play a vital role in the release of energy from proteins, fats, and carbohydrates. Without these two enzymes, the metabolism of the carbohydrates, fats and proteins is not possible. These enzymes catalyze the oxidation of glucose, glycerol synthesis and breakdown, the degradation and synthesis of amino acids, and fatty acid oxidation and synthesis within the body, among other functions.

A number of additional facts are known with respect to niacin. An excess intake of pure nicotinic acid in humans will cause a number of obvious symptoms, including severe flushing, itching, sweating, nausea, and abdominal cramps. An excess intake of nicotinamide will not cause the flushing, but will cause all of the other symptoms.

There are several known anti-nicotinic acid compounds that will destroy the effectiveness of this vitamin in the body. Also, niacin has been proven to be a part of the molecule of the Glucose Tolerance Factor, a vitamin that contains chromium as its basis. Finally, bacteria within the digestive tract of animals can synthesize niacin, and this is a noteworthy niacin source for some species. Though no information has been found regarding this bacterial niacin supply with regard to birds, experience with coprophagy in most cage birds indicates that this may also be true in the avian sphere. Only further detailed and controlled research will be able to prove or disprove this conclusively.

Niacin deficiency symptoms are well documented in chickens, and similar symptoms in any cage birds will be a definite indication of possible niacin deficiency. The primary symptoms in chickens are enlargement of the hock joint (the joint that connects the leg to the foot), bowing of the legs, poor feathering, and dermatitis or skin inflammation. In chickens, there also may be inflammation of the mouth and accompanying diarrhea. In young chicks, all of these symptoms will heal and become normal with additional niacin in the diet, including the bowed legs. Symptoms for ducks and turkeys are the same, but far more severe. Ducks have a niacin requirement about twice as high as chickens and in a severe niacin deficiency they will become so bowlegged and weak that they cannot walk.

As is true with most of the B complex vitamins, liver is an excellent source for niacin. Beans, peas, and peanut butter are also good sources for human nutrition. For cage bird diets, grains, peanuts, and sesame seeds are all good sources of niacin. Any refining will lower the niacin values of food, and white flour has only 19% of the niacin content found in whole wheat. Since this vitamin is water soluble, any wet cooking will dissolve it from the food. Fortunately, this is about the only loss of niacin that occurs. Niacin is probably the most stable of the vitamin compounds, and exposure to acids, alkalis, heat, light or oxidation will not destroy niacin.

Any appearance of the previously mentioned symptoms in your birds will signal that the avicultural diet is lacking in niacin. Either a radical change of diet will then be necessary, or you will have to add a balanced supplement of the B complex vitamins to the daily food items. A deficiency of one vitamin in the B complex surely signals the deficiency of others also, since all occur in similar food sources.

PANTOTHENIC ACID

Though pantothenic acid was isolated in 1938, the compound was known to exist as a vitamin before that year. Pantothenic acid is a water soluble part of the B complex, and in its pure form is a sticky, yellow oil. Very rarely, but occasionally, you will see this vitamin referred to in nutritional references as vitamin B_5. Pantothenic acid is usually seen outside of its natural state as calcium pantothenate, the calcium salt form of this vitamin. The pantothenic acid molecule is a combination of the amino acid alanine and pantoic acid. There is no scarcity of pantothenic acid in nature, and the name itself means an acid found everywhere.

The characteristics of pantothenic acid make the occurrence of any deficiency problem highly unlikely. It is stable in moist heat in neutral solutions, though it is unstable in acids or alkalis. Little is lost in normal cooking, but dry heat will destroy pantothenic acid completely. Refining removes much of the pantothenic acid content of foods, and half of this vitamin is lost in refining whole wheat into white flour. Though all plant and animal cells seem to contain some pantothenic acid, the richest known source of this vitamin is the royal jelly of honey bees. Other rich sources are liver, yeast, egg yolk, and green leafy plants.

Pantothenic acid is vital to all energy-requiring processes within the body as a result of its central role in the utilization of carbohydrate, fat, and protein. It participates in the release of energy from all three of these energy-yielding nutrient groups. Because of this, low intakes of pantothenic acid will slow down metabolic processes with general harm to the health of the cells. The highest concentrations of pantothenic acid are found in the most metabolically active body organs – the liver, adrenal glands, kidneys, brain, and heart. This vitamin is also required for the synthesis of fat, and it is important for coping with stress. Stress always increases the body's requirement for this vitamin. In addition, pantothenic acid seems to stimulate the vital spontaneous movement of the gastrointestinal tract, which is vital for the proper movement and absorption of the food. Chickens and other birds require pantothenic acid for normal egg production and hatchability. A lack of sufficient pantothenic acid in the diet will result in embryos dying in the shell before hatching.

Pantothenic acid combines with several other substances in the body to form a compound called coenzyme A. This is the form in which pantothenic acid occurs in microorganisms and animal tissues, and it is the form which the body cells use in most biological reactions. Coenzyme A apparently is synthesized within the cells, since it is found only in the cells and not in the blood. Pantothenic acid in this form is necessary for hemoglobin synthesis, and a deficiency of this vitamin also slows down the synthesis of insulin in the body. In addition, coenzyme A is required for the breakdown of the fatty acids within the body.

Researchers have examined the effects of pantothenic acid deficiency in experimental animals, and the results in chickens can safely be applied to all avian species kept in captivity. Any deficiency in the hen's diet will result in a shortage of pantothenic acid in the egg and will cause the death of the chick shortly after hatching. Chicks studied on a deficient diet will exhibit a severe skin inflammation, poor growth, broken feathers, and eventual death. Internal symptoms include spinal cord degeneration and fatty degeneration of the liver. Chicks will appear emaciated and crusty, scab-like sores will appear in the corners of the mouth. The margins of the eyelids will be granular, and small scabs will develop on them. The eyelids also may be stuck together by a sticky exudate.

On the feet, the outer layers of skin between the toes and the bottoms of the feet peel off and small cracks will appear in the skin. At times, the skin of the feet thickens and becomes horny with wart-like growths developing on the balls of the feet. These deficiency symptoms in chicks are very similar to those of a biotin deficiency, and only a close examination of the diet can reveal which of the two vitamins is in such severe deficiency. Ducks will develop anemia as a result of pantothenic acid deficiency, and in humans a feeling of burning in the feet is a symptom of a deficiency of this vitamin.

Such severe deficiency symptoms as those described for chickens will never occur on any natural, varied avian diet. Only purified diets in laboratory testing and experimentation will produce such severe effects. In addition, if the degenerative changes described have not progressed too far, the symptoms seem to be completely reversible. Since pantothenic acid occurs so widely in the food supply and the requirement is so small, the development of any deficiency in cage bird feeding is extremely unlikely.

PYRIDOXINE

This vitamin has been known as vitamin B_6 for a long period of time, but the chemical name of the compound, which is pyridoxine, is gradually replacing the older vitamin B_6 designation. The first identification of this vitamin occurred in 1934, and the compound was isolated in 1938. The term 'pyridoxine' is used to designate three separate substances, all of which are biologically active as vitamin B_6. These are pyridoxol, pyridoxal and pyridoxamine. You may occasionally see the term pyridoxine used synonymously with pyridoxol to refer to the primary form of vitamin B6. This vitamin occurs as pyridoxol in plant material as an alcohol bound to a protein. It is the primary form of pyridoxine, but unfortunately, it is not readily absorbable. Strict vegetarians who consume no animal material must be extremely careful to avoid a deficiency of pyridoxine caused by poor absorption. Pyridoxal and pyridoxamine, by contrast, are most prevalent in animal tissue and are easily absorbed in the digestive tract.

Vegetable pyridoxol is more resistant to losses from processing and storage than are the pyridoxine compounds from animal sources. Though pyridoxine is somewhat stable to heat, it is partly destroyed by cooking. Very high heat used in food preparation will destroy pyridoxine. Both irradiation and pasteurization deplete the pyridoxine content of milk, and freezing will cause a 25% loss of the pyridoxine value. The milling of cereal grains causes losses of as much as 80% to 90% of the pyridoxine value in them. White flour contains about 29% of the pyridoxine value of that in whole wheat. This vitamin is also rendered inactive by oxidation and ultraviolet light. Pyridoxine is unstable to alkalis, but all three forms are stable to acid exposure.

Though the National Research Council recommends two milligrams of pyridoxine per day for an average human adult, the requirement for pyri-doxine can vary widely, depending on a variety of factors, including biochemical individuality. Body size will alter the requirement, since a 250 pound adult male will obviously require a greater amount than will a 120 pound male.

The protein content of the diet is a primary determining factor in the amount of pyridoxine required, since there is a direct interrelationship between pyridoxine and all aspects of protein metabolism. Periods of rapid muscle growth will also increase the pyridoxine requirement. A diet high in the amino acid tryptophan will increase the need for pyridoxine, as will an abundance of the amino acid methionine in the diet. A high content of the compound sugar called sucrose in the diet will also increase the pyridoxine requirement for its metabolism. Finally, increased pyridoxine intake is needed during pregnancy and lactation, or from any exposure to radiation. Conversely, a high dietary intake of choline, the essential fatty acids, biotin, and pantothenic acid will reduce the requirement for pyridoxine.

Pyridoxine is essential in the body in a number of ways. It is vital to the proper functioning of the nervous system. Pyridoxine is vital to protein metabolism, but seems to play no direct role in the production of energy. In its protein-related functions, pyridoxine is necessary for the synthesis and breakdown of all amino acids. This vitamin is vital to the maintenance of the smooth integrity of the arterial walls and it is essential for the production of many enzymes. It also controls one of the intermediate steps in the body's production of niacin from the amino acid tryptophan.

It is interesting to note that normal dream recall in humans depends to a large extent upon the presence of adequate pyridoxine in the brain. With too little pyridoxine, there will be no dream recall. An excess of this vitamin will cause awakening after every dream with vivid recall of the dream sequence.

Pyridoxine is required for the proper absorption of cobalamin, and in its protein-related functions, it is necessary for the synthesis and proper functioning of both DNA and RNA. Finally, with magnesium, pyridoxine is essential for the synthesis of lecithin, and it has been proven to be effective in the reduction of tooth decay.

In the form of pyridoxal phosphate this vitamin functions in the body as a coenzyme for many biological reactions. Either zinc or magnesium can catalyze the formation of this coenzyme, which is especially important to protein and amino acid transformations. The body can form this compound from any of the three forms of pyridoxine. Pyridoxal phosphate catalyzes three main types of amino acid reactions, one of which is the removal of sulfur from the sulfur-containing amino acids. All of the amino acid transport systems seem to require this coenzyme. Pyridoxal phosphate also plays a vital role in the synthesis of the blood protein hemoglobin.

Pyridoxine is found in a wide variety of sources in both free and organically bound forms. These foods are common and include muscle meats, liver, vegetables, egg yolks, whole grains, and nuts. Bananas and pecans are respectable sources, and pyridoxine is synthesized in the lower digestive tract by microorganisms existing there. This intestinal microbial synthesis is an important source of pyridoxine for most species. Since pyridoxine is water soluble, virtually no storage of the pure vitamin occurs in the body.

However, the body can store some compounds containing pyridoxine. Fully one-half of the amount that the body can store is in the form of glycogen phosphorylase, an enzyme stored in the muscles, which facilitates the release of glycogen from the muscle tissues. Any excess over body needs is oxidized to pyridoxic acid, which is excreted in the urine. This acid will disappear from the urine entirely in cases of severe deficiency.

A variety of deficiency symptoms have been noted in animals suffering from a lack of vitamin B_6 or pyridoxine. Circulatory and nervous problems form a large group of these noted symptoms. Lesions in the artery walls are common; they fill up with fat and create all of the symptoms of arteriosclerosis. Also, a form of anemia will occur because of pyridoxine's role in hemoglobin synthesis. Nerve functioning is severely disrupted, to the point of death in severe deficiencies. Muscular twitching, irritability, and convulsive seizures are characteristic deficiency symptoms. Weight gains will cease in human infants, and anemia will develop. The severe convulsive seizures caused by pyridoxine deficiency will end in death.

Several other effects of pyridoxine deficiency have been documented. Animals suffering from deficiency will have four times as much dental decay as animals supplied with adequate pyridoxine. Utilization of the iron absorbed seems to be greatly decreased, and abnormal amounts of iron are stored in the body in cases of pyridoxine deficiency. The iron content of the blood will rise and the copper content of the blood will decrease in any dietary deficiency of pyridoxine. Needs for the essential fatty acids also will increase in any pyridoxine deficiency, and a skin eruption will occur in the area surrounding the nose in humans. Whereas young animals will suffer from convulsions from a pyridoxine deficiency, older animals will exhibit anemia.

A great deal of research on chickens and pyridoxine deficiency has taken place in the years since 1934. The resulting knowledge should be applicable to all birds maintained in captivity, though any direct research on any wild species seems to be non-existent. A deficiency in chickens will cause jerky, nervous leg movements, depressed appetite, and poor growth in growing chicks. Adult chickens will show the symptoms of reduced egg production, reduced hatchability, decreased feed consumption, loss of weight, shrinkage of sexual organs, and involution of the wattles and comb. Death is the final deficiency symptom in any chickens suffering from a pyridoxine deficiency.

Young chicks will be seized by extreme convulsions characterized by great activity with flapping of wings, running around, falling, and rolling around. These severe convulsions will end in death. Though anemia will occur in deficient ducks, this is not a strong symptom of deficiency in chickens or turkeys. A chronic borderline deficiency may cause one severely crippled leg with one or both middle toes bent inward at the first joint.

The first symptoms of deficiency in humans are varied and not all will occur in any one individual. Anyone suffering from at least two of these symptoms should begin taking a balanced B vitamin supplement immediately which contains 50 milligrams of pyridoxine, as outlined by John H. Ellis, M.D. Bursitis and pain in the shoulder joints is a strong symptom, frequently accompanied by cramps in the legs or 'charlie horses', particularly while lying on the bed at night. Awakening with a 'dead' arm with no feeling and dizzyheadedness at any time are two other symptoms. Swelling of the feet, hands, arms, or any other part of the body is a serious symptom of pyridoxine deficiency, particularly during pregnancy.

As important as these symptoms may be, the hands are the primary focus of symptoms of a deficiency of this vitamin. Swelling that masks the veins and tendons may be accompanied by tingling, numbness, prickling, and extreme sensitivity. Hands and fingers may be so painful and sensitive that a handshake is agony, with the joints particularly affected. The hand may go to sleep when writing and fingers will lose control and drop items held in the hand in a momentary, transitory paralysis. Frequently, the deficiency results in inability to make a fist with the fingers touching the palm of the hand. All of these symptoms are the result of the important role pyridoxine plays in the integrity of the nerves and circulatory system. These symptoms also correspond to the noted minor symptoms in chickens, particularly with reference to crippling of their feet.

Pyridoxine deficiency is a distinct possibility in cage birds. Their high protein requirements for their maintenance and breeding will demand a correspondingly higher amount of pyridoxine than is present in the cereal grains, for example. Though whole foods are expected to contain any of the nutrients necessary for their proper absorption and utilization, any cooking or processing will alter this balance. No bird in the wild ever cooks or processes its food in any way, and as a result, wild birds will not exhibit any deficiency of any vital nutrient. Cage birds under our care can and will show deficiency symptoms if their diet does not provide enough pyridoxine.

RIBOFLAVIN

In 1917 researchers realized that the substance they had designated as vitamin B was in part unaffected after heat had destroyed the anti-beriberi properties of the compound. For this reason, they listed the vitamin des-troyed by heat as vitamin B_1 and the one stable to the heat as vitamin B_2. Though vitamin B_2 eventually turned out to be six different vitamins, the designation B_2 remained with riboflavin.

Today, the terms riboflavin and vitamin B_2 refer to the same substance, a slightly water soluble orange-yellow fluorescent pigment. Initially, this vitamin also carried the name Vitamin G. It has in the past also been called by the names ovoflavin, uroflavin, lactoflavin, verdoflavin, and heptoflavin, depending upon the item from which it was extracted. This vitamin exists in two chemical forms in its biological functions.

Riboflavin is a relatively stable vitamin, quite resistant to acid, heat, or oxidation. However, it can be very unstable to both visible and ultraviolet light and to alkaline substances. This vitamin is not affected by light when it is dry, but light quickly destroys it when in solution. Heat in any acid solution will not destroy riboflavin, but any alkali will destroy it. Thus, baking soda used in cooking will destroy the riboflavin content of the food.

Riboflavin was isolated in pure form in 1932, and research then indicated that it was a combination of a protein and a pigment called flavin. Flavin compounds are substances that produce an intense yellow-green fluorescence in water. Riboflavin also contains a simple sugar called ribose, and this accounts for the first half of the name of this vitamin. Riboflavin was synthesized in 1935. Riboflavin is insoluble in fats and fat solvents, and it produces a strong, green fluorescence if irradiated with blue or ultraviolet light. The official British spelling of this vitamin differs from the American in adding a final 'e' to form 'riboflavine'.

Riboflavin is not abundant in the diet, and surveys have revealed there are substantial deficiencies in the American population. Part of this is due to the removal of riboflavin in the refining process, as 80% is removed in refining wheat into white flour. Neither the avian nor the human body is able to store riboflavin in any quantity, though the liver and kidneys do contain higher concentrations than the other tissues.

Yeast is the best source, and milk, liver, eggs, heart, kidney, cheese, green leafy vegetables, nuts, and grains also contain some amounts of riboflavin. Though riboflavin is widely distributed in both animal and vegetable sources, the quantities present are small. Any diet with an appreciable amount of refined foods is very likely to be deficient in riboflavin. The cereal grains are much richer sources of riboflavin after sprouting.

No animal has the ability to synthesize riboflavin, but all green plants, yeast, fungi, and some bacteria synthesize it routinely. Some intestinal bacteria can synthesize riboflavin, but this is not an abundant source of this vitamin. A diet high in starch stimulates this microbial synthesis, but diets that are high in fat or protein inhibit the existence of the producing microorganisms. In the ruminants, however, the entire riboflavin requirement is supplied by the microorganisms existing in the rumen, or first section of the stomach.

The absorption and excretion of excess riboflavin are controlled within narrow limits by the body's nutritional mechanisms. The body absorbs riboflavin through the intestinal wall, and it is attached there to a phosphate molecule. From this point, the blood carries the riboflavin compound to the tissues where it may be attached to a protein molecule. The compound formed in this way is called a flavoprotein. Most excretion of excess riboflavin occurs through the kidneys, and there is no evidence of human or animal toxicity, even at very high levels of dosage. Riboflavin is excreted when protein is broken down in the body and it is retained in the body when protein is being accumulated.

Riboflavin performs a wide variety of important functions within the body. It is essential to normal tissue growth and maintenance, and it also assists in the metabolism of amino acids, fatty acids, and carbohydrates. Riboflavin must be present for the amino acid tryptophan to be converted into niacin. The flavoproteins are important in the cells' utilization of oxygen, and they also work closely with the enzymes which contain niacin.

Riboflavin combines with a protein to form over a dozen known important enzymes in the body's metabolism. Before it can function as a part of these enzymes, riboflavin must have a phosphate group attached to it, which is usually added in the intestinal cells during absorption. Riboflavin's enzyme and coenzyme reactions are essential for the release of energy from glucose and the fatty acids. Riboflavin is also a part of enzymes involved in the transfer of hydrogen atoms in the metabolism of protein. As a part of several of these enzymes and coenzymes, riboflavin contributes to their ability to accept and transfer these hydrogen atoms. There are a number of known antagonists that will replace riboflavin in its functions and thus will prevent it from functioning usefully in the body. Also, research has indicated that riboflavin is probably required for the formation of melanin in the feathers of birds.

Deficiency of riboflavin has been termed by some experts as the most common vitamin deficiency in America, though this is certainly debatable. Riboflavin deficiency goes by the formal name of ariboflavinosis. In the human

147

population, the intake must be low for several months for the commonest symptoms of mouth abnormality to appear. The tongue will become smooth and sore with a characteristic purplish-red color. The lips may become noticeably red also, with cracks appearing in the corners of the mouth. A deficiency in animals also will cause a reduction in reproductive capacity. Pregnant animals will give birth to young showing abnormalities or will abort the embryos. Alopecia, or loss of hair, may also occur in these animals. Such congenital malformations as harelip and cataracts, clearly demonstrated in animal experiments, will occur if deficiency happens at a crucial embryonic stage of pregnancy. Growth of the young will also be retarded.

Problems with the eyes and skin can also be symptoms of riboflavin deficiency in humans. Eye fatigue, oversensitivity to light, blurred vision, and bloodshot eyes are all symptoms of riboflavin deficiency. A deficiency also causes a gritty feeling on the inside of the eyelids, burning eyes, and pupil dilation. Though the skin may become dry and scaly, a greasy skin inflammation on the face and ears, or particularly on the scrotum in males, is more likely. Animals will also experience abnormal growth of the blood vessels of the eye into the cornea, and the eye may eventually form a cataract.

Symptoms of deficiency in chickens are well known and should appear similar in all species of birds kept in captivity. In adult hens, egg production will not be affected in a riboflavin deficiency. Hatchability becomes poor within two weeks after hens are fed a deficient diet, and eggs from severely riboflavin deficient hens will not hatch. Hatchability will return to normal in about seven days with adequate supplementation of riboflavin in the hen's diet.

Chicks suffering from a deficiency will have a good appetite, but very slow growth. Gradually, they become weak and emaciated. The leg muscles are atrophied and flabby, and the skin is very dry and rough. Between the first and second weeks of a deficiency, the chicks will have diarrhea. They don't move around unless forced to move, and then they may walk on their hocks with the help of their wings. Malfunction of the sciatic nerve causes the toes to curl inward in paralysis, both when resting on the hocks and when walking. In an advanced stage of deficiency, the chicks lie with their legs extended. In a marginal deficiency, spontaneous recovery will occur, indicating a reduced requirement for riboflavin with age. If the deficiency is severe enough that the curled toes symptom remains over a long term, the damage to the sciatic nerve is irreparable, and then the deformity will be permanent.

On several occasions I noted this curled toe syndrome on fledgling Society Finches in my collection. At the time, as most breeders would, I attributed this to a genetic defect in the two pairs of my Society Finches that occasionally produced such offspring. The benefit of additional knowledge and experience has convinced me that this was definitely a riboflavin deficiency. Since less than one percent of the offspring of my strain of Society Finches showed this defect, there is little doubt that this reflected an unusually high riboflavin requirement in these few birds, governed by their biochemical individuality.

The information presented earlier in this section and my own experience indicate that a riboflavin deficiency is a strong possibility in any birds maintained in captivity. The only food commonly offered to cage birds that contains a reasonably good amount of riboflavin is hard-boiled egg, particularly the yolk. Yet, this source in abundance together with sunflower seed and millet, both common nutritional items that contain riboflavin, failed to supply enough riboflavin to prevent a severe deficiency symptom from appearing in my finches. The only real suggestion I can offer to the breeder is to mix a high potency, balanced B vitamin supplement with some soft food that the birds will eat if you should notice the appearance of any of the riboflavin deficiency symptoms noted in this section.

THIAMIN

Thiamin was the first of the B complex vitamins to be scientifically and chemically identified. It was crystallized in pure form in 1926, and its structure was established and synthesized in 1936. You will also see the name vitamin B_1 used for thiamin frequently, and it was called aneurin in years past. Thiamin is a water soluble, white, crystalline substance in its pure form. It is insoluble in fats and fat solvents. Thiamin hydrochloride and thiamin mononitrate are two more of the stable forms of this vitamin. Several thiamin derivatives have been synthesized, and they are absorbed in the body at a faster rate than natural thiamin. The spelling of the name thiamin frequently is seen with a final 'e', as 'thiamine'.

When food refining for increased storage life became common in the middle of the 19th century, thiamin deficiency in the form of beriberi then became a major health problem. Until the 1940's, beriberi was the main health problem in Java, Malaysia, Japan, and the Philippines. As late as 1947, thiamin deficiency was one of the two major causes of death in the Philippine Islands. Over 20% of the Japanese Naval personnel suffered from beriberi until 1882 when Tataki changed the diet of the Navy to include more protein, and at the same time inadvertently added additional thiamin to the sailors' diet. Beriberi was first recognized as a dietary deficiency disease in Java.

Thiamin is readily available in the food supply and is well absorbed in the body and easily transported. Brewer's yeast, pork, and liver are the three best sources of thiamin. Since these foods are something less than common in the average cage bird diet, whole grains, sunflower seeds, wheat germ, pecans, and other nuts are the best sources for avian nutrition. Most of the thiamin is in the outer coverings of the hulled grain, and the removal of this layer, particularly in rice, has caused an untold amount of suffering in the world. Even in wheat, as much as 77% of the thiamin content is removed when it is refined into white flour. Intestinal synthesis of thiamin does occur as a result of microbial action, but this is not an important source of thiamin in humans and occurs too far down in the digestive tract of birds to be absorbed and of value in avian nutrition. Here we have another clue as to why coprophagy is such a universal practice among our avian charges in captivity. Coprophagy would enable the bird to reclaim the thiamin synthesized by bacteria in the lower part of the digestive tract where it cannot be absorbed.

Absorption takes place in the first part of the small intestine, and this absorption requires an input of energy. A deficiency of folacin, another of the B complex vitamins, in the diet will hinder the absorption of thiamine. Also, analysis shows that human milk normally contains less than half the thiamin content of cow's milk, and breast-fed babies can get beriberi if the mother's milk is deficient in thiamin.

The body does not store thiamin in any quantity, but levels of this vitamin in the tissues will increase with supplementation. Any amount that is present over and above the body's needs will be excreted in the urine. A high fat and protein content in the diet reduces the amount of thiamin required, while an increased carbohydrate intake will increase the need for thiamin. Consumption of alcohol and sugar and also smoking greatly increase the thiamin requirement in the body. Alcoholics are particularly susceptible to severe thiamin deficiency. There is no indication of any toxicity from an excess intake of thiamin, even at very high levels.

The first symptom of a thiamin deficiency in humans is loss of appetite, technically called anorexia, and other symptoms appear rapidly. A deficiency of this vitamin has a more profound effect on the appetite than that of any other nutrient, as all interest in food is lost. Nausea, vomiting, constipation, and decreased muscle tone are also early symptoms of thiamin deficiency. In babies. Deficiency symptoms develop very rapidly and can cause death within hours. Excessive carbon dioxide in the blood causes a bluish color in the skin. Babies that are suffering from the onset of this severe deficiency have a very fast heartbeat and a very characteristic, loud, piercing cry. The administration of thiamin will relieve all of these symptoms within hours.

Adults will develop the disease symptoms called beriberi, which can come in two forms. In dry beriberi, the patient becomes thin and emaciated. This is also called wasting beriberi. The other form is wet beriberi, which is also known as edematous beriberi, in which there is a great swelling and accumulation of fluid beginning at the feet. The accumulation of fluid in the heart muscle leads to heart failure and death. In the wet form of beriberi, tissue wasting still occurs, but it is masked by the accumulation of fluids. Both forms share the same symptoms of irritability, along with vague uneasiness and disorderly thinking. The most acute symptom is mental confusion which rapidly leads to coma.

These symptoms of deficiency result from the functions and utilization of thiamin within the body. These functions are particularly concerned with the metabolism of carbohydrates, but thiamin is involved to a lesser extent in the metabolism of fats and amino acids. There is some evidence also that the

151

presence of thiamin is necessary for the synthesis of the amino acid glycine in the body.

For its utilization in the metabolism, thiamin forms a coenzyme that is vital to the metabolism of carbohydrates and fatty acids. Thiamin needs in metabolism will increase in proportion to the increase of carbohydrates that must be burned for energy within the avian body. In testing this increased need in pigeons, the pigeons that were kept experimentally in a cold room suffered from a need for this vitamin sooner than those that were kept in a warm area. Cold weather always increases the need for body heat through carbohydrate metabolism, which in turn increases the body's need for thiamin.

Thiamin also activates an enzyme necessary to oxidize glucose before it can be used to produce ribose, a simple sugar component of RNA, and before it can be used to produce an enzyme necessary for the synthesis of the fatty acids. Thiamin also has a strong effect on the nervous system, in addition to its coenzyme functions.

Symptoms of deficiency in chickens appear about three weeks after the beginning of a deficient diet. The onset of these symptoms in adult chickens is gradual. As in humans, loss of appetite is the first symptom, followed by loss of weight, ruffled feathers, weakness in the legs, and unsteady gait. Adult chickens may also show a blue comb and polyneuritis, the inflammation of many of the body's nerves simultaneously. Once the loss of neuromuscular coordination occurs, the chickens will die shortly.

Deficiency symptoms in young chicks may appear before two weeks of age, and the onset of such symptoms is sudden. The loss of appetite mentioned earlier is permanent, and the chicks will not resume eating until their thiamin requirement is restored. This thiamin must be either force-fed or injected in order to induce the chickens to resume eating. In a continuous deficiency, muscle paralysis occurs beginning in the toes and working upward. The result is contraction of nerves and muscles which causes a star-gazing position in the chicks. This star-gazing position is more pronounced than in the manganese deficiency symptom discussed later, with twisting of the neck. After this stage, the chicken loses the ability to stand, body temperature lowers, and breathing slows.

Several factors are important as destructive influences on thiamin. First, thiamin is the most vulnerable of all the B vitamins to destruction from heat. High temperatures used in drying food will destroy most of the vitamin B_1 in those food products. Oxidation, especially in the presence of alkalis, is also quite destructive of thiamin. In Japan the danger of thiamin deficiency in the past was great from the consumption of raw fish, as well as the consumption of large quantities of polished rice. Some raw fish contain an enzyme called thiaminase, which splits and thus destroys the thiamin molecule. Fortunately, thiaminase is inactivated by the heat of cooking.

For the nutritional needs of finches and other birds in captivity, millet and sunflower seeds are both good sources of thiamin. The thiamin contents of these seeds may vary widely, often depending upon the particular species of producing plants. Also, any whole grain that is included in the diet should supply an adequate amount of thiamin for seed eating birds. Since thiamin and the other B vitamins, excepting cobalamin and folacin, are not stored to any great extent in the body, a continuous supply of thiamin must be present in the diet of every avian species that is kept in captivity. Greens will supply some of the dietary requirement for this vitamin, and pecans and other nuts are also reasonable sources. Fruits as a rule, however, are poor dietary sources of this vitamin. Do not rely on any fruit included in the diet to contain enough thiamin for the daily needs of any avian species.

"The vitamins serve primarily as catalysts without which another chemical process in the body cannot occur."

CHAPTER 9

OTHER NON-MINERAL NUTRITIONAL FACTORS

AMYGDALIN

The controversy which surrounds this substance rivals that which erupts upon the mention of nuclear power. This is most unfortunate, since the controversy has virtually ended the possibility of serious research on this substance. Amygdalin has not been proven to be a vitamin as yet, though it is frequently referred to as vitamin B_{17} in many writings. Amygdalin is a principal component of the compound that is more well-known by its name in therapeutic doses, which is Laetrile. Need I say more about the controversial nature of Laetrile? Though this controversy has slipped somewhat into the background since the first edition of *Nutrition of Finches and Other Cage Birds* was published in 1981, the use of Laetrile is still prohibited in the United States.

Amygdalin has not been exposed to any extensive research, so its true nutritional value is largely unknown. The controversy over its use as a cancer treatment has served to thoroughly squelch any serious research into its true nutritional effectiveness. We will be lucky to hear anything but wild emotion concerning this compound for the next fifty years. Whether amygdalin will be classified eventually as a vitamin is open to question at this time. Too little is known about it to hazard even a guess.

155

The following presumed train of events is what has so divided the scientific community and condemned amygdalin to nonentity status, at least in the United States. The cyanide in amygdalin's chemistry is said to attack cancer cells selectively. In normal cells, the cyanide content of amygdalin is broken down through action of the enzyme rhodanese, and then the normal cells excrete it. However, cancer cells do not possess this necessary enzyme, but are surrounded by another enzyme that releases the cyanide from the amygdalin, and the cyanide destroys the cancerous cell through cyanide poisoning. How true or false this train of events may be will in all probability not be known until the next century is far advanced.

Though any benefit to the birds in your care is totally unknown at this point, for your own information, the best known source of amygdalin is apricot pits. Most whole seeds of fruits, as well as many grains and vegetables also contain amygdalin. Millet, buckwheat and flaxseed are good sources that are in common use in bird diets, and raspberries, cranberries, blackberries, and blueberries are also good sources of this compound.

BIOFLAVONOIDS

The bioflavonoids are a large group of water soluble substances that were referred to as vitamin P until 1950. Some writings still refer to them with this designation, and you will also see them referred to simply as 'flavonoids'. Research has identified more than 800 different bioflavonoids. They were first suggested as dietary factors in 1936, and hesperidin is probably the most active of these substances. Rutin and quercetin are also well known bioflavonoids. These are brightly colored substances found in the peelings and juice of citrus fruits, and in buckwheat, grapes, cherries, apricots, blackberries, and to a lesser extent in other fruits and vegetables. Buckwheat is a particularly good source of rutin. The bioflavonoids appear to be completely non-toxic.

Researchers to date have been able to uncover no specific biological role for the bioflavonoids, and there is no evidence of any specific dietary need for them. Nevertheless, the bioflavonoids can chelate copper, and they perform an antioxidant activity in the body. Specifically, research has proven them able to preserve the useful life of adrenalin by preventing its oxidation. Also, there are strong indications that the bioflavonoids may prevent the development of excess fragility in the blood capillaries.

These substances do exhibit some noticeable effects in the body with respect to enhancing the utilization of ascorbic acid. In some manner the bioflavonoids appear to assist in the proper absorption and use of vitamin C in the body. The exact way in which they work is unknown. The popular writings on nutrition list many health improvements resulting from an increased dietary intake of the bioflavonoids, but all of these seem to be the same as reported for increased vitamin C intake. It also seems that in some cases supplementation of either vitamin C or the bioflavonoids alone is largely ineffective, but together they will accomplish the needed result. Obviously, a large amount of serious research is still required on the bioflavonoids. I can find no information on the bioflavonoids with specific reference to avian nutrition.

ENZYMES

Though most of the sections in this book contain some information on individual enzymes, this section will cover enzymes in a more general way. A rather heated debate has raged for years over the subject of enzymes in the food supply. Some authorities, particularly in the health food industry, maintain that enzymes must be present in the food eaten. Other authorities hold that any enzyme entering the digestive system is broken down through digestion and utilized for its parts, and that the body manufactures any enzymes that are required internally for the body's metabolism. I suspect that the whole truth lies somewhere in between these two opposing views.

Enzymes are protein compounds that control all body processes. They function as catalysts in the body for all biochemical processes. Though they are probably synthesized by most of the body's cells, the liver and the pancreas are truly enzyme factories. The cells of these two organs produce a variety of enzymes that are necessary for the digestion and utilization of nutrients within the body.

The body contains and requires an untold number of different enzymes for its metabolic functions. The only figure noted indicates that over 700 different enzymes have already been identified, and there are quite probably thousands of them required by the body for various functions during every moment of physical life. Some of these work in an acid medium, such as pepsin in the stomach at a pH of 1.8, which is extremely acid. Others work in an alkaline medium, such as trypsin from the pancreas, at a pH of 8.2, which is quite alkaline. For this reason, the actions of many enzymes may be hindered or stopped if the body's tissues become too acid or too alkaline. One drop of blood contains over 100,000 enzyme molecules, in addition to all of the other blood cells and nutrient items that are circulating in that drop of blood. Over one-fourth of the enzymes active in the body also contain a metal ion. The sections on minerals go into greater detail on many of these metal-based enzymes.

All living things are rich in enzymes. Once the tissue dies, the enzymes gradually decompose. Whether they are totally digested when eaten, or absorbed and utilized without change, one primary fact must be paramount in your knowledge. *Any amount of cooking destroys all enzymes.* At temperatures of 125° Fahrenheit, all enzymes have been destroyed or rendered inactive. The ramifications of this fact are as yet almost totally unknown.

OROTIC ACID

This substance is popularly considered to be a vitamin and is referred to in a number of publications as vitamin B_{13}. Nevertheless, I can discover no scientific source in this country that yet accepts this view, though it has been synthesized and is used as a treatment for multiple sclerosis in Europe. The supplement form of this substance is calcium orotate.

Researchers have reported orotic acid to be necessary for a number of chemical reactions within the body. The body metabolism of folic acid and cobalamin is said to require orotic acid, and it is reported to be essential for the biosynthesis of nucleic acid. Its presumed necessity for the regeneration of the body's cells is the basis for its use in Europe as a treatment of multiple sclerosis. There are known human hereditary diseases in which overproduction of orotic acid occurs and the substance then appears in the urine. This is found primarily in the oriental races of humanity.

The best known sources of orotic acid are root vegetables and whey. There are no known specific deficiency symptoms caused by a lack of this substance, but a deficiency may cause liver disorders, cell degeneration, premature aging, and overall degeneration, as in multiple sclerosis. Obviously, a great deal of additional research is necessary to determine the exact body requirement and nutritional effects of this substance. At least, at the state of current knowledge, there is no known toxicity of orotic acid. I have not as yet discovered any information regarding the possible need of orotic acid in avian nutrition.

PANGAMIC ACID

Pangamic acid is referred to in many places as vitamin B_{15}, and you will also see it referred to as 'pangamate' and 'calcium pangamate' in some nutritional references. However, its nature and composition are still under debate, though scientists in Russia and other countries now definitely classify this substance as a vitamin. Since the publication of *Nutrition of Finches and Other Cage Birds*, research has proven that this substance can improve the vital, basic functions of each cell. This is because it improves the oxygenation of the cells and in the process greatly prolongs the life of each individual cell. Prolonging the life of each cell is obviously of considerable benefit to the whole organism, whether it be avian, animal, or human. Fewer cells to replace after their death means less nutrients required, and more of the body's metabolism and energy available for the maintenance and health of all of the cells of the body.

The scientists of the Soviet Union took an early interest in vitamin B_{15} because of its reported ability to increase oxygenation of the cells for greater stamina and to retard the aging process at the cell level. Perhaps the advanced age of the Politburo members at the time had something to do with this interest. Even decades ago, scientists and nutritionists in the Soviet Union used pangamic acid widely in health care, and the nutritionists of other countries rapidly followed their lead. The Russian research was translated into English many years ago, and it is readily available for anyone who cares to do the research into the early history of this substance. The Russians definitely regard pangamic acid as a vitamin and claim that it is of vital importance in maintaining health and full activity into old age.

The isolation of dimethylglycine or DMG as the active ingredient in pangamic acid has resulted in a resurgence of research into pangamic acid and its characteristics. This new research has proven that DMG definitely has the ability to boost the activity of the body's immune system. Pangamic acid can increase the body's ability to fight off invading microorganisms four-fold, and even in a body already weakened by disease, the immune reaction from pangamic acid supplementation enabled the body to fully double its immune response.

Another field of research that has shown a great deal of promise is in the control of epileptic seizures. Supplementation with the concentrated DMG or dimethylglycine caused a noticeable reduction in epileptic seizures. The probable rationale behind this improvement was increase in the body's ability to metabolize homocysteine, a chemical which is present in the body and is known to cause seizures. Further research with mice confirmed that reduction in seizures was produced as the supplementation of dimethylglycine increased.

As this substance does not seem to be synthesized within the body, there seems little doubt that in time DMG, if not the entire pangamic acid molecule, will be classified as a vitamin. Research that indicates its beneficial effects within the cells of the body continues to mount, and most researchers have now become convinced that this substance is as beneficial in the body's metabolism as the Russian researchers reported 20 years ago.

At this point, with both Russian and American research confirming the value of this substance in the nutrition of the human race, and further research with mice confirming their need for it also, there is little doubt that birds will soon be included in the research into the effects of pangamic acid and its active ingredient, dimethylglycine, on their metabolism.

For your own interest in avian nutrition, a number of items that are frequently used as foods for birds in our cages and aviaries are known to be good sources of pangamic acid. Brewer's yeast, pumpkin seeds, sesame seeds, nuts, and the whole grains are all good sources of pangamic acid and its active constituent, dimethylglycine or DMG.

RNA AND DNA

The formal names of these complicated substances are ribonucleic acid and deoxyribonucleic acid. They are not nutrients, but cell components. Since any nutritional study will encounter these names frequently, and this book also has referred to them frequently, they are covered here in a basic form to answer any question that the beginning student of nutrition might have. Nucleic acids are structural components of the cells, and living cells produce them. A detailed, scientific examination of these substances is available in the *Review of Physiological Chemistry* listed in the bibliography. For reasons of brevity, all publications refer to these substances as RNA and DNA.

RNA is a single-stranded molecule built on a base of ribose, one of the simple sugars, a monosaccharide. There are three different classes of RNA which differ in size, function, and stability. These are messenger RNA, shortened to mRNA; transfer RNA, usually written tRNA; and ribosomal RNA, written as rRNA.

Messenger RNA shows the most variation in form of the RNA's in size and stability. The mRNA transfers information from the gene which carries the genetic material to the cell's internal machinery for making proteins. The tRNA serves as an adaptor for the translation of information from the mRNA into the specific structure of the amino acid that is being produced. The rRNA acts as the machinery for the synthesis of proteins from the mRNA patterns. As you might suspect from the complexity of this process, the rRNA is extremely complex, and its molecules are groups of at last four other RNA molecules plus nearly 100 specific protein molecules.

RNA is the user of the genetic information, and the DNA is the storage house of that information. The primary function of DNA is to provide the progeny with the genetic information possessed by the parent. This holds true from the simplest bacterium and actinomycete to an organism as complex as the physical body of the human being, though a human cell will contain about 1000 times more DNA than the bacterial cell. The complete set of chromosomes contains enough DNA to code for one million pairs of genes.

DNA is a very long, complex, double-stranded molecule. In construction, it looks much like a spiral staircase with no center pole. The two strands on the outside run in opposite directions, and each side seems to contain all of the stored genetic information. These strands unwind and separate, apparently in small sections, when the cell begins to divide, which is only at very specific times. When the cell divides, both halves of the DNA molecule still possess the entire genetic pattern. Each half of the DNA molecule rebuilds the side that was lost to the other new cell into a once again complete DNA molecule.

161

In reproduction, the male sperm carries one side of the DNA molecule with its full genetic pattern of the male's body structure, and the female egg carries one side of the DNA molecule with its full genetic pattern of the female's body. When the sperm unites with the egg, the genetic patterns of both parents are merged and shared. The genetic characteristics that are dominant in both parents will manifest in the offspring, and the offspring will share the full genetic pattern of both parents, even though many of those characteristics may be recessive and will not manifest as physical attributes in the offspring.

This chain of predestined events is the reason why excessive radiation can be such a disaster to the reproductive process. Remember that the basic cell has a full DNA molecule, with a complete pattern on each side of the full physical form and characteristics of the total organism. Should radiation strike and destroy a pattern on one side of the molecule, that pattern will be resupplied and reestablished from the other side of the DNA molecule to make the pattern whole once more. Believe me, this is not a rare occurrence; it happens a thousand times in every second of every day. The body continually struggles to repair and replace the damage done by the natural radiation that constantly surrounds us. A number of nutrients are vitally important in the ability of the body and its cells to repair and rebuild their structure under this constant bombardment of radiation. If you haven't noted this in the sections on vitamins, go to the index and look up the entry on radiation to find the page number for each reference to radiation and the nutrients that protect against radiation's effects.

However, the sperm and egg carry only one-half of the DNA molecule of the parent. Radiation that strikes and destroys a tiny part of this pattern means that this particular part of the genetic pattern is lost completely. As an example, if the part of the pattern destroyed is the genetic ability to form a vital enzyme, the body of the offspring may lose the ability to form this vital enzyme. Yet, the genetic patterns do have a fail-safe mechanism, since even if the enzyme pattern is destroyed by radiation in the male DNA molecule, it will still exist and can be replaced when the male and female DNA patterns unite.

As another example, if a pattern for an outward physical characteristic, such as blue eyes, is destroyed by radiation striking the DNA in the female egg, and the male sperm carries no gene for blue eyes, then this possible characteristic will be completely lost in the pairing of the male and female portions of the DNA.

Somehow, it seems very hard to conceive of all of this incredible complexity and organization in such a microscopic package simply occurring by chance without the guidance of a supremely wise Intelligence.

*   *   *   *   *   *   *   *   *   *   *   *   *   *   *

Three men in the 1970's and 1980's studied avian specimens from two entirely new perspectives: protein electrophoresis and DNA analysis. Charles G. Sibley and Jon E. Ahlquist in 1975 began making major revisions in the existing taxonomic structure of the birds of the world, based on their techniques of protein electrophoresis and DNA-DNA hybridization. Though their discoveries are now history, the ramifications of these discoveries will continue to reverberate throughout the ornithological community through the next century.

In 1983, Burt L. Monroe, Jr., began correlating and computerizing this information, which was published in a 1990 volume as Sibley and Monroe's *Distribution and Taxonomy of Birds of the World*. They followed this in 1993 with *A World Checklist of Birds*. Though the family Psittacidae (the parrots), as an example, remained relatively stable with only a few minor changes, the families set up to classify the finches and other seed-eating birds that are so popular in aviculture were completely transformed, expanded and reorganized into only two new families: Passeridae and Fringillidae.

There is still a huge amount of controversy surrounding this checklist, since a traditional softbill family, the Motacillidae (the wagtails and pipits), has also been placed in the family Passeridae, along with the traditional finch families Estrildidae, Prunellidae and Ploceidae. Other families of soft-billed birds, the Icteridae (the orioles, blackbirds, meadowlarks, cowbirds and others), the Thraupidae (the tanagers, euphonias, chlorophonias and others), the Parulidae (the warblers), the Coerebidae (the conebills, bananaquit, flowerpiercers, dacnis and others), the Tersinidae (the swallow-tanager) and the Zeledoniidae (the wren-thrush) have also been placed in the Sibley-Monroe family Fringillidae, along with the four traditional finch families Emberizidae, Fringillidae, Drepanididae, and Catamblyrhynchidae. Thus, Sibley and Monroe have discarded any distinctive family classifications for the seed-eating birds alone. Obviously this lumping together of so many different, dissimilar species based on their DNA and protein similarities, has caused, and will continue to cause extreme controversy. When the dust finally settles, a compromise in this part of the avian taxonomic reorganization seems likely.

UBIQUINONE

The discovery of ubiquinone, perhaps more commonly called coenzyme Q, is one of the more recent nutritional advances. This discovery took place only in 1961. The structure of ubiquinone is very similar to that of vitamin E and vitamin K. Still, since it is synthesized within the body, it is not technically considered to be a vitamin. Coenzyme Q serves as an essential link in the respiratory chain in which energy is released from the energy-yielding nutrients. Without this link in the metabolic chain, the release of the energy would be incomplete.

Ubiquinone is found in nearly all living cells. Vitamin C and selenium function to maintain high tissue concentrations of this substance, and any excess can be excreted in the urine. Synthesis of ubiquinone depends on the presence of two of the amino acids – tyrosine and phenylalanine, and five of the vitamins – niacin, folacin, cobalamin, pyridoxine, and pantothenic acid. A pantothenic acid deficiency will depress the synthesis of coenzyme Q by 50%.

PART THREE

THE MINERALS

AND OTHER NUTRITIONAL ELEMENTS

"The body has mechanisms for controlling the absorption and excretion of essential minerals, and all body tissues and internal fluids contain varying levels of these minerals and other elements."

CHAPTER 10

INTRODUCTION TO THE MINERALS
AND OTHER NUTRITIONAL ELEMENTS

Minerals and other non-mineral elements exist in the avian body in both organic and inorganic combinations. About five percent of the body weight is in the form of minerals. Analysis of the residual ash of all living things reveals twenty to thirty minerals present, over and above all of the minerals and elements that are known to be essential. These additional minerals may be simply body contaminants, or they may have an as yet unestablished role in nutrition. The term 'minerals' will be used frequently in these chapters to refer in general to both the actual metallic elements and the non-metallic elements, which are equally as vital in the nutritional process.

The body has mechanisms for controlling the absorption and excretion of essential minerals, and all body tissues and internal fluids contain varying levels of these minerals and other elements. The controlling forces and factors for the levels of these minerals within the body are called the body's homeostatic mechanisms. The homeostatic mechanisms for some minerals are very effective and exacting, but virtually nonexistent for others.

Minerals in nature exist as combinations of isotopes. The nature of the mineral is dictated by the number of protons in the nucleus, but the number of neutrons may differ. These different numbers of neutrons are the different

167

isotopes of the mineral. The body apparently cannot use all isotopes indiscriminately, as will be covered in the discussions of biological transmutations in Chapter 13.

Mineral elements in the body fluids occur primarily as salts. These salts in solution will separate into their component ions, or electrically charged particles, and they are in this form called 'electrolytes'. The ions that are positively charged are referred to as 'cations', while the negatively charged ions are called 'anions'.

Eight essential minerals exist as cations: calcium, sodium, potassium, magnesium, manganese, zinc, iron, and copper. Cations have a deficiency of electrons, and this accounts for their positive charge.

Five of the essential minerals are anions or are found in anionic groupings: chloride, iodide, phosphate, molybdate, and selenite. Bicarbonates and sulfates are also anions. The anions and cations are exactly balanced in all body fluids to maintain osmotic pressure. The main cation of the intra-cellular fluids is potassium, while the main one of the extracellular fluids is sodium.

Minerals are vital to the overall physical and mental health of a living organism. Though the term mineral is used for all of these elements, as previously mentioned, some are not metals, such as chlorine and fluorine. All of these elements serve many functions within the body, and for purposes of organization are divided into bulk essential minerals and trace essential minerals. In order of their quantity found within the body, the bulk minerals, or 'macro-minerals', are calcium, phosphorus, potassium, sulfur, sodium, chlorine, and magnesium. These are present in relatively high amounts in body tissues. Silicon is on the borderline between essential bulk minerals and essential trace minerals. All others essential in nutrition are generally classified as trace minerals and trace elements. The bulk elements are measured in grams and milligrams, though it might be better to refer to the body contents of calcium and phosphorus in humans in terms of pounds or kilograms. They are by far the two most abundant minerals in the body. The trace elements, their requirements and their functions in metabolism, are measured in milligrams or micrograms.

Four basic elements form the vast bulk of the body and most organic compounds contain at least three of them. These four are carbon, oxygen, hydrogen, and nitrogen. Carbohydrates and fats are made up of carbon, hydrogen, and oxygen, and the proteins contain nitrogen, in addition. Water is a combination of hydrogen and oxygen, of course, and by the measurement of the body's water content, these two gaseous elements would be by far the most abundant elements in the body. Oxygen is also required as a gas to metabolize all food products and maintain life in most living things. Only certain anaerobic microorganisms are able to exist without oxygen.

These four elements form about 95% of the substance of the avian or human body. No physical life would be possible in their absence. These four elements are so basic to nearly all biological life that they are normally ignored in discussions if nutrition. Other than the need for gaseous oxygen for the energy metabolism of the cells, I have encountered no reference to any specific individual need for carbon, hydrogen or nitrogen in the body in their basic, elemental form, other than the uses in biological transmutations, for which Chapter 13 is now the area of coverage.

The absorption of minerals in the digestive system is not completely understood, but it now appears that the chelates formed of minerals may be the most important factor in their absorption. When a mineral atom is attached to one of the amino acids or to any other chelating agent, which are collectively called ligands, a chelate is formed. The chelates will form because of the peculiarities in the electron shells of the transitional metals. Amino acids, particularly cysteine and histidine, are excellent chelating agents. Peptides, which are linkages of two or more amino acids, and whole proteins can also serve as ligands.

Chelates have two primary metabolic functions in the body and one deleterious effect. First, they transport and store the metal ions of the essential minerals. Second, they can be essential in such functions as the formation of heme, the iron chelate portion of the hemoglobin molecule. This essential function is also evident in the formation of cobalamin around the cobalt molecule as a cobalt chelate. Chelates can be so stable that the metal ion becomes nutritionally unavailable. This can have an unfortunate effect on nutritional requirements, since these chelates are able to tie up an essential mineral completely and prevent its absorption and/or utilization within the body. This occurs with phytic acid, which attaches itself to zinc so securely that the zinc is rendered unabsorbable. Oxalic acid will do the same to calcium, rendering it insoluble as calcium oxalate. This will be covered fully in the sections on the individual minerals.

One of the primary body functions of minerals is in the maintenance of the acid-base or acid-alkaline balance in the body. Those minerals which form an acid medium in solution are chlorine, sulfur, and phosphorus. The acid-forming minerals are found mainly in protein foods from animal sources and in cereal grains. Take care not to confuse this acid reaction in the body with the acid taste of foods. These acids in foods are broken down in the digestive cycles with no effect on the acid-base balance. The minerals that will form a basic or alkaline medium in solution in the body are calcium, sodium, potassium, and magnesium. These occur predominantly in fruits, nuts, and vegetables.

If foods contain acids that the body cannot metabolize, such as benzoic acid, oxalic acid, and tannic acid, the acid potential of these overbalances the

169

alkalinity of their base-forming mineral constituents. These non-metabolizable acids occur in such foods as cranberries, rhubarb, cocoa and tea. Milk, pure carbohydrates, and fats will have no effect on the acid-base balance of the body.

Should the acid-alkaline balance begin to shift in either direction, the body has a variety of ways to bring the balance back to the required level. Since excess acidity is more often the danger, both the excretion of carbon dioxide through the lungs and the slight acidity of the urine that is excreted through the kidneys will rid the body of excess acidity under any normal conditions.

When normal excretion is insufficient, the body can neutralize either acids or bases by use of the carbonates, phosphates, and proteins that act as buffers in the blood. Even the bones are able to release phosphates to act as buffers and remove hydrogen ions, which are the basis of acidity, from the body fluids. If these buffers are not sufficient to handle excess alkalinity, the body is able to combine water and carbon dioxide, which are normally excreted, into carbonic acid. This carbonic acid will neutralize the excess alkali-forming elements.

In the same manner, the body can form a base from a nitrogen-hydrogen compound formed during protein breakdown to prevent excess acid from forming and causing a problem. In addition, the body can break down carbonic acid through the action of a zinc-containing enzyme that is called carbonic anhydrase. With this variety of means for neutralizing both the excess acidity and excess alkalinity of the body's fluids, it is quite rare to encounter any excess of either acidity or alkalinity that is caused by dietary intake.

When feeding any of the avian species, take care not to offer the birds exclusively animal products, such as eggs along with the cereal grains. This combination without any other foods to modify the balance will eventually cause an excess of body acidity. Likewise, if the birds are fed exclusively fruits, nuts, and vegetables, they will soon show an excess of body alkalinity. All wild birds instinctively will vary their diet to include a variety of both animal and plant sources to forestall any body imbalance. You must do the same when feeding birds in captivity. This also explains one reason besides nutritional deficiencies as to why birds maintained strictly on diets of cereal grains soon sicken and die.

Minerals in general perform a very wide range of functions in the human or avian body. They act as catalysts for many reactions in the body. In this function, they are not a part of the initial compounds nor of the end products, but they must be present for a reaction to take place. At least nine different minerals are required to catalyze the breakdown of fatty acids to energy, carbon dioxide, and water. The minerals are components of essential body compounds as parts of hormones, enzymes, and other compounds, and they are an essential part of several vitamins. Minerals are important in the maintenance of water balance in the body, with water movement governed by the concentration of minerals on either side of the cell membrane as electrolytes. Minerals are also required for the transmission of the nerve impulses, the regulation of muscle contraction, and the growth of body tissue.

Though minerals are not destroyed in food preparation, processing, or storage, the refining of food products removes substantial quantities of both the bulk elements and the trace elements from the food. This aspect will be covered fully with the discussion of each individual mineral and element. As previously mentioned, minerals can be rendered insoluble by a variety of factors.

Other elements in the same periodic group act as antagonists to the essential minerals and will displace them in a biological reaction. The best description I have seen of this is in describing the minerals as keys. Those in the same periodic group will all fit the same biological lock. But the displacing mineral can neither perform the required function nor get out, so it is similar to the wrong key in a lock. The antagonistic mineral will not work, but it prevents the right mineral from getting in to do the job. And consequently, the necessary biological job simply doesn't get done.

This general introduction to the minerals has laid the foundation for a better understanding of the biological functioning of each mineral. All of the essential minerals have unique functions to perform, and all are necessary for life and health. I have also included a short section of the additional minerals that may be proven essential in the future and those that are found consistently within the body.

"One of the primary body functions of minerals
is in the maintenance of the acid-base or acid-alkaline
balance in the body."

CHAPTER 11

THE ESSENTIAL BULK ELEMENTS

CALCIUM

Calcium is the most abundant mineral in the body with as much as two percent of the body weight consisting of calcium. Calcium is usually associated with phosphorus in its biological functioning, and fully 99% of the calcium in the human body is in the bones and teeth. The percentage of body calcium found in the bones of birds is less, but still represents over 90% of the body's content. Obviously, calcium is an essential bulk element in nutrition, and much more remains to be learned about it, as the remainder of this section will point out. The earth's crust contains calcium in the amount of about 36,300 parts per million, and it is present in sea water at the rate of around 400 parts per million. These are average amounts, taking the entire planet into consideration.

Food sources of calcium are irregular, and most foods of plant origin are low in calcium. For human consumption, milk is one of the very best sources for those who can digest it properly. Substantial portions of our black population and most of the oriental populations cannot digest milk because of the lactose content. Fortunately, processing of the milk does not reduce the availability of its calcium content. The calcium content of the food is only a part of the body's calcium sources, as will be detailed in Chapter 13.

173

Though its function in bone structure is the biggest calcium use in the body, the remaining amount performs a wide variety of functions. The parathyroid hormone controls the calcium in the bloodstream to maintain a normal saturation level. Calcium, along with sodium and potassium, controls the contraction and relaxation of the heart muscle, or more plainly stated, calcium, sodium and potassium function to control the heartbeat. Calcium is also essential for the clotting of the blood, for the maintenance of acid-base equilibrium, for contraction and relaxation of muscle fibers, for permeability of the cell membranes to fluid passage, and for the activation of many enzymes involved in the release of energy from carbohydrates, fats, and proteins. Calcium is also necessary for the formation and breakdown of a substance called acetylcholine, which is necessary for the transmission of nerve impulses from one nerve fiber to the next. Irritability of the nerves increases when the amount of calcium in the blood is below normal, and all of these functions will be maintained at the expense of the calcium in the skeleton.

The skeleton is by any estimation an engineering marvel. Without its function in the bodies of birds, animals, and humans, we would be forced to move and exist as amoebas, or develop an exterior skeleton as have the lobsters and kindred creatures. Calcium in a complex compound with phosphorus gives rigidity and hardness to the bones and teeth. The bones are composed of complex crystals of calcium and phosphorus in a honeycomb structure, set around a framework of softer protein material, called the organic matrix. About two parts calcium to one part phosphorus are incorporated into this structure. This honeycomb structure gives strength and at the same time a huge surface area. Connecting canals of blood, lymph, nerves, and marrow pass throughout this structure, though in birds the bones are mostly hollow. The fluids surrounding these bone crystals supply the materials needed for growth and repair, and they withdraw material as necessary. The basic structure changes constantly in response to body changes. Bone tissue is not permanent, and about 20% of bone calcium is replaced every year.

Calcium and phosphorus occur together, circulate together, and work together in the body. When discussing bones, in particular, it is impossible to discuss one without the companion functions of the other entering in. Decalcification, for example, involves the removal of both the calcium and phosphorus from the bones. Also, bones can accumulate a reserve supply of both calcium and phosphorus. If this available reserve within the bones is used up, the minerals will be removed from the structure of the bone itself. This removal usually occurs first from the spine and pelvic bones. 30% of this structure or more can be withdrawn before the loss will even show up on an x-ray of the bone tissue. The bones will also lose calcium simply from inactivity of the body.

Of course, vitamins are necessary for the proper utilization of calcium within the body, as are a variety of enzymes. Vitamin D is of particular importance, and its functioning with calcium was fully covered in the section on vitamin D in Chapter 7. Vitamin A is of crucial importance in depositing the minerals within the bones. Vitamin C is required for formation of the connecting material between the cells and the walls of the vessels in the bones.

A variety of factors affect calcium absorption in the digestive system. Calcium dissolves best in an acid solution, such as the stomach contents, and it is absorbed as it moves into the small intestine. When the intestinal contents become alkaline, absorption is poor. Though the affinity of strontium, particularly radioactive strontium[90], for the bones is well known, the body preferentially will absorb calcium at a nine to one ratio over strontium, providing that the calcium is available. Strontium is also excreted preferentially over calcium. Calcium must be separated from the food mass and ionized before it can be absorbed, and still only 40% to 60% will be absorbed. Though rats usually absorb 100% of their dietary intake of calcium, humans may absorb as little as 10%. In humans, this low rate of absorption may well be as the result of the common deficiency of adequate vitamin D in many human diets.

The best dietary ratio to promote the highest rate of absorption is one part calcium, to one part phosphorus. Lactose is an excellent promoter of calcium absorption in the humans that can tolerate the lactose content, so the calcium in milk is very well absorbed. An increased bodily need for calcium will increase the level of absorption, also, as will an adequate amount of vitamin D. Anything that speeds up the movement of the food mass through the intestine will decrease the calcium absorption rate. Laxatives will have this effect in humans, and a high fiber diet will also decrease the absorption of calcium. For this reason, the calcium from vegetables with their high fiber content is more slowly absorbed than is the calcium from animal sources. The presence of dietary fat also lowers calcium absorption. The more stress is experienced, the less calcium will be absorbed. Also, calcium ions are needed for the proper absorption of cobalamin, also called vitamin B_{12}.

Two naturally occurring acids are detrimental to calcium absorption, in addition. Cereal grains, such as wheat, contain a substance called phytic acid, which combines with phosphorus to form phytates. These phytates inhibit calcium absorption in humans, though some other species possess phytase, the enzyme needed to break this compound apart and utilize its components. Nutritionists state that the body seems to be able to adapt to high phytic acid intake and still absorb calcium. See chapter 13 for further information that calls this assumption into question.

Oxalic acid is present in spinach, beet greens, chard, and rhubarb, and this combines with calcium to make calcium oxalate. The intestines cannot absorb this compound from the intestinal fluids, and it is eliminated.

Calcium is so easily excreted that there is no evidence of bad effects from even excessive calcium intake. Any excess is excreted through the kidneys, though other factors do enter in. If vitamin D is in excessive supply, for example, too much calcium can accumulate in the blood. This will cause accumulation of calcium in the kidneys. If too much phosphorus is in the blood with too little calcium, the result will be muscular twitching. In addition, excess calcium in the diet decreases the absorption of zinc.

There is rather intense controversy among nutritionists as to what level minimal daily requirements should be set for calcium. This controversy seems to an outside observer to be an exercise in futility, for a variety of reasons. First, even in areas where calcium intakes are low, calcium deficiency does not occur. There is no evidence of adverse effects from low calcium intake on any human diet. Second, there is now strong evidence that no relationship exists between calcium intake and bone loss as in osteoporosis. Also, there is no evidence that low calcium intake is a deterrent to growth. And finally, *no clinical condition has ever been classified as a calcium deficiency*. This is remarkable when considering that the United States Department of Agriculture reports that 30% of American diets are calcium deficient. These are strong statements, all based on thorough research. Calcium deficiency, by these known facts, seems to be nonexistent. The answer to what actually seems to be going on within the living body is covered in Chapter 13.

It is possible to induce a calcium deficiency in chickens and other animals by strictly controlling the diet. A severe deficiency of calcium and phosphorus can cause permanent stunting of size or malformations of bones, and also of the teeth in animals. The symptoms of deficiency are slowed growth, lower food consumption, abnormal posture and walking, and shortened life span. Adult chickens will produce thin eggshells, egg production will be reduced, and the chickens will experience painful muscular spasms.

Where the nutrition of birds in cages and aviaries is concerned, calcium supply need not be of great concern. However, the ratio of calcium to phosphorus in the diet is crucial. A ratio of as much as 3.3 parts of calcium to one part phosphorus is sufficient to produce rickets and other leg abnormalities in chickens. However, in most cage bird diets, the problem is the reverse – phosphorus exceeds calcium in most diets in captivity, and the birds must be given every opportunity to restore this balance in order to maintain their health at an optimal level. An available calcium source is always necessary for cage birds because most plant foods are very high in phosphorus, while the bird's body needs a much higher proportion of calcium. This additional calcium available constantly is crucially important to enable the birds to balance the calcium:phosphorus ratio in their diets and in their bodies. Crushed eggshells, with a calcium content of over 98%, are an ideal source of calcium. If you feed a hard-boiled egg mix, crush the leftover eggshell, and feed it separately as an excellent and free calcium source for all of your birds. All birds that I have kept love these crushed eggshells, and they will not cause any bird to start eating its own eggs. They will eat this calcium supplement instinctively whenever they feel the need to balance their intake of calcium and phosphorus, and they will never overeat of this particular food item.

PHOSPHORUS

The earth's surface has a phosphorus content of about 1,180 parts per million, and sea water contains around 70 parts per billion. Phosphorus is the second most abundant mineral in the human and avian body, making up about one percent of the body's weight. This amounts to well over one pound of phosphorus in the human adult, and phosphorus is a part of every cell. It is an essential bulk element in nutrition, and about 22% of the body's mineral content is in the form of phosphorus.

From 85% to 90% of the phosphorus content of the human body is as calcium phosphate to give rigidity to the bones and teeth. This function of phosphorus is discussed thoroughly in the section on calcium, since both minerals work together so closely in this function. The rest of the body's phosphorus content is distributed through all of the cells and fluids of the bodies of birds, animals and humans. The egg's mineral contents are over 25% phosphorus, making this the most abundant mineral element in the avian egg.

Virtually all foods from the plant kingdom that are rich in protein are also rich in phosphorus. For avian nutrition, peanuts, eggs, black walnuts, some other nuts, and sunflower seeds are rich in phosphorus. Most fruits and vegetables, by contrast, are low in phosphorus.

Many factors influence the absorption of phosphorus in the digestive system. Though about 70% of dietary phosphorus is absorbed, 100% of the phosphorus from animal food sources is available, while only 30% of the phosphorus from plant sources is available. Almost all of this is absorbed as free phosphorus. An overabundance of either calcium or phosphorus in the diet will interfere with the absorption of the other in the digestive tract. For chickens, a calcium:phosphorus ratio of from 1.5:1 to 2:1 seems best, while laying hens have a wider tolerance. A similar ratio should be the best for birds maintained in our cages and aviaries, also.

Phosphorus occurs in whole grains as phytic acid. This compound will bind calcium and make both the phosphorus and the calcium completely unabsorbable. Phytic acid may account for 86% of the phosphorus present in seeds. About 80% of the phosphorus in corn exists as phytate, a compound of phytic acid and phosphorus. Phytic acid occurs in wheat, oats, flax, rye, rice, soybeans, and peanuts, any of which may be used in the feeding of birds in captivity.

A number of other facts about phosphorus are of interest. The presence of beryllium in the diet prevents phosphorus absorption, and this will cause rickets. Beryllium seems to form an insoluble compound with phosphorus called beryllium phosphate, which is not absorbable. Also, high levels of calcium phosphate in the diet will aggravate a manganese deficiency, and high phosphate levels also reduce iron absorption. In addition, phosphates are used to remove excess fluoride from water supplies, since fluorides have a strong affinity for phosphates.

Phosphorus has an essential role in virtually all body processes. It is vital to any reaction that involves the uptake or release of energy, and it is an important structural component in the skeletal system. In the form of phosphate, phosphorus is responsible for the controlled release of energy resulting from the oxidation of carbohydrates, fats, and proteins. It is a part of the adenosine triphosphate which stores body heat energy in a high energy bond for slow release as necessary. Phosphate also attaches itself to many nutritional substances to facilitate their passage through membranes of the cells. It transports fats and fatty acids in the bloodstream as phospholipids, since they are insoluble in the blood fluids in their basic forms. Phosphorus is an integral part of both DNA and RNA and is also a part of many coenzymes.

Any excess of phosphorus in the body is excreted through the kidneys, and needed supplies of phosphorus are resorbed through the kidneys. The presence of vitamin D increases this rate of phosphorus resorption. Also, the parathyroid hormone affects the level of phosphorus in the bloodstream and its rate of kidney resorption. It is interesting to note that hens excrete phosphorus from the body at a much higher rate when they're laying. Even during starvation, there is a continuous loss of phosphorus from the body.

As previously mentioned, no dietary deficiency of phosphorus is known in humans. Symptoms of deficiency have appeared in chickens on strictly controlled diets, however. Either a deficiency or a wide variance in the calcium:phosphorus ratio will cause rickets. Growth failure will always result from a phosphorus deficiency. A severe deficiency causes a loss of appetite, weakness, and death within ten to twelve days.

The aviculturist need have no concern with regard to phosphorus. A natural phosphorus deficiency is unknown, and only a gross imbalance in the calcium:phosphorus ratio or a vitamin D deficiency in the diet is likely to cause any problem with regard to phosphorus. If you supply one of the foods with a high phosphorus content mentioned previously, plus a good calcium source, such as eggshells, cuttlebone, or mineral block, you are free from any problem of mineral imbalance. The birds will balance their own intake with no conscious thought on your part.

POTASSIUM

Potassium is a vital bulk element in the nutrition of birds, animals, and humans. Plants also require potassium as a bulk mineral, and both plants and animals have high potassium requirements. Potassium is a bulk element in sea water, with about 380 parts per million, and the earth's crust contains potassium in great abundance with about 25,900 parts per million. The chemical symbol for potassium is K, derived from the Latin name for this mineral, Kalium. Research has proven that rubidium will displace potassium in metabolic functions.

About 5% of the total mineral content of the body is potassium, and it is the third most abundant mineral in the body after calcium and phosphorus. The human body can contain as much as 300 grams of potassium, well over half a pound. This amounts to about 2,000 parts per million of the body contents, on an average.

The body uses potassium in a variety of ways. Since this mineral cannot be conserved or resorbed in the body, it is fortunate that the dietary supplies are so widely available. Potassium is rapidly absorbed in the small intestine, and humans need an intake of from two to six grams a day. Any body excess is excreted through the kidneys. Within the body, potassium acts as a catalyst and enzyme activator within the cells in many reactions, especially in the release of energy and in glycogen and protein synthesis. It is a major factor in maintaining osmotic pressure within the cells. Though potassium is not so easily mobilized as sodium for the purpose, it is important in maintaining the cell's acid-base balance by offsetting excess acid-forming elements. It also seems to increase the permeability of the cell membranes. Potassium speeds up the intake of neutral amino acids, such as glycine, and it is important in the breakdown of lysine. The radioactive isotope potassium[40] can be used to determine the amount of body fat relative to lean tissues. In addition, potassium plays a role in the transmission of nerve impulses. Finally, this mineral is important in maintaining the healthy body's electrolyte balance.

The body's cells and tissues are very high in potassium, while the body fluids are contrastingly high in sodium. The muscle and nerve cells are especially high in potassium. Within the cell, there is one part of sodium to ten parts of potassium. Potassium works with sodium in the body fluids to regulate the blood and water balance, urinary acidification, nerve conduction, and muscle contraction. Sodium and potassium are antagonists and as such they regulate the necessary equilibrium between the fluids within and outside of the cells. An abnormal balance of these two nutritional elements will result in paralysis of the nerves of the heart and lungs. An increase in the sodium level within the cell can counteract potassium's important effect as a catalyst and thus interfere with cellular metabolism, especially in the important function of protein synthesis.

Potassium also has a number of known relationships with magnesium and calcium in the normal functioning of the body's tissues. First, a magnesium deficiency can cause decreased retention of potassium. Potassium also acts with magnesium as a muscle relaxant in opposition to calcium. Surprisingly, though a magnesium injection will cause an animal to fall asleep, a potassium injection will awaken it. An adequate supply of magnesium is needed in the body to retain the correct amounts of calcium in the cells. Potassium is required for normal heart activity and acts in a manner opposite to calcium. Potassium favors the relaxation of the heart muscle, while calcium favors its contraction. Therapeutic doses of potassium have even been used to slow the heartbeat in cases of serious injury.

Deficiencies of potassium can be induced in experimental animals, and diarrhea can cause a deficiency by hindering the absorption of potassium. Symptoms of such a deficiency are overall muscle weakness, heart weakness, intestinal distension, and the weakness and ultimate failure of the respiratory muscles. Humans will show mental apathy, fatigue, constipation, and muscle cramps in the calf muscles. Chicks that are deficient show high mortality rates and slow growth. Chicks seem to require about 0.4% of the diet as potassium, about the percentage contained in millet. Rabbits and turkeys seem to require more, at least 0.6% of the diet. In cases of actual starvation, some potassium can be derived from metabolized tissue protein. Also, the protein deficiency disease kwashiorkor cannot be cured by increased dietary protein intake alone. Potassium must also be added to the diet.

Potassium is widely distributed in food sources, and plant material is especially rich in this mineral. All vegetable matter contains it, especially green leafy vegetables, whole grains, fruits, nuts, and dates. Potassium is the second most abundant mineral in the contents of the egg. Only phosphorus is more abundant. However, refining whole wheat into white flour will remove about 77% of the potassium content. In addition, potassium in foods occurs in a very soluble form, and it can be lost in cooking with water.

Though the importance of potassium in the avian diet is undeniable, the bird breeder does not need to be overly concerned about the dietary content available to the birds. Any varied diet of plant products should provide a sufficient amount of potassium for even the most discriminating avian taste.

SULFUR

Sulfur is classified as a major bulk mineral in the nutrition of plants, animals, and birds. It occurs in sea water at the rate of about 885 parts per million and in the earth's crust at the rate of about 5,200 parts per million. Sulfur is found in every cell of both plant and animal bodies. It is the fourth most plentiful mineral in the body after calcium, phosphorus and potassium.

Sulfur is found virtually everywhere in nature and all food sources will contain some. For avian nutrition, the cereal grains, nuts, and eggs are among the highest sources. Eggs, in particular, are very rich in sulfur. The characteristic odor of rotten eggs is caused by the formation of hydrogen sulfide gas in the decaying process. Over 15% of the mineral content of an egg is sulfur, some of it in an unbound, inorganic form. It is the most abundant mineral in the albumen of the egg and one of the four most abundant in the total contents of the egg, excluding the shell. The inorganic sulfur in the egg is the reason for the formation of the dark stains of silver sulfide on silverware used for eggs.

Keratin is the primary protein that forms feathers, hair, claws, nails, and beaks. It has a very high sulfur content, which produces the odor of sulfur dioxide gas when feathers are burned. The amino acid cysteine, one of the sulfur-containing amino acids, is found in abundance in keratin. The wool of sheep is also extremely rich in sulfur, with a sulfur content of five percent. Many of the strong odors found in nature are caused by sulfur-containing compounds.

Half of the sulfur in the body is in the muscles. Most of this sulfur content is in the amino acids cystine, cysteine, taurine, and methionine. The body is capable of synthesizing the first three of these amino acids if it has a sufficient supply of sulfur. Methionine is an essential amino acid that must come from the diet. Since sulfur is a part of these amino acids, it is a necessary part of any protein containing them.

Sulfur also serves a variety of other functions in the body. There are at least four vitamins which have been proven to contain sulfur. These are all within the B complex – thiamin, pantothenic acid, biotin, and lipoic acid. Sulfur is required for the formation of melanin pigment, which forms in the presence of sunlight from sulfur and two amino acids. Several hormones contain sulfur, including insulin, the hormone that regulates carbohydrate metabolism. An adequate supply of sulfur also appears to be necessary for the synthesis of collagen, the protein that forms such an integral part of the cell structure. Also, there is a possible sulfur antagonism by vanadium.

As a result of the wide and abundant distribution of sulfur in virtually all living things, there is almost no chance of any deficiency ever developing in birds maintained and bred in captivity. No deficiency symptoms as such are known, since it is impossible to formulate a diet devoid of sulfur. It is certain, however, that such a diet would cause almost immediate death from lack of the amino acids, vitamins and hormones previously mentioned that contain sulfur as an integral part of their structure. No supplementation with sulfur should ever be necessary in the diets of any birds maintained in your cages and aviaries.

SODIUM

Though salt has been important in human life since the dawn of time, it was only in 1937 that research indicated the role of sodium in nutrition as a dietary essential. Salt is a compound of sodium and chlorine, technically called sodium chloride. Sodium occurs in sea water at the rate of 10,500 parts per million and the earth's surface contains about 28,300 parts per million. All living things require sodium, but most do not get their dietary sodium in the form of salt.

Sodium is present in the body mainly in the fluids outside of the cells. About 50% of the body's sodium content is in these fluids where sodium serves as a cation. However, up to 10% of the body's sodium is in the cells. The remainder, which will range from 30% to 45% of the body content, is in the skeleton in humans. Some mammals carry a much higher amount of body sodium in the bones with as much as 55% located there. About half of this skeletal sodium is present as a body reserve. The body can draw upon this reserve when less sodium is available in the diet or when body losses are high. The absorption of sodium is mostly in the small intestine, with a small amount absorbed in the stomach. This absorption is an active process that requires energy.

The kidneys filter the blood constantly to maintain normal blood levels of sodium. Aldosterone, a hormone secreted by the adrenal glands, controls the regulation of blood sodium. The kidneys can either resorb or excrete sodium, as the body's needs demand. If the need for sodium increases, the secretion of aldosterone will increase. This increase in the aldosterone level will stimulate both absorption and resorption of sodium. If the intake of sodium is high, the secretion of aldosterone decreases, and less sodium is retained. When the dietary intake of sodium exceeds the kidneys' ability to excrete it, the blood and fluid levels of sodium will rise. This rise in blood sodium stimulates thirst, and the increased water intake then enables the kidneys to excrete more sodium.

Loss of sodium from the body can occur in ways besides the urinary excretion with a number of effects. Any kidney damage or adrenal damage can

183

cause excessive losses of sodium through the urine. The urinary level frequently reflects the dietary intake of sodium. Excessive amounts of sodium can be lost in sweating, and this will cause muscle cramps. In cases of diarrhea, there is also a major sodium loss through the intestines. In addition, large losses of sodium may cause excessive vomiting. A low level of sodium in the fluids causes potassium and water to leave the cells. This cell dehydration causes the feeling of fatigue that goes along with sodium depletion.

Sodium serves a variety of functions within the body. Since sodium accounts for 90% of the basic or alkaline ions in the fluids outside of the cells, it counteracts the acid-forming elements to maintain body neutrality. It is essential for the absorption of glucose and for the transportation of other nutrients across the cell membranes. Sodium is involved in the contraction and relaxation of muscles, and it both stimulates the nerves and enables the transmission of nerve impulses. Also, sodium is very important in the maintenance of the body's fluid volume. As a part of bile, pancreatic, and intestinal juices, about twenty grams of sodium per day are secreted into the digestive system. However, most of this is later resorbed.

Sodium in the body appears to come primarily from dietary sources. The largest amounts of sodium in the diet are found in animal products, rather than in foods of plant origin. For cage bird nutrition, eggs, kale, spinach, celery, carrots, and Swiss chard contain appreciable amounts of sodium. Over 14% of the mineral contents of an egg is also in the form of this element. Most other grains, vegetables, fruits, legumes and nuts, however, are low in sodium. Oils contain no sodium at all.

Deficiencies of sodium have been caused in chickens and other animals for experimental purposes. In a deficiency, the bones will soften, growth failure shows up with a variety of internal disorders, and the utilization of protein and energy is greatly reduced. A sodium deficiency also interferes with reproduction. A deficiency in chickens will cause reduced egg production, poor growth, and cannibalism.

An excess of sodium is also possible, but extremely unlikely, since such a large amount of sodium or salt is absolutely unpalatable. If sodium concentrations in the cells rise too fast for the cells to pump it out, the result is water taken in to dilute it, and the cells become swollen. Less than one per cent salt content in the diet of chicks will cause watery droppings, decreased growth, loss of appetite, and some mortality. Extended wings, poor feathering, constant drinking, and dehydration are among other symptoms of excess salt. Chicks are not seriously affected, however, and there is no mortality increase until salt becomes 7.5% of the diet. This amount exceeds the ability of the chicks to consume enough water to flush out the excess salt.

184

No dietary supplementation with any sodium compound should ever be necessary for cage bird diets that contain a small amount of salt. Many of the commercially available vitamin-mineral supplements do contain salt. Vionate®, for example, contains from 0.5% to 1.5% salt in its contents. In cage birds, too much salt is as great a danger as too little, since they cannot excrete excess sodium through sweat. There is little danger of either a deficiency or an excess on any normal cage bird diet, however.

CHLORINE

Chlorine is also classified as a major element in nutrition. When considering the amount contained within the body, it ranks sixth after calcium, phosphorus, potassium, sulfur, and sodium. The elemental form of chlorine is a greenish-yellow gas which is extremely poisonous. In sufficient concentration in the air, chlorine gas is deadly. In its inorganic form, chlorine will destroy vitamin E on contact. It occurs in sea water at the abundant rate of about 19,000 parts per million and in the earth's crust at the rate of about 200 parts per million. Bromine will replace chlorine in chemical reactions within the body. Since chlorine is highly reactive, it forms compounds readily and occurs primarily as chlorides in nature.

The commonest form of chlorine is in the compound sodium chloride, common salt. Without sodium chloride, animal life is not possible. However, an excess of salt can be as deadly as a lack of it. For this reason, all birds and animals are able to excrete excess salt to a certain extent. Many sea birds and fish have special organs for eliminating excess salt that they ingest. This sodium chloride content of the body is found in the extracellular fluids, the fluids of the body found circulating outside of the cells. It controls the volume and pressure of those fluids.

The primary function of chlorides in the body seems to be in the regulation of the body's acid-alkaline balance. Since sodium is alkaline and chlorine is acidic, the kidneys can excrete sodium to increase body acidity and chlorine to increase body alkalinity. Also, chlorine is a highly important and necessary ingredient for the formation of hydrochloric acid for digestion in the stomach. Though chlorine also occurs in the body as calcium chloride, these seem to be the only functions of chlorine in the body. No other role for chlorine in nutrition has yet been discovered.

Chlorine is one of the four most abundant minerals in the contents of a chicken egg. Over 16% of the mineral content of an egg is chlorine. In any state of chloride deficiency, chicks will show a specific nervous reaction. With any sharp noise, scare, or handling, the chicks will fall forward with legs stretched out behind them in a state of paralysis. They will recover after a couple of minutes and it will be a while before this characteristic symptom can be repeated.

Sufficient chloride content should be present in most common cage bird food items to prevent any deficiency or deficiency symptom. In addition, any commercially prepared food or vitamin-mineral supplement will contain supplementary sodium chloride. Any deficiency of this nutrient in the maintenance and breeding of birds is highly unlikely.

MAGNESIUM

Magnesium is an essential bulk mineral in nutrition. All birds, plants and animals, including algae, fungi, and bacteria, require magnesium for the maintenance of biological life. Magnesium is abundant in the earth with 20,900 parts per million in the crust on the average and 1,350 parts per million in sea water. The human body can contain as much as 28 grams of magnesium. It is found in all of the cells of the body. In the plants, magnesium is an essential part of chlorophyll. This green compound is similar to the hemoglobin in animal blood, but magnesium replaces iron in the structure of the chlorophyll molecule.

The presence of magnesium in living organisms has been known since 1859. It was identified as a dietary essential for mice in 1926 and for rats in 1932. Nevertheless, most of the information on magnesium's biological functioning has been learned since 1950. Between 50% and 60% of the body content of magnesium in humans is in the bones. The balance is concentrated within the cells, including the red blood cells. Magnesium is alkaline in cell solution. The body can mobilize magnesium from the bones to maintain normal blood and tissue levels. The body's ability to absorb and excrete this mineral as necessary to maintain a correct balance is quite well developed. The kidneys resorb magnesium as necessary to prevent the body loss of excessive amounts in the urine. Any actual excess of magnesium to body needs is excreted either by way of the urine or through the bile and the intestines.

Absorption of the dietary intake of magnesium occurs primarily in the small intestine. Normally, about 43% of the magnesium intake is absorbed. In low dietary levels, as much as 75% of the magnesium may be absorbed. Absorption will also increase as the levels of protein and calcium in the diet increase. Raising either the calcium or phosphorus content of the diet will increase the magnesium requirement of chicks. It appears that a common carrier transports both calcium and magnesium across the intestinal wall. Absorption will be reduced in diets high in phytic acid, a compound which is found in abundance in cereal grains.

One of the primary functions of magnesium in biological activity seems to be in the functioning of the muscles and nerves. Increased blood levels of magnesium have a definite anesthetic effect. Low blood levels will cause irritability and nervousness with convulsions in severe cases. These convulsions are caused by increased transmission of nerve impulses and increased muscular contraction. In the nerve cell fluids, magnesium is involved in the conduction of nerve impulses. In the functioning of the muscles, calcium and magnesium are strong antagonists. Calcium will stimulate muscular action, and magnesium acting with potassium will relax muscular action. Because of its anesthetizing effect, a magnesium injection can be used to cause animals to fall asleep. At the highest levels in the blood, magnesium will cause coma and eventual death.

Hundreds of enzymes have been found to be activated by magnesium. Because of this biological effect, magnesium is important in almost all of the functions of the body. It is also needed for the synthesis, breakdown and stability of DNA. Magnesium is necessary for the activation of amino acids so they can be incorporated into the protein molecules. Magnesium is important in cellular respiration and is vital to cell metabolism by its function of catalyzing several reactions involving the release of energy, synthesis of body compounds, absorption and transportation of nutrients, and any muscular physical activity.

The magnesium content of eggs and the rate of egg production are important results of the content of this mineral in the diet of chickens and other birds. The mineral contents of the egg are 5% magnesium, and eggshell contains about 1% magnesium. By far the largest part of the magnesium in the egg is in the shell and shell membrane. In laying hens, the magnesium required may be drawn from the bone at times of dietary deficiency. Egg size, magnesium content of the egg, and weight of the shell will all decrease due to deficiency of magnesium in the diet. Any increase in calcium at the same time will make the effects of a magnesium deficiency even more pronounced.

Magnesium is the only bulk element which plays an active role in the enzyme systems involved in the metabolism of foods. For this reason, the dietary need for magnesium is greater whenever the diet is rich in carbohydrates. About 300 to 350 milligrams of magnesium per day are required for human health, and research has proven that beryllium will replace magnesium in its biological functions.

The best sources of magnesium in the diet for birds in captivity are found in the nuts and whole grains. Soybeans are also rich in magnesium, and green, leafy vegetables with a high chlorophyll content are also rich in magnesium. Any refining, processing, or cooking will reduce the content of magnesium in the food. From one-half to three-quarters of the magnesium content is lost in vegetables cooked in water. As much as 80% of the magnesium content is removed in the refining of whole wheat into white flour.

In a severe dietary deficiency of magnesium, muscle control will be lost. This uncontrolled neuromuscular activity will result in tremors first and then convulsive seizures. There will be calcification of the soft tissues as more calcium is absorbed. Newly hatched chicks fed a diet with no magnesium will live only a few days. Low magnesium levels will cause as their symptoms slow growth, lethargy, panting, and gasping. When disturbed, the chicks will have brief convulsions and go into a comatose state which is sometimes only temporary, but also is often fatal. Even a marginal magnesium deficiency with nearly normal growth will result in a high rate of mortality.

Severe deficiencies of this type are only found in experimental nutritional testing, and certainly not on any normal avian diet. Also, an excess of magnesium on any normal diet is equally unlikely. In nutritional testing, a rate higher than 1% in the diet will cause some reduction in egg production and a decrease in eggshell thickness in laying hens. In growing chicks, a 1% dietary magnesium content slightly depresses growth and causes very wet droppings.

The chance of a deficiency of magnesium occurring in cage birds on any normal feeding program is minimal. This mineral occurs widely in food sources and is unlikely to be in short supply in any diet of whole foods. A diet high in refined food products, however, would probably be less than adequate in magnesium content.

SILICON

Silicon is the second most abundant element in the earth. Over one-fourth of the known earth surface is composed of silicon, and only oxygen is found in greater abundance. Even in sea water, silicon occurs at the rate of about four parts per million. The body contains fairly large amounts of silicon, and research has proven it to be an essential mineral required for the maintenance of life. It is on the borderline between trace elements and bulk elements in nutrition, since it seems to be required in daily amounts of up to one gram. It is most unfortunate that many of the standard nutritional sources fail even to list silicon as a necessary nutrient. Nevertheless, research has proven silicon to be a necessary mineral in the nutritional process.

The likelihood of any silicon deficiency developing is negligible, since silicon is so plentiful on the earth's surface. Researchers feeding purified diets to determine silicon necessity and deficiency symptoms have proven that silicon is essential for both growth and skeletal development in rats and chicks. Supplementation has resulted in significant increases in growth rate of these test animals. Symptoms of a deficiency in chicks were a reduced growth rate, atrophied organs, and very pale legs and comb with no wattles. Skeletal development was significantly retarded.

Silicon is an integral component of both cartilage and collagen, and any deficiency will show up in abnormal cartilage and connective tissues. These connective tissues have a high silicon content, as it is a part of the essential structure of these tissues. In the collagen molecule, there seem to be from three to six atoms of silicon for each protein chain.

Research has indicated that silicon is needed as the bone material is formed and hastens the rate of bone mineralization. This need apparently slackens off as mineralization proceeds to the point at which very little is needed for the completion of bone mineralization. It also seems probable that silicon is involved with phosphorus in some manner in the formation of the bone tissue. Chapter 13 also presents a different viewpoint of the uses of silicon in the body.

Foods from plant sources are usually much richer in silicon than those from animal sources. Whole cereal grains are an excellent source, and the high fiber grains, such as oats, are much higher in silicon than the low fiber grains, such as wheat and corn. As might be expected, there are substantial losses of silicon in any refining process. Cage bird diets that contain cereal grains, fruits, or greens should supply an adequate amount of silicon for any avian nutritional needs.

CHAPTER 12

THE ESSENTIAL TRACE ELEMENTS

ARSENIC

Arsenic is one word calculated to strike terror into the heart of the wife-beater. Yet, arsenic is not nearly so poisonous as its reputation would suggest. At the time of this writing, enough good effects have been reported from its supplementation in trace amounts that there seems no doubt that it is an essential trace element in nutrition.

Arsenic occurs naturally in sea water at the rate of about three parts per billion. The earth's crust contains it in the amount of two parts per million. Some shales are especially rich in arsenic, and the source of the arsenic in air pollution is coal burning. There are relatively large amounts of arsenic in sea foods, and it seems to be completely non-poisonous as found in the natural foods. Arsenic is found throughout the human body in low concentrations with higher concentrations in the skin and nails and the highest amount in the hair.

Organically bound arsenic is readily absorbed in the body and rapidly eliminated, primarily in the urine. As far as the positive effects of arsenic research are concerned, in the days before antibiotics, arsenic was used as a common treatment for syphilis and yaws, a tropical skin disease characterized by multiple red pimples.

In research on chickens, arsenic compounds added to the diet have caused improvements in growth and market grades. Arsenic supplementation promotes the longevity of rats in experimentation, and arsenic supplementation also can alter the sex ratios of the offspring of both mice and rats. In an experimentally induced deficiency, rats will exhibit rough coats, significantly lower growth rates, and enlarged, blackened spleens.

An excess of arsenic in the diet is also possible, and an excess has caused a reduction of egg laying in chickens, and decreases in body weight gains in turkeys. Also, experimentation has shown that arsenic is toxic to mice at the continued dosage rate of five parts per million in their drinking water. Arsenic can replace phosphorus in biological reactions, and an excess can also cause skin lesions in people.

Some arsenic compounds, such as arsenic trioxide, are definite poisons, since they are readily absorbed and retained in the body. As little as thirty milligrams of arsenic trioxide is deadly to a human being.

At the present time, supplementation with arsenic in any form would seem to be unnecessary for the diets of birds, animals and humans. In aviculture, the traces needed for an adequate nutritional supply should be provided easily by a normal avicultural feeding program, since arsenic occurs in the necessary trace amounts in fruits, cereal grains, and most other common food items that are found in most cage bird diets.

BORON

Though boron has been known for decades to be a required nutrient for the growth of plants, it was only in 1982 that researchers definitely identified boron as a necessary growth factor for warm-blooded animals. Boron was proven to help in reducing calcium loss from the body, and in this capacity it may prove to be a factor in preventing osteoporosis, the loss of calcium from the bones.

Boron occurs in sea water at the relatively huge rate of 4,600 parts per billion. Many soils are deficient in boron, particularly along the Atlantic Coastal Plain, in Wisconsin, and in the northwestern Pacific Coast States. Boron occurs in air pollution as the result of coal burning.

Many specific deficiency symptoms have been noted and verified in a variety of crops, and boron is known to be required in plants for flavonoid synthesis. Since boron is required by plants, foods from the plant kingdom, seeds, and particularly green, leafy vegetables, should have an adequate amount of boron for any minimum needs that birds in captivity may have.

No definite need for this nutrient has yet been proven for birds, though research in the future will undoubtedly prove that trace amounts of it are needed in avian diets. Eggs contain consistent traces of boron, at the rate of about 40 micrograms for one chicken egg. Also, boron is found throughout the bodies of both birds and animals, and it is stored primarily in the bones. Boron is almost completely absorbed from the food and is excreted in the urine.

An excess of boron in the diet is also possible, and research has proven that boron is toxic to mice and rats at the rate of ten parts per million in continuous dosage. In the diets of birds in aviculture, however, there is virtually no possibility of any natural food containing an overabundance of boron that would be sufficient to cause illness or death.

Plant materials have much higher concentrations of boron than do animal materials. The best known sources of boron for any possible need in birds that are maintained and bred in captivity are peanuts, prunes, dates, raisins and honey. For your cage birds, any varied diet should supply enough boron for their health and breeding, and this is certainly not a nutrient that needs to be of concern to the aviculturist.

CHROMIUM

Research on chromium is a relatively new development in the field of nutrition. Virtually all nutritional knowledge of this essential trace mineral dates from 1959 to the present. I can find no mention of chromium in any book on the subject of nutrition before that date. Obviously, research work has a long way to go with respect to the importance of chromium in nutrition. However, at this point, there can be no doubt that chromium is an essential trace nutrient in the nutrition of humans, animals, and birds.

Chromium occurs naturally in sea water at the average rate of two parts per billion and in the earth's crust at the rate of about 200 parts per million. The amount that is locked up in the earth's crust is insoluble, however. Chromium is also present in air pollution as a by-product of coal burning and can accumulate in the lungs in insoluble forms. One form of chromium has been proven to cause cancer in metal workers. Otherwise, chromium toxicity is unknown. Inorganic chromium is only one percent absorbable, but better digestive absorption is found in the organic compounds of chromium. Nevertheless, inorganic chromium compounds have been found to be effective in treating the protein deficiency disease called kwashiorkor.

Modern refining methods are nothing short of a disaster for their removal of the chromium content of our foods. Refining whole wheat into white flour removes 83% of the chromium content of the whole wheat. Sugar refining is even more destructive, removing 92% of the chromium content in the transition from raw sugar to white sugar. In addition, 75% of the chromium content of whole brown rice is lost in polishing the rice.

Chromium has been proven to play a vital role in the body's glucose metabolism. An adequate supply of chromium is essential for the effective use of insulin in the body. In its known body use, chromium is bound into an organic compound referred to as the Glucose Tolerance Factor, called GTF for short. See the section on vitamins for a more thorough discussion of the Glucose Tolerance Factor. Chromium seems to be the basis of GTF, just as cobalt is the basis of cobalamin or vitamin B_{12}. Chromium in the GTF form works so closely with insulin in glucose metabolism that either one is almost completely ineffective without the other.

Feeding glucose after a complete fast causes three changes in the blood. First, blood sugar levels will rise. Second, insulin levels will rise, and third, chromium levels in the blood will rise as chromium is drawn from tissue storage. The chromium level of the blood always rises with the glucose level. This increased blood level causes a resulting significant increase in chromium excretion in the urine. Initial credit for this series of discoveries goes to Klaus Schwarz and Walter Mertz. In 1959, they discovered that chromium was the deficient factor in reduced glucose tolerance, also called mild diabetes.

In western countries, the chromium content of the human body decreases with age, but this does not occur in eastern countries. The most probable cause for this difference is the far higher consumption of refined carbohydrates, in particular white sugar and white flour, in the western countries. Chromium accumulates in the body in the liver, corneas, and skin. It has been shown to increase growth, to stimulate the formation of cholesterol and fatty acids, and to be necessary for the maintenance of normal cholesterol and sugar metabolism. The bile also contains chromium. Vanadium can antagonize and replace chromium in the body. An acute infection will cause a decrease in the amount of chromium in circulation. An adequate supplement of chromium has been reported authoritatively to cure both hypoglycemia (low blood sugar) and hyperglycemia (high blood sugar) overnight.

Tests with rats and mice prove that two to five parts per million of chromium as a drinking water supplement will result in significantly better growth in male mice and rats, but curiously, no change in females. Any deficiency of this mineral in the diet is characterized by impaired growth and reduced longevity, plus disturbances and changes in the glucose, lipid and protein metabolism. Chromium has been proven to be very important to eye health in rats, also, with a chromium deficiency causing opacity of the corneas which will not be reversible upon chromium supplementation. In experiments conducted by Dr. Henry A. Schroeder, rats grew faster, survived longer, and at death showed no atherosclerotic plaques in their aortas. In a low chromium diet, elevated blood cholesterol and sugar levels were evident, while chromium supplementation resulted in low cholesterol and sugar levels in the blood. Though old rats developed corneal opacity under low chromium diets, the significant finding was that chromium deficiency is an instrumental factor in the development of atherosclerosis.

At present, there is no evidence of any natural chromium deficiency in man or animals. As previously stated, the low chromium levels in the human life of western nations are attributable to the high degree of food refining in those countries. It now seems certain that any deficiency in the levels of chromium in the diet will contribute materially to the development of both atherosclerosis and arteriosclerosis over the long term. A deficiency can also inhibit protein synthesis in the body. A severe deficiency will cause immediate hyperglycemia or hypoglycemia, as soon as the body's chromium reserves are exhausted. It is highly significant that a fully developed deficiency of this type can be cured completely by one adequate dosage of an absorbable chromium supplement.

The two best sources of organically bound chromium in the diet are not common in cage bird feeding. Those two are brewer's yeast and sugar beet molasses. Beef liver is also an ideal source with 1,000 parts per million of chromium. Nuts and cereal grains are good sources, in addition. Whole wheat is a particularly good source of biologically active chromium. The vegetable oils have some chromium, but animal meats and fat have several times as much chromium as any of the plant sources. Surprisingly, seafoods are not a good source of chromium. Eggs have a high chromium content, but unfortunately, it occurs in a form that is predominantly not absorbable. Though inorganic chromium compounds are poorly absorbed, the natural organic complexes, such as occur in brewer's yeast, are absorbed much more easily.

The content of chromium in food is dependent upon its existence in the soil upon which that food is grown. Research in several European countries has shown the extreme value of a chromium addition on deficient soils. As little as 100 grams per acre on deficient soils has increased the crop yield on those soils by more than forty percent! There can no doubt that continual farming over the centuries depletes the soil of chromium and results in poorer growth in the crops. The ultimate human consumption of those crops means that the human

195

population is then getting lower values of chromium in the food than are needed for optimal health.

Nutritional authorities state that the nutritional significance of chromium in birds is not yet established. Though this may be technically true, the fact that no major differences in the nutritional needs of humans, birds, and animals, has yet been discovered will certainly mean that chromium is also a vital nutrient in the nutrition of birds. It would be the greatest of surprises to find that birds have no need for chromium when it is a vital nutrient for all other higher life forms on the earth. The unity of all nature dictates that all animal metabolism will depend upon the same systems and nutrients, albeit in differing ways and in different quantities. Since chromium has been proven to be an essential nutrient in humans and rats, it would be shortsighted in the extreme to suppose the same will not prove true in birds.

The best sources of chromium in cage bird nutrition will be the whole cereal grains. Any whole seed, fruit, or vegetable grown in a soil with adequate chromium content will contain a sufficient amount of chromium for that food's metabolism in the body. Insects will also contain a sufficient amount of chromium. As previously stated, no natural chromium deficiency has been noted anywhere.

COBALT

Cobalt is present in the earth's crust at the relatively abundant average rate of 23 parts per million, yet soils deficient in cobalt occur in wide areas. Cobalt occurs in sea water at the rate of about one part per ten billion. As early as 1935, researchers had listed cobalt as a vital trace element in human and animal metabolism. Though little research is available to me on birds at this time, the functions of cobalt indicate that it is also an essential trace mineral for all birds, as a component of cobalamin, vitamin B_{12}.

I find diametrically opposed views as to cobalt's use in plant nutrition. Some claim a vital role, though I have seen no convincing discussion concerning this role. Others claim that though cobalt is found in many plant sources, there is no evidence that it plays any part in plant metabolism, but is there only as a contaminant absorbed from the soil. As no plant nor animal is known to be able to synthesize cobalamin, and only certain soil bacteria and actinomycetes can perform this synthesis, the second hypothesis seems the more likely to be true.

Cobalt forms an integral part of cobalamin, which in pure form is a red, crystalline compound. Approximately four percent of the dry weight of cobalamin is cobalt. No other function of cobalt in animal or man is yet known. Other possible functions are suspected, but are as yet unproven. Cobalt does exist in the body separately from cobalamin, but any possible functions it may have in nutrition are as yet unknown.

Unrefined foods seem to contain adequate amounts of cobalt. However, refining foods removes very substantial portions of the cobalt in their composition. Cooking alone causes losses from one-third to 90% of the cobalt content in many raw vegetables. Polished white rice has lost about 38% of its cobalt content. Up to 98% of the cobalt is removed in refining raw brown sugar to white sugar. A maximum of only 12% of the cobalt is left in white sugar.

Good sources for dietary cobalt are cereal grains, oils, fats, oily seeds, and nuts. Whole wheat is an especially good source, if it is grown on soil that is adequate in cobalt content, but milling whole wheat into white flour removes up to 89% of the cobalt content. The best sources of cobalt for human consumption are the seafoods. Eggs are also an appreciable source, with the yolk containing twice the cobalt of the egg white. Any excess is excreted, primarily in the urine.

Deficiencies of cobalt have occurred only in experimental or domestic animals. Ruminants on pasture deficient in cobalt will suffer from wasting disease, also called by the name 'salt sick'. This disease is characterized by loss of weight and appetite, anemia, and general wasting away. The symptoms are similar to starvation, with the additional symptoms of pale skin, and blanched mucous membranes. The ruminants seem to have a higher cobalt requirement than other animals, probably because it is less well absorbed in this group of animals. Too little cobalt inhibits the synthesis of vitamin B_{12}. Cobalt is fairly well absorbed in the digestive system, but it is not readily stored in the liver nor elsewhere in the body, except when it is a component of cobalamin.

Human research has proven that cobalt deficiency results in vitamin B_{12} deficiency and pernicious anemia. Never fear, however, as was pointed out in the section on cobalamin, plenty of raw liver in your diet will protect you completely from pernicious anemia. Not an appetizing thought, and we are fortunate that other sources of cobalamin are available.

Folic acid, another of the B complex vitamins, can also mask a cobalt deficiency, leading in the worst cases to death from cobalamin deficiency. In addition, rhodium, in the same periodic group of the elements, can displace cobalt in its metabolic functions.

Too much cobalt in the diet is definitely toxic. Deliberate administration of a large excess has caused polycythemia in mammals and birds, a condition resulting from too many red blood cells in the blood. Yet, people have taken continually one thousand times over the amount of cobalt necessary for health without ill effect. An excess of cobalt in beer to maintain the foamy head has caused heart failure in heavy beer drinkers at the intake rate of about 1.2 parts per million. Though cobalt chloride can stimulate red blood cell production in cases of anemia, the large twenty to thirty milligram doses necessary often prove toxic. Also, a high quality protein diet has proven to offer considerable protection against cobalt toxicity.

If your birds are eating a diet of whole grains, any oily seeds and nuts, or eggs, no supplementation with cobalt should ever be necessary. For cobalt's functions within the cobalamin molecule, however, remember that only eggs and other animal products are dependable sources of this vitamin.

COPPER

The human race has known of and used copper for untold thousands of years, but it was not until 1833 that Boutigny demonstrated the presence of copper in mammals. In 1928, copper's true importance was recognized when it was discovered to be an essential trace mineral. Sea water contains about ten parts copper per billion, and the earth's crust has a content of around 45 parts per million. This copper-rich ground is unevenly distributed, however, and many areas and soils are seriously deficient in copper.

So far as can be determined, all living things require copper. All plant life requires it, including bacteria, fungi, and algae, as do animals, insects, and birds. In some sea life, such as mollusks, copper serves as the oxygen carrier, though it has only one-half of the carrying capacity of iron, which serves this oxygen-carrying function in birds and the other higher vertebrates. The National Research Council recommends two milligrams of copper daily for human needs. Absorption of copper in the diet is normally only about thirty percent of the amount ingested. The copper is absorbed in the stomach and the first part of the intestine. Only here is the food mass acid enough to allow good absorption.

Copper eaten will show up in the bloodstream within fifteen minutes after being consumed. A high ascorbic acid content in the diet seems to reduce intestinal absorption, and it will increase the severity of a copper deficiency in chicks.

One of copper's most important functions appears to be its work in the blood in the prevention of anemia. Copper assists in the formation of hemoglobin, the oxygen-carrying blood protein found in the red blood cells, facilitating iron absorption in some manner. Copper is not a part of the hemoglobin molecule, but it is vital to the normal formation of that molecule by influencing the iron in the synthesis of the hemoglobin. Though the final decision is not in, most research indicates that copper aids in the release of iron from storage in the liver. At any rate, anemia cannot be prevented or cured by iron alone. Copper must be present in addition to the iron.

Copper also performs a vital function with ascorbic acid in the synthesis of elastin. Elastin is the connective tissue of the blood vessel walls. If the copper present is insufficient, the tensile strength of the elastin and the blood vessels will be flawed and weak. This vascular weakness will cause a variety of circulatory problems.

Copper serves a variety of other functions in the body in its primary actions as a catalyst. Copper is necessary for the maintenance of normal nervous functioning, and it is required for the formation of the phospholipids which form the myelin sheath for the protection of nerve tissue. Copper is necessary for the production of ribonucleic acid, commonly called RNA, and it is involved in protein metabolism and healing. It is present in many enzymes performing these varied functions within the body, and copper is necessary for proper bone formation and maintenance. Many other metabolic functions of copper have been identified, but at this time these cannot be adequately understood because of the complex interactions of copper with other trace elements.

Copper is required for the formation of the dark color pigment called melanin, and it is a part of the enzyme tyrosinase. This enzyme is needed for the conversion of the amino acid tyrosine into melanin. The absence of this necessary enzyme has been associated with albinism. Copper is responsible for the black wool on sheep, and with inadequate copper in the diet, even a black sheep will produce white wool.

An unusual pigment in one species of the turacos, the Knysna Turaco, *Tauraco corythaix*, is called turacin. This pigment contains a copper salt whose color depends upon the amount of moisture present in the feather. As a consequence, the normal dry feather color of this bird is purple-red, but in a rain, the bird assumes a blue color. Turacin is a unique pigment, since it is unlike either the melanin pigments or the lipochrome pigments that are found in avian feathers. Thus far, I have encountered no other species that has developed this unique turacin pigment for the coloring of feathers.

The copper content of the soil will affect the content in any products coming from that soil, but it is difficult to create a copper deficiency on a varied diet. The mineral is too abundant and widespread not to be in adequate supply in most diets. Nuts, fats, meats, cereal grains, and seafoods are notably good sources of copper, but all living things will contain some copper. Soybeans, peanuts, and onions are excellent sources. By far the most abundant source of copper seems to be oysters, with the relatively huge content of 137 parts per million. The copper content of a hen's egg according to one authority is about 30 milligrams, and less than one percent of that amount according to another authority. I have been unable to resolve the contradiction, but a misprint is probable, as .3 milligrams seems to be the logically correct amount for a trace element.

Unrefined foods will contain sufficient copper for all normal health needs, but refining removes a great deal of the copper content of the food. Around 68% of the copper is removed from whole wheat in processing it into white flour. Significant amounts of copper are dissolved from copper pipes, particularly if the water is acid.

A natural deficiency of copper is unknown in humans, but has been documented in livestock grazed on pastures deficient in copper with no outside food source. Many Florida soils fall into this category. Still, deficiencies are very unlikely and will occur only in experimental or domestic animals, as far as is known. Lest that statement be lost on your consciousness, however, don't forget that cage birds classify under the heading 'domestic animals'. In livestock, a copper deficiency will cause diarrhea, loss of appetite, and anemia. There is a wide range of possible symptoms, depending on the species, but the symptom that is common to all species is anemia. Depressed growth, bone disorders, depigmentation of wool or fur, or abnormal fur growth are also possible symptoms. Chicks will become lame after two to four weeks on a deficient diet. Bones will be fragile and easily broken. Adult birds that are deprived of copper will show depigmentation of feathers with abnormal feather growth, and hens will also show reduced egg production.

There is some body storage of copper, and this will also make a deficiency highly unlikely on a varied diet. The highest copper concentrations found in the body will be in the liver and brain primarily, but with large amounts also found in the kidneys and heart. The bones and muscles have lower concentrations of copper, but their content totals from 50% to 75% of the total body copper content. Ceruloplasmin is a copper-containing protein that stores copper in the blood. Any excess intake of copper to a certain point can be excreted by the liver through the bile into the intestine.

Several other minerals are antagonists of copper in the body. For example, copper occurring with large amounts of sulfur, as it does in eggs, may be partly or totally unabsorbable. The sulfur combines with the copper in the inactive and relatively insoluble form of copper sulfide. An overabundance of molybdenum will create a deficiency of copper, since molybdenum inactivates the copper for biological functioning. There is also a biological antagonism between copper and zinc, as copper will make the zinc unavailable for biological activity. Finally, it has been reported that silver in the diet antagonizes copper, and an excess of silver will result in copper deficiency symptoms.

Copper in excess of the amount the body can use or excrete has a definite toxic effect. Copper in inorganic form acts as an enzyme inhibitor. Ingestion of ten times the amount of copper normally found in the diet will cause nausea and vomiting. Many human deaths have been reported from copper poisoning, but only one is known from a great excess of copper in the drinking water, that of an infant in Australia. Chronic, long term toxicity occurs only in a recessive hereditary condition known as Wilson's disease.

For cage bird nutrition, the copper content of the food variety normally offered will be sufficient to prevent any deficiency from developing. A diet of predominantly refined foods might be low in copper, but even the purified diets used in nutritional research usually contain enough copper impurity to prevent any deficiency symptom from developing. The greater concern with respect to this mineral should be in the possibility of an excess from the amount dissolved from copper pipes in acid water. This water sits overnight in the pipes accumulating an ever greater quantity of dissolved copper. In general, however, copper is not a nutrient about which the average aviculturist need have any concern.

FLUORINE

The necessity of writing about this trace element does not fill me with the greatest of joy. No other nutrient is surrounded by so much emotion and accompanied by such uncompromising attitudes. Its value in nutrition is controversial, and the available literature on fluorine is contradictory.

Nevertheless, a number of definite statements can be made safely about this nutrient. Fluorine occurs in all body tissues at the rate of about 37 parts per million as fluoride compounds, with a very high proportion of the body's content found in the skeleton. The earth's crust contains a relative abundance of fluorine with about 700 parts per million. Sea water contains it at the rate of 1.3 parts per million. All known life seems to have evolved from sea water containing fluorine in this amount, so such a concentration cannot possibly be of any danger to any living species.

Elemental fluorine is a greenish-yellow, highly poisonous gas. It is an extremely reactive element and will instantly form a compound with a wide variety of other elements. Fluorine gas is so active that it will etch glass. Air pollution contains fluorine as a by-product of coal burning.

Fluorine in nutrition is invariably in the form of a compound with other elements, usually as a fluoride, so that term will be used freely in the subsequent discussion. Most of the fluorine in sea water is in the form of sodium fluoride. Much of the fluorine in the body is in the form of either calcium fluoride or magnesium fluoride.

In nutrition, fluorides have never been proven to be essential for life. However, though they are not vital, their absence will result in ill health. Up to ten parts per million have resulted in substantial increases in the growth rate of rats in experimentation. Fluorine is also important for normal reproduction. Fluorides are important in bone and tooth structure in mammals, but in human nutrition, as little as two parts per million in the food and water supply over a twenty year period will produce symptoms of toxicity. Fluorine is cumulative in the body at any level of intake. The fluoride content of eggs from hens on a high fluoride diet will be much higher than normal. Nevertheless, research has shown that without adequate fluoride content in the diet, animal and human bones and teeth will be soft and brittle.

Though this may be worthless information for your birds, it is vital for your children. My own teeth were so poorly formed from malnutrition and nutritional ignorance that dental bills now cost me thousands of dollars every year. Don't put your own children through this for the rest of their lives. Believe me, it's no fun at all. By contrast, however, a friend of mine had parents who were quite well informed concerning nutrition, and his teeth were perfectly formed. When I last talked with him, he was 26 years old, and had NEVER even had a cavity.

An excess of fluoride is as bad as a deficiency of this element. An excess during tooth formation will make teeth so soft they will wear away. Fluorides in excess act as enzyme inhibitors. Fluorine readily binds magnesium into a relatively insoluble form, which occurs with calcium fluoride as a constituent of bone. Excess fluorides are excreted primarily in the urine. Also, vitamin C will nullify fluoride toxicity and will carry excess fluorides from the body via the urine. With either an adequate ascorbic acid intake or synthesis internally, a noticeable fluoride toxicity is highly unlikely.

Organically bound fluorine occurs in many whole foods. Fish, cheese, and meat are all good sources. Seafoods are also good sources, but by far the richest source is tea, with up to 398 parts per million. Heavy tea drinkers should be especially careful of the cumulative effects of the high fluoride content found in tea leaves. Molybdenum is another trace mineral which will increase fluorine absorption and retention in the body, especially in the muscles and brain.

With particular reference to birds, feeds from a variety of geographical areas should contain sufficient fluoride content for good health. Since a deficiency is possible, however, keep in mind that there is a dietary necessity for fluorine, particularly in any problem that involves weakness of the bone structure. With the exception of a diet of foods grown exclusively in the most deficient soils, no fluoride supplementation should ever be necessary. This is not a nutrient that should cause the aviculturist any concern.

IODINE

Whether or not a severe iodine deficiency will cause death is still debatable, but the effects can be worse than death. Iodine is an essential trace nutrient. The element itself was first discovered in Napoleon's time, though written knowledge of the treatment of goiter by foods that are rich in iodine goes back to about 2700 years before Christ, to the reign of the Chinese emperor Shen-nung. He mentions seaweed as an effective remedy for goiter, and we now know that seaweed is rich in iodine. In 1820 the Swiss physician Coindet recommended iodine specifically as a remedy for goiter. This was periodically rediscovered by physicians for the next 100 years, but only in the 1920's was this treatment widely accepted. People never seem to be able to learn from the discoveries of others the first time around.

Though iodine occurs in the earth's crust at the average rate of about three parts per ten million, wide areas of the land have soils with little or no iodine. Near the coastlines, rains and storms lift some sea water and carry enough iodine inland for trace needs, since it occurs in sea water at the rate of about 50 parts per billion. Soils in the United States Great Lake Basin are especially deficient in iodine. In addition, in Switzerland the iodine available naturally is locked up in rock formations and is unavailable for nutritional purposes. This lack of natural iodine available in the soils has made Switzerland a notable area for the study of iodine deficiencies over the years.

Iodine has a very worthwhile use in relation to the unsaturated fatty acids in research work. Each open double bond in these fatty acids will take up two atoms of iodine. Iodine can be used in this way to measure the degree of unsaturation in mixed fats. The mixed lipids showing the highest iodine values are the most highly unsaturated fats. This type of test provides no information on the specific type or arrangement of the unsaturated fatty acids, however.

Iodine occurs in foods mostly as inorganic iodide. Any uncombined iodine in the diet must be changed to iodide, which is iodine joined to another atom or group of atoms, before it can be absorbed in the digestive tract. Iodides are freely absorbed at all levels of the digestive tract. The primary organ for iodine storage in the body is the thyroid gland, but small amounts are also found in the kidneys, salivary glands, skin, hair, and female reproductive system. A chicken's body stores iodine extensively enough that a full year's deficiency after an abundant supply causes no strong deficiency symptoms. Any excess of iodine in the body is excreted, primarily in the urine.

Once the iodide absorbed into the blood from the intestine reaches the thyroid gland, it is oxidized and converted to organic iodine in the form of the hormone thyroxine by combining with the amino acid tyrosine. This is the only known function of iodine in the body. Each thyroxine molecule contains four atoms of iodine, and it controls a wide variety of the body functions. Chief among these functions are control of the rate of metabolism, control of growth, muscular control, and mental capacity.

A deficiency of iodine in the diet will cause first an enlargement of the thyroid gland, as it attempts to keep up the production of its hormones with an insufficient supply of iodine. The resulting swelling is called a goiter, and goiter is now extremely rare with the current wide available knowledge of iodine requirements in nutrition.

In chickens and probably in all cage birds, an iodine deficiency will cause a reduction in the iodine content of the egg, decreased hatchability, and prolonged hatching time. Iodine deficiency is a primary cause of embryos dead in the shell, and will also cause an increase in the size of the embryonic thyroid glands. Lack of thyroid activity will cause hens to become very fat and to cease laying.

A deficiency in mammals interferes with conception and reproduction. Young will be born weak or dead. Pigs will be born hairless and bloated, with thick skins and puffy necks.

My own experiences and those of many other breeders have proven beyond doubt that iodine deficiency in some species is quite common in the avicultural community, and it is usually not recognized as the basic cause of the problems that appear. The Lady Gouldian Finches have a particularly high requirement for iodine in their diets. Insufficient iodine in the diet will result in baldness, as the birds fail to regrow their head feathers when they are lost in a molt. When a sufficient amount of iodine is added to the diet, the birds will develop a headful of pinfeathers within two weeks.

Apparently the native Australian areas of the Gouldian Finches are very richly supplied with iodine compounds in the local foods. Normal quantities of iodides in the avian food items in North America, though they are perfectly adequate for most of our birds, are simply inadequate for the Gouldian Finches and some of the other colorful Australian species.

In order to solve this problem and to supply these finches with the full amount of iodide compounds that they require for their health, you will need to supply a supplemental amount of iodide to their diet. Potassium iodide is the compound used for human supplementation, and it is also the preferred form for birds. Potassium iodide is available in some drug stores, and through some avian supply outlets and farm stores. These compounds come in all strengths and dilutions. You can usually tell the strong solutions by the odor, which is very powerful. In supplementation with one of these strong solutions for birds that are already suffering from a deficiency serious enough that their head feathers will not regrow, use one drop of the strong solution in two ounces of the birds' drinking water for the first day. This will shock the bird's system to begin forming thyroxine again in adequate quantities. For the following week, supplement at the rate of one drop per half pint of water. As a regular supplement, use one drop per pint of the birds' drinking water. A number of breeders have used potassium iodide in these concentrations and have reported excellent results with these supplemental concentrations.

After iodine supplementation to correct a deficiency, sufficient vitamin E must also be in the diet to promote healing of the scar tissue that has formed in the thyroid gland. Without a sufficiently nutritious diet, healing of the damaged thyroid will be slow and incomplete. Remaining scar tissue will prevent the return of the thyroid gland to full function until that scar tissue is dissolved and replaced by healthy thyroid tissue.

A large excess of iodine in the diet can be toxic and will also cause goiter. In chickens with a severe excess, over about 300 parts per million, egg laying will cease, early embryonic death will be evident, and eggs will show reduced hatchability and delayed hatching. These adverse effects are only temporary in nature, and will revert to normal when the excess intake of iodine ceases. Laying by hens will resume within seven days of stopping the dietary excess. You will note that these symptoms of excess iodine in the diet are substantially similar to the symptoms of deficiency. As much as iodides are needed in nutrition, crystalline iodine is extremely toxic – it is poisonous in any quantity.

A really severe deficiency in humans results in myxedema, a disease characterized by greatly decreased thyroid activity, dry skin, swelling around the nose and lips, and mental deterioration. At its worst, iodine deficiency in child development results in cretinism. Symptoms of this are arrested physical and mental development and complete idiocy. To get an idea of the curse of cretinism and the heart-rending disasters caused by acute iodine deficiency, you need only read chapter 9 of Dr. Lionel James Picton's book, *Nutrition and the Soil*. This excerpt is quoted as the final paragraph of chapter 9 and gives an idea of the extremely fine line between iodine sufficiency and iodine deficiency in areas located far from an iodine-rich ocean:

> "A notable example of the narrowness of the margin between just enough and only a little less but disastrously too little was disclosed in 1927 in Switzerland. In view of the European menace, a review of the manpower of the country was undertaken, and it was found that goitre occurred much more often in the cantons speaking German than in those that speak French or Italian. Though the speech was different, the race was the same. No difference in the hygiene or sanitation of the different districts nor in the mineral content and purity of their water supplies could be found; the suggestion that the mere articulation of the guttural language might be responsible was quite untenable – there was no similar frequency of goitre in Germany. At last the true explanation dawned on the investigators: the cooking customs went with the language. The German-speakers threw away the water in which their vegetables had been boiled, and with it went the iodine-containing salts which the boiling water had extracted from them; but the French and Italian-speakers were fond of soup for which

they used all the vegetable water. Thus they commonly got enough iodine to protect them against the development of goitre."

For the nutrition of our birds maintained and bred in captivity, supplies of the iodide compounds are normally adequate in a varied diet of seeds, greens, fruit, nuts, eggs, and other whole, unprocessed foods that come from a variety of geographical areas. In addition, all standard vitamin-mineral supplements have iodine added to insure the minimum needed in the nutrition of birds in captivity. However, certain species, notably the colorful birds from Australia, seem to have a much higher requirement for iodine in their diet, and keeping them in perfect health and condition will require supplying a higher amount of the iodide compounds in their diet.

IRON

The knowledge of iron as an essential trace mineral reaches back farther than the specific knowledge of any other known nutrient. The ancient Greeks knew of iron as a treatment for anemia over 2,000 years ago. As early as 1746, Manghinis discovered that iron is a constituent of the blood. Iron is vital for all plants and animals, and iron is a necessary ingredient in the process of photosynthesis. Mollusks, such as snails, which live out of water, need iron, as do all insects. Most life forms on earth would cease to exist without iron.

Fortunately, the earth's crust has a relative superabundance of iron, with about 50,000 parts per million. Most of the soils have an adequate iron content, and iron occurs in sea water at the average rate of 3.4 parts per billion.

Iron occurs in most foods, and an iron deficiency is the next thing to impossible on a diet of unrefined foods. Meats; eggs; dark green, leafy vegetables; and whole grains are all good sources of iron. For avian nutrition, the whole grains, greens, fruits, and nuts should provide an adequate amount of iron in the diet for any normal maintenance and breeding. Egg yolk, in particular, is an excellent source of iron, and one average chicken egg will contain about one milligram of iron. Refining removes much of the iron from foods. For example, 76% of the iron content is removed in the milling of whole wheat into white flour.

Assimilation is the major roadblock to adequate iron content in the body. Generally, 10% or less of the iron in foods is absorbed through the intestinal wall. The stomach's hydrochloric acid dissolves iron to make it available for absorption. The presence of ascorbic acid, vitamin C, or other acids greatly increases the percentage of absorption. Even an iron deficiency can be partly corrected by simply supplying additional vitamin C to the human diet, since vitamin C is necessary for the optimal absorption and utilization of iron. Iron deficiency can still remain unless the body also has traces of both copper and vitamin B_{12} available, both of which are essential for the efficient conversion of iron into hemoglobin. Nickel also seems to aid in the absorption of iron. Any excess build-up of iron in the tissues is prevented in the intestinal wall as the saturated cells slow down the iron absorption.

Some researchers have claimed that vitamin E is a strong antagonist of iron, but other sources have contradicted this and have indicated that there is no foundation for this belief. At any rate, it is positively confirmed that inorganic iron, such as is found in iron-rich water, will destroy vitamin E on contact.

The function of iron is to carry and exchange oxygen in the blood. The human body contains 60 parts per million of iron, and the relative body content of a bird will be similar. The red blood cells contain 57% of the body's iron in the protein compound called hemoglobin. Female mammals need far larger amounts of iron than males because of three exclusively female functions: menstruation, gestation, and lactation. Female birds will need much more than males to supply the iron that is necessary for egg production. Iron is absolutely vital to the life of all higher species. Death will result without it.

A number of other functions of iron in the human and avian body are known. For example, a number of the necessary enzymes in the body's metabolism contain iron. Another essential use of iron in the body is in the formation of myoglobin. This is a muscle protein which carries oxygen in the muscle cells. The body cannot form myoglobin without iron, and this is why an iron deficiency will cause such chronic fatigue. Seven percent of the body iron in a dog is in the myoglobin, compared with about 3% in an adult man.

Iron is of special interest in its relationship to feathers. The turacos or plantain-eaters of Africa use iron in the formation of a pigment in the turacos' feathers. The technical name for this pigment is turacoverdin, and it has been found only in this avian family. This iron-containing pigment is the basis for the green coloring of the feathers of turacos. The turacoverdin pigment is unique to this avian family, Musophagidae.

It is also interesting to note that iron is required for the formation of the coloring in the feathers of New Hampshire Red chickens. In an acute iron deficiency while they are molting, their new feathers will contain no red pigment.

The utilization and control of iron levels in the body are one of the keys to maintaining good health. Copper has been proven to be necessary to the proper utilization of iron. Pyridoxine or vitamin B_6 appears to be essential in the regulation of iron levels in the body. If the control mechanisms fail, iron toxicity can be the result. Iron salts, such as ferrous sulfate, are toxic, and have been fatal in overdose many times. This is another example of the many ways in which nutrients work together in the body to ensure the functioning of the metabolism and the maintenance of good health.

Iron is stored in the liver primarily. A brown protein called ferritin is one storage form, and a brownish-yellow phosphate called hemosiderin is another. If the body's control mechanisms have failed, excess iron can overwhelm the capacity of the liver. Siderosis is one disease caused by the toxic nature of excess iron in the body. In siderosis, up to 18 times the normal body storage of iron is maintained with toxic effects.

Iron and manganese have a very close biological relationship. For example, an excess of manganese will impede the assimilation of iron. Other information regarding this relationship is included in chapter 13.

Recent experience has shown that toucans in captivity are susceptible to problems caused by excess storage of iron. As this is not known to occur in the wild populations, there is apparently a dietary factor missing that would normally enable the toucans to control this iron storage and excrete any excess. Only thorough study of the diet from a nutritional viewpoint will be able to pinpoint the cause and control of this unusual phenomenon.

For other birds, iron need not be of concern to the bird breeder and aviculturist. Since it is so widely distributed in nature, a deficiency on any diet of unrefined foods is highly unlikely. Any varied diet of natural, unprocessed foods should supply a sufficient amount of iron for any avian need. Only on diets with a high percentage of refined foods is there a possibility of iron deficiency.

LITHIUM

Since the original publication of *Nutrition of Finches and Other Cage Birds*, where lithium was listed as a mineral that was found in the living body consistently, research has advanced our knowledge of this mineral to a considerable degree. Lithium is an alkaline metal that is similar to and thus can be antagonistic to both sodium and potassium. Lithium has been used in the treatment of human psychiatric disorders, where it has had very beneficial effects. However, intakes from 92 to 200 milligrams per day will prove to be a toxic excess for humans.

Research has now confirmed beyond doubt that lithium is a required trace element in the nutrition of goats. On a diet that is too low in lithium content, goats will gain body weight much more slowly, conception rates will be lower in the breeding stock, and mortality rates will be significantly higher. All research is now indicating that lithium will be proven to be essential for all mammals and birds, though excess amounts tested in both animals and chickens still prove to be toxic. Any amount needed in the diet for optimal health will therefore be quite small and should be supplied in any varied diet of unrefined, whole foods.

Natural sources of lithium are difficult to locate, as food testing in the past has not included testing for this mineral. However, it is known that cereal grains, onions, and apples are low in lithium content, while lettuce is an excellent source of this mineral.

MANGANESE

Manganese was one of the earliest trace minerals to be proven essential in nutrition. That early discovery took place in the year 1931, and since that date research has proven manganese to be essential to all life forms, both plant and animal. Every living thing from the lowest bacteria and fungi to birds and human beings requires trace amounts of manganese for life. Manganese is found in sea water at the rate of only about one part per billion, but the earth's crust contains a relatively abundant supply of manganese, with about 4,000 parts per million. The bodies of primitive man contained far more manganese than does the body of modern man, and wild animals also retain in their bodies far more manganese than humans retain in their tissues. This may be the result of our high degree of food processing and also by the fact that so many of our agricultural soils in the world have been depleted of manganese. Should these possible causes of low manganese levels prove true with future research, then modern man is suffering from a constant deficiency of this vital trace mineral.

The absorption of dietary manganese in the digestive system seems to be very poor. As little as one percent of the amount ingested may be absorbed, and absorption appears to depend on the formation of natural chelates. The effect of the other dietary metals on the absorption of manganese does not appear to be severe, except in the case of iron. A high iron content in the diet will reduce the absorption of manganese, and a high manganese content will cause a decrease in the iron absorption in test animals. Also, a high calcium and phosphorus intake in the diet will interfere with manganese absorption and will aggravate any existing deficiency. Fortunately, the absorption of manganese takes place throughout the small intestine, and any changes in the acid-base balance do not affect absorption of the manganese in the diet.

Though manganese is widely distributed on the earth's surface, plant deficiencies of this mineral may occur even though the soil is not deficient in this mineral. This deficiency in the plants happens when the soil is too alkaline. Alkaline soil causes the oxidation of manganese into a form that the plant roots cannot absorb. This results in a bleaching or chlorosis of the leaves, which is a known symptom of manganese deficiency in plants. Merely returning the soil to a more acid state is sufficient to cure any deficiency of manganese in such plants. In areas of highly alkaline soils, a favorite gardening trick to make the soil compatible with the acid loving plants, such as azaleas, camellias, and gardenias, is to pour diluted pickle juice or vinegar around them every few months.

In spite of the many years of research that have been done on the metabolic functions of manganese, its actions within the body are still not well known. Even the proven effects of a manganese deficiency frequently cannot be related to a specific function of manganese in the body.

Nevertheless, a number of known and proven functions of manganese in the body have been confirmed. Manganese takes part in many of the known enzyme reactions in the body, and it is essential for the activation of several of the body's enzymes. In this capacity, manganese stimulates the formation and synthesis of cholesterol and fatty acids in the liver, and manganese is also essential for the release of energy within the cells. In addition, manganese is important in the formation of the vital thyroid compound, thyroxine, and it is required for the metabolism of both lipids and glucose. Manganese functions closely with vitamin K in that vitamin's blood clotting function, and vitamin K alone will not act without adequate manganese in the body at the same time.

Several other functions of manganese are known, but again the exact basis for these actions has not yet been discovered. Manganese is also essential for the development of the organic matrix for bone tissue, though it does not seem to be directly involved in bone calcification.

Perhaps the most puzzling function of manganese is in the contribution it makes to motherly love in mammals. Female rats deficient in manganese will abandon their offspring, and whereas adoption of orphaned babies is usually almost automatic, healthy females will refuse to adopt babies that are suffering from a known manganese deficiency in over 90% of the cases studied. The physiological basis for such actions at this point is totally unknown. Diabetics have been shown to have very low manganese levels, so a dietary deficiency of this mineral may well be a contributing cause of this human disease. Also, symptoms of multiple sclerosis have appeared in rats that have been fed a manganese deficient diet.

Manganese is found throughout the body, but the bones, liver, kidneys, and pancreas contain higher concentrations of the manganese found in the body. Also, the pancreas seems to rely particularly heavily for normal functioning on an abundant supply of manganese. A female animal whose diet is deficient in manganese will produce young with an abnormal pancreas, or occasionally will produce young with no pancreas at all.

At any rate, it is somewhat comforting to learn that such deficiencies, severe enough to cause these noticeable deficiency symptoms, have occurred only in experimental or domestic animals. Yet, the aviculturist should never forget that all birds in captivity are also classified as domestic animals and may be subject to a manganese deficiency, as is described later in this section.

Manganese deficiency will completely destroy the reproductive process. Male rats reared on a manganese deficient diet will be sterile. In the first stage of such an induced deficiency, females will give birth to living young, some or all of which will show a lack of muscular control. In a more serious manganese deficiency, the young ones will be born dead or will die shortly after birth. Poor lactation will also become a prevalent symptom in female animals. In the most severe manganese deficiency, animals will not mate and will also be sterile, with testicular degeneration in the males. There will be a high rate of mortality by the time this stage of deficiency is reached.

Severe manganese deficiency will show up in both chickens and mammals with similar symptoms in some areas. In chicks, the main symptom of severe manganese deficiency is a disease called perosis, a deformity characterized by great enlargement of the tibiometatarsal joint, which connects the leg to the foot. This is accompanied by twisting, thickening, and shortening of the bones. The tendon will slip from its proper position, which gives the common name 'slipped tendon' to this serious deformity. Mammals will exhibit reduced bone mineralization and defective bone structure, along with their reduced growth.

Hens that are suffering from a manganese deficiency will have reduced egg production, decreased hatchability, and an increase in eggs with thin shells or with no shells at all. All of these problems are also common in the birds kept in aviculture. The embryos from eggs laid by deficient hens will have a deformed appearance referred to as chondrodystrophy. Among the symptoms of this deficiency disease are shortened and thickened legs along with shortened wings. The chick embryos will have a shortened lower mandible, giving them a beak resembling a parrot's. The abdomen will protrude and the growth of the down and the body will be retarded.

With a less severe deficiency, chicks that have hatched will be deformed in that the head and beak will point straight up, in a posture that is referred to as 'star-gazing'. This is a sure symptom of severe manganese deficiency, which also occurs in mammals. In a case of manganese deficiency, this condition is also apparently irreversible. Research has also indicated that this particular deformity is probably caused by a structural defect in the inner ear. Though star-gazing may also be caused by thiamin deficiency, once adequate thiamin is included in the diet, the symptoms are completely curable and will disappear.

A number of years ago, I noted this symptom of star-gazing in my Society Finch fledglings. Unfortunately, at that time my library did not contain the specific nutritional information that is now available for my research. At that time, I presumed this was merely a genetic defect, since it occurred only in two or three of my eighty breeding pairs, and only in a minority of their offspring. Now, of course, I can be certain that this problem was the result of the biochemical individuality of these few birds, each of which had a much higher manganese requirement than my diet could provide. Though the star-gazing posture is also a symptom of thiamin deficiency, the particular characteristics displayed in my finches pointed more towards a manganese deficiency.

Experience is obviously the best teacher in such cases, but it is a merciless master, unforgiving of ignorance. Perhaps the information in this volume will help you spot similar deficiencies in your own breeding stock and recognize them as such, allowing at least an opportunity for correction.

Chickens seem to require about 50 parts per million of manganese in their diet. Growing chicks seem to need about 40 parts per million. The manganese levels in the eggs of chickens and other birds vary greatly, depending upon the amount consumed in the diet. The concentration in the egg yolk is four to five times as high as that in the egg white. The 50 parts per million needed by chickens when translated into simpler terms, is only one part in 20,000 of the food that needs to be manganese to constitute an adequate dietary supply.

Nuts are probably the best source for manganese, along with green, leafy vegetables. Whole grains are good sources, and buckwheat, soybeans, peanuts and wheat are all excellent sources of manganese. Several human specialties, such as tea and spices, are especially rich in manganese, with cloves probably the highest available source.

As previously mentioned, refining removes a great deal of the manganese in whole foods. In the processing of whole wheat into white flour, 80% or more of the manganese content is removed. Whole wheat with an average value of 31 parts per million of manganese may have 160 parts per million in the germ, 119 parts per million in the bran, but only 5 parts per million in the white flour. Refining raw sugar into white sugar removes around 89% of the manganese that is available in the raw sugar.

Up to a certain point, the body can excrete an excess intake of manganese through the bile into the intestinal tract. The excreted manganese can then be resorbed, excreted again, and then resorbed several times before finally being eliminated. However, the body's ability to excrete an excess of manganese can be overwhelmed. A toxic excess of manganese occurs only rarely and this is in miners and metal workers in the manganese industry from inhaling a toxic excess of manganese dust. This will result in a form of severe pneumonia and a nervous disease that is similar to Parkinsonism.

Though a deficiency in cage bird diets is a definite possibility, as proven by my own experience with Society Finches, it is not likely. Every aviculturist should be aware of the symptoms described herein to be able to spot any such problem in its early stages. Supplementation, if necessary, is simple, and there is little likelihood of feeding your birds a toxic excess. Fortunately, manganese is among the least toxic of the trace minerals to birds. Hens in experimentation will tolerate as much as 1,000 parts per million with no toxicity. Levels higher than this may be toxic, especially to chicks, so a degree of caution is advisable. Just because one part per thousand is good in the diet definitely does not mean that ten parts per thousand is better! That would constitute a sufficient amount to be deadly in its toxicity.

MOLYBDENUM

Molybdenum is a silvery gray metal which looks something like lead in its pure metallic form. There is a relative shortage of molybdenum in the earth's crust in comparison with the known quantities of other nutritionally important metals, only one part per million. Molybdenum occurs in sea water at the rate of about fourteen parts per billion.

Molybdenum is an essential trace mineral in nutrition. Research has proven it essential to all mammals, and further research with chickens indicates molybdenum as also essential in the nutrition of birds. Molybdenum is found in low concentrations in all of the tissues and fluids of the body. It is a proven constituent of several necessary enzymes that the body constantly requires in its metabolism. One of these enzymes is xanthine oxidase. This enzyme is an essential catalyst for the oxidation of a number of substances in the body's metabolism. Aldehyde oxidase performs similar catalytic functions within the body, as another molybdenum-containing enzyme. A great deal of research remains to be completed to determine the true functions of these enzymes in the avian body, however. These may be somewhat different from the uses in the body of a mammal, though the unity of nature argues against this possibility.

Molybdenum is readily absorbed in the digestive tract, and a higher dietary intake of molybdenum will result in higher concentrations of molybdenum in the body. Tungsten can replace the molybdenum in some of the enzymes in mammals, which will result in weak biological activity in those enzymes. When more molybdenum is absorbed than the body needs, the kidneys filter out the excess, and it is excreted in the urine. Sweat is also a route for excretion of excess molybdenum in those animals having this excretory function.

Both deficiency and toxicity symptoms are known for molybdenum in both birds and animals. A deficiency of molybdenum will cause a reduction in growth in chickens, but little is known about any other effect of a deficiency. Supplementation of the diet of chicks with trace amounts will result in an increased growth rate, and all species studied seem to have an extremely small requirement for this nutrient.

Researchers have proven that an overload from excess molybdenum in the diet is possible. An excess in the diet at the rate of 2,000 parts per million will decrease the growth rate severely in chicks, and anemia will also develop at dietary levels of 4,000 parts per million. Though toxicity shows up even at levels below 200 parts per million, confirmed cases of molybdenum poisoning have never been reported on natural diets. Nevertheless, toxicity symptoms will occur regularly on pastures that are overly abundant in molybdenum. Cattle are affected first and seem to be the most sensitive domestic animal to an excess of molybdenum in the diet. Horses are not affected at all, even at much higher levels of dietary intake. Whole liver in the diet has been reported to counteract any molybdenum toxicity in humans.

Plants cannot take up molybdenum from the soil if the acidity of the soil is too high. Most plant deficiencies, characterized by dead leaf edges, occur in soil with a pH lower than 5.2. Simply raising the soil pH to 7 with the addition of lime is usually sufficient to alleviate any deficiency symptom in plants. Still, plants take up molybdenum in the least amounts of any trace mineral.

Molybdenum is vital to legume plants in particular. The nitrogen-fixing bacteria associated with these plants must use the molybdenum as a catalyst for synthesizing the absorbable nitrates that the plants must absorb and use in their building of the proteins. Vanadium can substitute for molybdenum in some of these nitrogen-fixing bacteria. One writer has flatly stated that any soil lacking all molybdenum will be completely barren. Obviously, any molybdenum deficiency in the soil will cause a corresponding deficiency in the plants grown in that soil, and consequently also in the animals consuming those plants.

Molybdenum strongly antagonizes copper absorption. Since copper is the vital mineral for the production of the black wool of a black sheep, the addition of molybdenum to the diet of black sheep will cause them to produce white wool. Alternating a high molybdenum intake with a high copper intake in black sheep will cause the production of wool that is banded black and white. Sulfur is also involved in this process, but the molybdenum is the decisive factor. An excess of copper can be corrected by the simple addition of molybdenum to the diet. Likewise, a molybdenum excess can be alleviated by additional copper in the diet.

The best sources of molybdenum for the nutrition of the seed-eating cage birds are the whole cereal grains. Milling wheat to make white flour will remove about 48% of the molybdenum in it. Dark green, leafy vegetables are also a good source of molybdenum, as is liver. Dairy products, fruit, and eggs also contain a respectable amount of molybdenum. There is a tremendous variation, frequently over a hundred-fold variation, in the molybdenum content of vegetables, depending upon the molybdenum content of the soil on which they were grown.

Fortunately, this mineral is widely enough distributed in the natural food supply that there is very little likelihood of a deficiency developing in a varied diet. This is not a mineral that you need to be particularly conscious of in avian nutrition, as long as you feed a variety of whole, natural foods.

NICKEL

Nickel is relatively abundant in the earth's crust, which has a content of around 80 parts per million. Sea water also contains nickel in the amount of about three parts per billion. Nickel is widely distributed in human and animal tissues and only seems to be in any concentration in the pancreas. Within the individual cells, however, there are significant concentrations of nickel in both RNA and DNA. Human tissues have been shown to contain nickel at the rate of about one part per ten million.

Research over the years in the field of nutrition indicates that nickel is an essential trace mineral for chicks, rats, and pigs. The future research into the requirements for this mineral will very likely indicate its vital necessity for humans and all birds as well. The need for nickel in the metabolism of living things is extremely small. It is truly a trace mineral, and it has been difficult to formulate diets for testing that are sufficiently low in nickel to cause symptoms of deficiency.

With respect to the human nickel metabolism, it is puzzling that the levels of nickel circulating in the blood will double after an acute heart attack and are also abnormally high after an acute stroke or after an individual suffers severe burns. The reason for this increase in circulating nickel and the source of the additional nickel definitely does not come from the heart itself, however, since the reserves of nickel in that organ are simply not that extensive.

Nickel is poorly absorbed in the body, and less than 10% of the nickel contained in the diet will be absorbed. Retention of nickel in the body is also poor, as the body has efficient mechanisms for excreting excess nickel. These facts are a further indication of the extremely small amounts of nickel necessary for optimal nutrition. Human sweat will contain about twenty times as much nickel as is found in normal concentration in the blood.

Though concentrated amounts of nickel can be toxic, this metal is fairly safe at quite high levels. Chicks in testing are unable to tolerate a dietary intake of 700 parts per million in the food supply, however, without exhibiting symptoms of toxicity. These symptoms will take the form of a lower growth rate, reduced consumption of the food, reduced energy metabolism, and a large reduction in the retention of nitrogen. However, rats that are fed 1,000 parts per million showed no ill effects even after several months of continuous feeding. This would indicate that the excretion process for excess nickel in mammals is more efficient than that of chickens and probably more efficient than that of most other birds, also. Air pollution contains considerable amounts of nickel, as the by-product of the burning of coal and petroleum. Breathing nickel dust will cause cancer in the nose, sinuses, and lungs of humans, with skin irritation appearing in some sensitive individuals.

Though the need for nickel is extremely small, all species tested will show similar deficiency symptoms. Chicks in testing on specially nickel-free diets will show a number of deficiency symptoms within three to five weeks on the deficient diet. They will exhibit color changes in the skin and skin eruptions in certain areas, thicker legs, and swelling in the hocks. There will also be both structural changes along with a change in appearance of the liver, and also biochemical changes within the body. Rats will show similar symptoms with impaired growth and reproduction. Fetal death, less active offspring during the suckling period, rougher fur, and less weight at weaning will also be evident. Pigs will suffer from the same symptoms with higher mortality in the piglets.

Any deficiency of nickel in rats will have a very adverse effect on iron absorption, which will result in severe anemia and greatly reduced storage of iron in the tissues. Even a doubling of the iron content of the diet will not restore normal iron levels in the tissues nor will it completely cure the anemia. The exact biological role that the nutritional nickel plays in these changes is not yet understood.

The best dietary sources for nickel have not been determined, since research on this mineral in its biological functions is so recent. Green, leafy vegetables contain considerable amounts of nickel, and a varied diet of whole seeds, greens, fruit or nuts should contain sufficient nickel content for any avian need. Soybeans and peanuts are both excellent sources of nickel. There is virtually no possibility of any serious deficiency of nickel occurring in birds maintained and bred in captivity. Nickel as a nutritional trace mineral should not be a cause of concern for any aviculturist.

SELENIUM

A Swedish chemist, Baron Jöns Jacob Berzelius (1779-1848) discovered selenium as an element well over a century and a half ago. The earth's crust contains selenium at the rate of about nine parts per 100 million, but selenium is very unevenly distributed in the crust of the earth. The soils of South Dakota are very high in selenium, for example, while Ohio soils are very low in their selenium content. Sea water contains selenium at the rate of four parts per billion, on the average. Selenium is also a component of air pollution, as it is a by-product of coal burning.

Any mention of selenium before 1950 was in relation to its toxicity. Only its poisonous aspect was known before that date. Cattle that were grazed on land with an overabundance of selenium showed typical toxicity symptoms – brittle hair, hooves that were brittle and fell off, and serious wasting disease.

In humans, when the ability of the body to excrete selenium via the urine is exceeded, the excess selenium is excreted through the lungs as a gas, giving a characteristic garlic odor to the breath. Elemental selenium has little toxicity, but selenium oxides are very toxic. An intake level of 10 to 20 parts per million will produce toxicity symptoms, and selenium in that concentration can cause cancer if consumed in excess over a lifetime.

The properties of selenium are similar to those of sulfur and tellurium. For this reason, selenium will displace sulfur in the metabolism of the body. This displacement of sulfur is the cause of the wasting disease that occurs in cattle. With specific reference to birds, an excess of selenium in the diet will also cause malformation in bird embryos.

A revolution in our knowledge of selenium occurred in the 1950's through the work of Klaus Schwarz. In 1957 his efforts resulted in the reclassification of selenium as an essential trace mineral. The level needed varies from 0.05 to 0.2 parts per million, and this is the level of the selenium content in the human body. Apparently, death will not result from a serious deficiency of selenium, though impairment of the health of the body will be severe. Nevertheless, a total lack of selenium in the diet will cause destruction of the pancreas, and this will result in death. Also, research has proven that selenium works very closely with vitamin E in its metabolic functions.

Selenium deficiency has been studied extensively in chickens, and the resulting information should apply to all birds maintained and bred in captivity. First, a selenium deficiency is unlikely in birds that are fed a varied diet of whole, unrefined foods. Selenium is widely available in the seeds and other foods that we feed our cage birds, and the amounts required in the diet are very small. However, you should be aware that a deficiency of selenium in the diet has been directly related as one of the nutritional causes of muscular dystrophy, atrophy of the pancreas, liver necrosis, and infertility.

There is a spontaneous swelling and hemorrhage disease of chickens that is called exudative diathesis. This disease is directly caused by a deficiency of selenium in the chickens' diet. Since selenium and vitamin E are so closely linked nutritionally, though either additional selenium or additional vitamin E in the diet will cure most deficiency symptoms in other diseases, the addition of selenium alone to the diet of chickens on experimental diets will completely prevent exudative diathesis.

Degeneration of the pancreas is the most serious effect that occurs when there is a selenium deficiency in the diet of chickens. This degeneration results in a lack of the pancreatic enzymes in the digestive system. This enzyme lack, in turn, will result in the body's inability to absorb the vitamin E in the diet from the foods passing through the intestinal tract. In cases of a severe selenium deficiency in the diet and the resulting emaciation of the pancreas, however, research has shown that dietary supplementation with selenium will cause the pancreas to return to normal within ten to seventeen days.

The degeneration and emaciation of the pancreas will cause the growth of chicks to slow noticeably or to completely stop. When selenium is added to the diet of these chicks, normal growth will also resume. The effect of selenium supplementation alone on growth is greater than the effect of vitamin E alone, and it is equal to the effect of vitamin E and selenium provided together in the chicks' diet.

Reproductive failure is certain in selenium deficient birds. Selenium is especially abundant in the male reproductive system, and males seem to have a higher selenium requirement than females. Hatchability of the eggs will drop to zero by the 17th week in chickens that are suffering from selenium deficiency. When selenium is added to the diet through supplementation at this point, the hatchability of the eggs will return to over 90%.

Research has shown that additional vitamin E intake in the diet can partly relieve a selenium deficiency, and as previously mentioned, these two nutrients have a strong interactive role in nutrition. There are at least three ways in which selenium has been confirmed to spare vitamin E in the functions of the body. First, selenium preserves and protects the activity of the pancreas, thus allowing for normal absorption of vitamin E in the intestinal tract. Second, selenium is an integral part of an enzyme called glutathione peroxidase, which destroys peroxides that form in the body by converting those peroxides to harmless alcohols. This in turn reduces the amount of vitamin E that is required for the body to maintain the lipid membranes of the cells and to prevent the destruction of those membranes through the action of the peroxides. Third, selenium aids in an as yet unknown way in the retention of vitamin E in blood plasma. See the section on vitamin E for more information regarding this close nutritional interrelationship between selenium and vitamin E.

Researchers have also discovered a number of other nutritional functions of selenium. Adequate selenium in the diet can reduce the toxicity of excess amounts of arsenic, mercury, silver, and copper in the body. Selenium also protects the body against cadmium toxicity, and it serves as an antioxidant in the body. Selenium is also necessary for the synthesis of protein in the body. In addition, research indicates that selenium may also be required for normal body growth. In the feeding of livestock, a trace supplement of selenium added to the diet will prevent both still births and the wasting that occurs in the young animals that survive.

With specific reference to human nutrition, we may require more selenium than other mammals or birds. Human milk contains up to six times as much selenium as that contained in a cow's milk. The cancer rates among human populations are significantly lower in areas where selenium occurrence rates in the diet and in the water supply are higher.

Good food sources of selenium are brewer's yeast, eggs, liver, and garlic. Nuts are also a good source of selenium. The food sources from animals are generally higher in selenium than the food sources from plants. Again, a variety of whole seeds, fruits, insects, and other whole foods should supply all of the selenium needed in avian nutrition, providing they do not all come from an area that is well known for selenium deficient soils.

All foods will lose selenium in processing. Whole brown rice, as an example, has fifteen times the selenium content of milled white rice. The processing of raw sugar to create white sugar, and the processing of whole wheat to create white flour also substantially reduces the amount of selenium in the content of those refined foods.

When the content of selenium in the diet is sufficient, the body will store the amount of selenium that is over and above the daily needs. The body stores selenium in all of the body organs to some extent, but the primary area of selenium storage seems to be in the liver.

No selenium supplementation should ever be necessary for any birds in captivity when they are provided with a varied diet that includes whole, raw foods from a variety of sources and growing areas.

TIN

Information on the nutritional aspects of tin is extremely hard to find. Very little nutritional research has been done on tin as an essential trace mineral, and the available material is quite recent. Until the late 1960's, tin was considered strictly as a relatively harmless contaminant in the food supply. It is found in large amounts in many processed foods as a by-product of the canning and processing of foods. Asparagus packaged in glass has traces of tin added to make it taste like the product from a metal can. Tin occurs in sea water at the rate of three parts per billion.

Research has proven tin to be an essential nutrient for the growth of rats, but the exact biochemical functions of tin within the body are not yet known. In experimental dietary testing with rats, the growth rate of the rats improved by nearly 60% when one to two parts per million of tin were added to their highly purified diets. Researchers achieved this successful demonstration with the use of stannic sulfate and several other tin compounds as the source of the dietary tin. Other than the slower growth, no other deficiency symptoms caused by a lack of sufficient tin in the diet were noted. The latest information available on the research involving the dietary need for tin still does not seem to include birds. The expansion of knowledge regarding this trace mineral is going very slowly, indeed.

Tin is found in most human and animal tissues. Tin is poorly absorbed from the digestive tract and poorly retained within the body. This would account for tin's low degree of toxicity. Any excesses are excreted through the colon. Considering the large amounts of tin occurring in many diets, it is fortunate that this metal has only a low level of toxicity. Five parts per million of tin in the diet resulted in the production of completely normal mice and male rats. Female rats did show a shorter life span with fatty degeneration of the liver at this dietary concentration. This would indicate a greater sensitivity on the part of females to dietary tin. In higher concentrations in the diet, these animals will exhibit slackened growth and reduced hemoglobin synthesis.

Though no information seems to be available on the need for tin in avian nutrition, any trace requirement should be easy to supply from the cereal grains, fruits, nuts, and vegetables. At this point, there is no reason to consider any supplementation of tin to be necessary in the diet. Cage birds and all birds kept in aviculture will get any traces of dietary tin that their bodies may need in any regular, varied diet that you are feeding to your birds that includes foods from both plant and animal sources.

VANADIUM

Research has proven vanadium to be an essential trace mineral for humans, rats, and chickens. It is therefore logical to presume that vanadium is also an essential nutrient for all of the birds that are kept in our cages and aviaries, though no specific research in this regard seems to have been done yet. The earth's crust contains a relative abundance of vanadium at an average rate of 110 parts per million. Sea water carries vanadium in the amount of about five parts per billion, and vanadium is detectable in most of the tissues of the body. In addition, research has proven all other elements with the same properties as vanadium, such as zinc, to be essential in nutrition.

Almost all nutritional knowledge of vanadium seems to be a product of research in the 1970's. Only one reference to vanadium was available for an earlier year, and that was in 1962, though surely research work was in progress before that date with some published research papers presumably found in the periodical literature. Future research and experimentation undoubtedly will be able to increase our knowledge of this mineral's nutritional value.

Vanadium serves the same purpose in sea squirts that iron serves in the blood of higher vertebrates. Up to four percent of the content of the blood cell material of a sea squirt is vanadium. It serves to transport oxygen for the life processes of the creatures in this family. Vanadium is an effective substitute for iron in these organisms, but it is not a very efficient substitute. The most unusual feature to human eyes is that this vanadium base in the blood cells gives the sea squirts green blood.

The food items with the highest levels of vanadium are not normally used in avian feeding. They are black pepper, soybean oil, corn oil, olives, and gelatin. Vanadium is more highly concentrated in fats and in vegetable oils. Consequently, nuts will contain a good quantity of vanadium within their fat content. Marine life is the most consistently reliable source of vanadium. At a

223

maximum possible intake from both dietary sources and from air pollution, there is no known toxicity of vanadium. Any excess over body needs will be excreted in the urine. The source of the vanadium in air pollution is from burning both coal and the Venezuelan and Iranian low-sulfur petroleums. A living body stores this mineral in the fatty tissues.

Researchers have been able to establish a definite correlation between vanadium deficiency and heart disease. Vanadium is abundant in the drinking water supplies of those United States areas where heart disease is the lowest. Relatively high levels of vanadium help to lower serum cholesterol levels. The vanadium in the diet acts similarly to chromium and zinc in this regard. Other research results indicate that the vanadium circulating in the body also speeds the destruction of existing cholesterol. Changes in vanadium levels in any given area are proven to show up in the hair, and presumably also will be detected in the feathers of birds.

Animal research has brought forth a number of facts about vanadium in the diet that may be of interest to aviculturists. Deliberately generated deficiencies of vanadium in young chickens on purified diets will cause a significant decrease in the growth of the feathers. A dietary deficiency also decreases the reproduction rate in rats and increases mortality in their offspring. Vanadium has been proven essential to the growth of rats in laboratory experimentation. Also, vanadium deficient diets in testing have resulted in increased triglyceride levels in chickens. Also, chromium has been demonstrated to be an antagonist of vanadium in the study of nutrition in chickens. Sulfur may also be such an antagonist, counteracting or neutralizing the effect of the vanadium present. In addition, niobium can displace vanadium in metabolic reactions, since both minerals are in the same periodic group.

Vanadium poisoning is possible, but has been reported only in petroleum workers inhaling vanadium-laden dust directly into the lungs. Other workers in the vanadium industry who absorb considerable amounts of the metal will get green tongues and little more. This is the same effect the tongue shows from a synthetic crème de menthe the morning after.

In many areas, vanadium deficiency may be a problem, as evidenced by the research on heart disease reported in this section. Insufficient vanadium in the diet should not be a concern for aviculturists, since whole, unprocessed seeds, particularly the fatty seeds, should contain vanadium in sufficient quantity for any needs in the avian body. Nevertheless, research on vanadium needs in living organisms is too recent and too incomplete to allow even preliminary estimates of the amounts that are needed in nutrition at this time. As with all other aspects of nutritional study, keep an open mind with regard to vanadium. Be prepared to change your views and expand your knowledge with every new research development.

If you feel the necessity to supplement your birds' diet with vanadium, kelp is a readily available source of vanadium and of all of the other necessary trace elements. Supplementation with purified sea water is another possible source for all of the essential trace elements. Mix one part of purified sea water to ten parts of regular drinking water. This will not overload the birds with the salt that occurs so richly in sea water, and will supply the birds with all of the trace elements that are dissolved in the sea water. In my own personal experience, this is a perfectly safe, though somewhat expensive method for supplementing the trace elements in an avian diet, and it is of considerable value for long term supplementation.

ZINC

The importance of zinc in nutrition cannot be overstressed. Zinc is vital to life, and it is more abundant in the cells than any other trace element. All birds and animals, as well as all plants, including algae, fungi, and bacteria, require zinc for life. Zinc has been recognized as an essential nutrient for fungi for over a hundred years. Zinc is found in the earth's crust at the rate of about 5 parts per million, and sea water contains zinc at the rate of around fifteen parts per billion. Zinc will be found in human tissues at an average rate of 33 parts per million and in animal tissues at the average rate of about 30 parts per million.

In 1934 researchers discovered zinc to be an essential trace mineral in the nutrition of rats and mice. Additional information has been accumulating since that year regarding its importance in nutrition, and the future will undoubtedly hold more information yet to be discovered. Absorption of zinc occurs both in the proventriculus and in the small intestine of birds. Pyridoxine must also be present in the body for the utilization of zinc. The colostrum of all mammalian species is three to four times richer in zinc than the later milk.

Zinc occurs in higher accumulations in several parts of the body. Twenty percent of the zinc present in the human body is found in the skin. Because of this high skin content, the body can lose large quantities of zinc in the sweat, especially in the tropics. The human hair, nails and eyes also contain high concentrations of zinc. The skin and fur of rats combined contain 38% of the zinc in their bodies. The protein keratin contains zinc as one of its constituents, which accounts for the high zinc content in the hair and feathers. Copper, nickel and zinc are all proven to be involved in taste, but zinc is the main factor. This is one specific area where zinc works very closely with pyridoxine. A severe zinc deficiency will cause anemia among other symptoms that will be discussed later, and zinc is required for the synthesis of nucleic acids and the protein portions of some vital enzymes. Stress will deplete the body tissues of zinc and for this reason, stress will greatly increase the requirement for zinc in the diet.. Approximately 85% of the zinc content of the blood is found in the red blood cells.

Zinc apparently plays a very important role in the health and proper functioning of the eye, since the retina of the eye is very high in zinc content. The visual parts of the eye can contain up to 4% zinc. In dogs and foxes, these zinc values can rise as high as 85,000 parts per million, or 8.5% of the choroid tissues. The actual function of these extremely high levels of zinc is unknown. Nevertheless, these high levels occur in the eyes of all species tested, including fish. The fluorescent reaction of many animals' eyes to light at night depends upon zinc-containing enzymes.

A substance called phytic acid exists in cereal grains which will bind zinc in an unusable form. Diets exclusively of cereal grains will bind so much of the zinc content that severe zinc deficiency will result. If the zinc is in a chelated form, however, the phytic acid cannot bind the zinc, and it will be available for absorption and use in the body's metabolism. Also, the zinc requirement in the diet is partly dependent upon the calcium content of the diet. An increase in dietary calcium will increase the zinc requirement.

The first obvious symptoms of a zinc deficiency in humans are fortunately highly noticeable and relatively harmless. A borderline deficiency will cause white spots or lines on the fingernails or sometimes a milky, opaque appearance on the whole fingernail. This will be accompanied by poor growth in both the hair and nails. White spots will occur most frequently on the index finger and the little finger of the dominant hand, that is, on the right hand for right-handed people. Brittleness will accompany this discoloration, and the spots will not disappear with zinc supplementation. They must grow out over a period of months. A deficiency is also noticeable by the development of stretch marks in the skin from exercise or rapid growth.

In 1961 zinc deficiency was definitely linked to retarded growth, delayed sexual maturity, and delayed wound healing. These effects are not surprising when you consider that zinc is a constituent of at least 25 different enzymes in the body that are involved in digestion and metabolism. One of these zinc-containing enzymes plays an important role in the calcification of bone tissue and in the formation of eggshells. Calcium will displace zinc in many of its metabolic functions and will inactivate many of these zinc-containing enzymes. The major organ involved in the living body's zinc metabolism is the liver. Supplementary zinc in the dietary intake will increase the efficiency of feed utilization up to 25%. Healing is speeded by an adequate dietary intake of zinc, and in a severe dietary deficiency of zinc, healing will not occur until the zinc content of the body is increased.

A zinc deficiency in chicks will cause poor growth, abnormal bone development with shortening and thickening of the leg bones in proportion to the degree of zinc deficiency, and enlargement of the hock joint. Changes and disproportionate growth will occur in other bones, also, with resulting spine curvature and fusing of the vertebrae. The skin will show scaling, especially on the feet. In addition, very poor feathering will be evident along with loss of the appetite and finally death. Chicks that are hatched from hens that have been fed a deficient diet will be weak and will not stand up, eat, or drink. An accelerated respiratory rate and labored breathing are other symptoms of a deficiency. If the chicks are disturbed, the symptoms are aggravated and the chicks often die.

Embryos in the eggs laid by hens suffering from a severe zinc deficiency will exhibit grossly impaired skeletal development. Toes will often be missing, and in extreme cases the embryos will have no lower skeleton or limbs. The eyes occasionally will be absent or undeveloped.

In any dietary zinc deficiency there are changes in both the carbohydrate metabolism and the fat metabolism. Any deficiency during the critical period of brain growth will permanently affect brain function with reduced brain size and reduction in the total number of brain cells.

Zinc deficiencies will be most likely to show up in humans consuming foods grown on soils that have been depleted of their zinc content. This is particularly true in areas such as Egypt, Iran and Iraq, where agriculture for thousands of years has completely depleted the soil of this mineral. Zinc deficiency has been studied intensively in both Egypt and Iran, where soils and the foods grown on those soils are severely deficient in zinc. The symptoms are dwarfism, rough and hyper-pigmented skin, underdeveloped sexual organs, and also a lack of secondary sexual characteristics. These deficiency-related malformations respond well to treatment with supplementary zinc, if caught in time. One might also note that the fragility of the red blood cells increases in any period of zinc deficiency.

The previous section of this chapter that discussed iron covered the unique female requirements for iron, and in this section, we must turn to zinc as the mineral with unique functions in the male reproductive system. The highest concentrations of zinc in the male body occur in the reproductive system, and any sexual activity causes great body losses of zinc which must be replaced in the diet. These concentrations of zinc obviously serve a vital purpose in the male, but this has not yet been pinned down to specifics. The prostate gland, seminal fluid, and spermatozoa are all very high in their zinc content, and any prostate problem invariably shows a subnormal level of zinc concentration. Men should be aware of this constant zinc loss and the need for its continual replacement. This increased need for zinc is as important to the life and health of the male as an abundance of iron is to the female. Fortunately, any zinc deficiency in the male reproductive system does not result in any permanent damage. Complete recovery will occur with the resumption of adequate zinc intake. Nevertheless, you should be aware that all stages of reproduction in both the male and female will be harmed by any zinc deficiency.

Zinc is available in a wide variety of foods, but in general the zinc content of plant protein is less than that in animal protein. By far the richest known source of zinc is oysters, with herring in second place, far behind. Oysters may contain as much as 1,000 parts per million of zinc. Other seafoods, meats, maple syrup, liver, wheat, buckwheat, oats and other cereal grains, nuts, and eggs have appreciable amounts of zinc. Nuts are a better source than meat. One chicken egg will contain up to one milligram of zinc, most of which will be found in the yolk of the egg. Sunflower seeds and pumpkin seeds are also excellent sources of zinc. The refining of foods removes a great deal of the zinc content, and at least 78% of the zinc is removed in the processing of whole wheat into white flour.

Of all the trace minerals, zinc is the least likely to produce toxic effects. Though it is relatively non-toxic, a consistent zinc intake of over 1,000 parts per million can cause depressed growth, depressed appetite, arthritis, and internal hemorrhages. However, no known diet could possibly provide nutritional zinc in this concentration. An excessive intake at one time can cause diarrhea at first, followed by nausea and vomiting. Yet, in one recorded instance of a deliberate ingestion of 12 grams of elemental zinc, a little less than half an ounce, this excessive amount produced only intense difficulty in staying awake, with the individual constant falling asleep even over meals for several days, but no other noticeable effects. An excess of zinc will also cause a large loss of iron from the liver and a later loss of copper from the liver, both of which will cause anemia.

Zinc is a trace mineral that must be of primary concern to the aviculturist. Research testing has indicated that even the widely varied American diets are frequently deficient in zinc. If you doubt this, look around at the number of individuals with white spots on their fingernails, a dead giveaway of zinc deficiency (not a sign of frequent lies, as old wives tales would have you believe). I can recall that my own fingernails showed this symptom back when

I was a normal, oversexed teenager. Of course, at that time, as is true of most teenagers, I was also a total nutritional illiterate.

All of this means simply that the limited variety of foods in the average cage bird diet is more likely than not to be deficient in this vital trace mineral. It is the rare aviculturist that feeds his charges oysters, herring, or pumpkin seeds, probably the three richest sources of zinc. Much of the zinc in cereal grains will be rendered unavailable by the phytates contained in these foods, as the phytates bind the zinc content of the foods in an unabsorbable form. This leaves sunflower seeds, eggs, and nuts as the only likely sources of zinc in any quantity in most cage bird diets. The result is every likelihood of a deficiency and resulting breeding failure caused by the concentrated needs for zinc in normal sexual functioning. In any suspected mineral deficiency, zinc is the first mineral that should be supplemented in the dietary intake, since it will be the most likely to be deficient.

OTHER MINERALS FOUND CONSISTENTLY IN THE BODY

BARIUM

Barium is abundant in the earth, and the human body contains .3 parts per million of this element. Barium occurs in sea water at the rate of about six parts per billion. About 93% of the barium in the human body is found in the bones, with the remainder distributed throughout the body. Barium is detectable in the body tissues of all newborn infants. Brazil nuts are very rich in barium, and there is apparently no toxicity at any normal level of intake.

Though evidence exists of a possible body requirement for barium, there is still no conclusive evidence that it performs any essential biological function in birds or other living things.

BROMINE

Bromine seems at this point a likely element to be proven nutritionally essential in trace amounts at some time in the future. Bromine occurs in sea water at the substantial rate of about 65 parts per million. Whereas the body content of primitive peoples is only one part per million, the body of modern man contains about 2.9 parts per million.

Experiments with chicks have shown that bromine can substitute for part of their nutritional chloride requirement. The addition of trace amounts of bromine to purified diets for chicks results in a small, but significant, increase in their growth.

All animal tissues except thyroid tissues contain from 50 to 100 times more bromine than iodine. Those proportions are reversed in the thyroid tissue. There are no large accumulations of bromine in any part of the body. An increase in the dietary intake of bromine will result in an increase in tissue levels of this element. Any excess in the body is filtered out by the kidneys and excreted in the urine.

CADMIUM

Cadmium is a serious pollutant in modern life and is extremely toxic in excess amounts. However, research has shown indications that cadmium may be essential in trace amounts. I stress that no need for this element has yet been proven, but that possibility does exist. Cadmium occurs in sea water at the rate of about .03 parts per billion. Most intake comes from the food supply, but sizable amounts of cadmium enter the human body from smoking. Fortunately, cadmium is poorly absorbed, with only from 3% to 8% of the ingested amount entering the bloodstream. However, the excretion of excesses is very slow. Oysters are a very rich source of cadmium with a content of three to four parts per million.

Cadmium toxicity has been reported many times. The toxic effect of an excess of cadmium will affect all parts of the body and will cause reproductive failure. Part of the toxicity of cadmium is caused by antagonism to copper, iron, and zinc. At the current state of our nutritional knowledge, cadmium is not considered a necessary trace mineral in the nutrition of cage birds or other higher life forms.

RUBIDIUM

Though there is currently no information that proves rubidium to be necessary to biological functioning, there are some indications that it might one day be classified as an essential trace mineral. Rubidium is closely related to potassium, and it is found in living tissue in higher concentrations than in the environment. Rubidium is abundant in the earth, and sea water contains about 120 parts per billion. The human body contains rubidium at the rate of about 4.6 parts per million. Meats are high in rubidium content, as are soybeans. Grains, fruits, and vegetables also contain appreciable amounts of rubidium.

All plant and animal cells freely allow the passage of rubidium through the cell membranes. Also, experimentation has shown that rubidium can replace potassium as a nutrient for the growth of yeast. The body does not accumulate rubidium in any particular organ or tissue, and no cases of rubidium poisoning are known. As much as 200 parts per million of rubidium in the diet are not toxic, but a quantity as high as 1,000 parts per million causes a decrease in growth, reproduction, and lifespan. No research at this time has shown any dietary requirement for rubidium in poultry nor in any other birds that are maintained in aviculture.

STRONTIUM

Strontium has received a very bad press over the years because of its wayward isotope, strontium[90]. This element is not always such a villain, however. Strontium is common in sea water at the rate of about 8 parts per million. The human body contains over four parts per million of strontium, and there is strong evidence that it is required by the body in trace amounts. Since this evidence is not yet conclusive, strontium has not yet been classified as an essential trace element. It seems likely that its designation as essential will occur in time with further research. Plant sources are generally richer in strontium than animal sources, except for the higher amounts that are found in the bone structure of animals.

There is no evidence of strontium accumulation in any particular tissue other than bone, and strontium does seem to have an affinity for the bone tissue. Absorption of the strontium in the diet ranges from 5% to 25% of the dietary content. Absorption is reduced with age. The amount of calcium in the body strongly influences the effects of strontium. The less calcium is present, the more toxic will be the strontium. Any excess of strontium in the diet will cause incoordination, weakness, posterior paralysis and bone deformation. I have encountered no information with relation to strontium in the nutrition of birds.

OTHER MINERALS

A fairly large number of elements occur in trace amounts in all human tissues. No biological function is known nor suspected for any of them in either humans or birds. The fact that they occur consistently in the body, however, means that there is the possibility they may one day be proven essential in trace amounts. Of this list, lead in particular is a highly toxic pollutant. It would be a great surprise to discover that lead is necessary for nutrition, even in trace amounts. These are the elements that are found in the body consistently:

| aluminum | bismuth | gallium | gold | niobium | silver | uranium |
| antimony | cesium | germanium | lead | radium | titanium | zirconium |

Of the minerals on this list, germanium is the one element that is most likely to eventually be classified as essential in nutrition in trace amounts, since it has the chemical structure necessary for such functioning.

TISSUE SALTS

In any extensive nutritional research, sooner or later you will encounter the tissue salts. These are also called cell salts or biochemical tissue salts. A virtual cult has been built up around the use and curative powers of these twelve mineral salts. Yet, if you have learned anything from the previous sections on vitamins and minerals, you now know that there is no such thing as a panacea in nutrition. The bodies of birds and animals are simply too complex in their structure and nutritional needs to permit us to believe that these twelve salts are a cure-all. Without the vitamins and trace minerals, nutrition is incomplete, and death will be sure to result from malnutrition. Though all of these salts are found in the living body, nothing in my research has yet indicated that the body's cells do not synthesize all of these in adequate quantity, if they are provided with the necessary raw materials, with the single exception of sodium chloride, common salt. The twelve tissue salts and their reported functions are listed below. Only sodium chloride is dealt with in detail in the sections on sodium, potassium and chlorine.

Calcium fluoride	-	gives elasticity to body tissues
Calcium phosphate	-	promotes health and nutrition of cells
Calcium sulfate	-	serves as the blood purifier
Iron phosphate	-	serves as the oxygen carrier
Magnesium phosphate	-	acts as anti-spasmodic and supplements the action of potassium phosphate
Potassium chloride	-	cures sluggish conditions
Potassium phosphate	-	serves as a nerve nutrient
Potassium sulfate	-	acts with iron phosphate as an oxygen carrier
Sodium chloride	-	serves as the body's water distributor
Sodium phosphate	-	acts as an acid neutralizer
Sodium sulfate	-	maintains proper density of Intercellular fluids
Silicic Oxide	-	acts as a cleanser and eliminator

There may be more value in this knowledge than meets the eye or the mind at this point, however. You will find that each of these elements is also discussed in chapter 13. As I mentioned in the foreword, our current knowledge of nutrition is very limited, and it is advantageous to keep a completely open mind regarding any items that may turn out to be of value in biological functioning.

"Though minerals are not destroyed in food preparation, processing, or storage, the refining of food products removes substantial quantities of both the bulk elements and the trace elements from the food."

CHAPTER 13

BIOLOGICAL TRANSMUTATIONS

The study of nutrition presents the reader with many totally incomprehensible and conflicting statements and research results when these concern the intake and utilization of minerals in the living body. Particularly with reference to calcium, the available information was simply not logical nor believable. However, the new scientific study of biological transmutations has explained these inconsistencies to my satisfaction, and a thorough reading of Louis C. Kervran's *Biological Transmutations* will be sufficient to convince most readers that the living body does possess the capability to transmute elements from one basic form to another. Nutritionists easily accept that the body routinely takes methyl groups, tears them down and rebuilds them into other compounds. It is only one small step farther to accept that the living body also has the routine capability of moving some protons and thus transmuting one basic element into another.

The periodic charts of the elements deal with atoms as a whole and elements as a mixture of isotopes, while biological changes are presumed to be accomplished at the level of the atomic nucleus. Each element may have one or more isotopes, having the same number of protons in the nucleus, but differing numbers of neutrons. Only certain of these isotopes can be used by the body in biological transmutations, and organisms seem to succeed better in transmutation with the heavier isotopes. Naturally occurring elements are mixtures of isotopes, and as outlined in the periodic charts have no biological value for transmutations. How living creatures and plants, apparently by enzymatic action, can move particles from one atomic nucleus to another is at present a complete mystery. Yet, there can be no doubt that these changes occur.

In inorganic chemistry, any transmutation of elements occurs only at extremely high temperatures and/or pressures. The sun, for example, with its incredibly high temperatures and pressures, routinely transmutes the elements in its nuclear furnace and in the process releases tremendous amounts of energy. This energy, even after traveling some 149,600,000 kilometers to reach the earth, is still strong enough to support physical, biological life in virtually every square kilometer of this planet's surface.

Biological life, by contrast, seems to have been blessed by the Creator with the ability to transmute basic elements internally with virtually no release of energy and with a great deal of benefit to the organism. The wild, native, North American daisies, for example, will only germinate and grow in areas where the soil is very deficient in calcium. Yet, the daisy plant is very rich in calcium content, so rich that when the season ends and they die and decompose, the soil has a measurably greater calcium content than it had before the daisies grew there. Daisy seeds that contain no calcium can be germinated in a prepared medium that contains absolutely no calcium, but when these new plants are dried and analyzed, they will always contain measurable amounts of calcium. The only logical conclusion is that the daisies have the ability to transmute other elements into calcium; indeed, that may be their primary purpose in the scheme of nature.

This knowledge is not a recent development, since as far back as 1880, Von Herzeele established beyond doubt that germinating seeds with no source of calcium contained calcium after germinating. Von Herzeele was the first to conclude that there was an actual transmutation of the elements in living things. However, as with so many other initial discoveries, this information has been largely ignored for over a century.

The reader will need to approach this chapter with a very open mind, for much of the information presented here will contradict the textbooks, schooling and teachings of the last 200 years. Yet, despite any ridicule that may come my way as the result of including this information in a book on the nutrition of birds, I feel that everyone needs to see that biological transmutation is not only a possibility, but a probability. Nothing else will adequately explain the presence and utilization of minerals in the living body.

CALCIUM

The contradictory information that has been published concerning calcium needs and calcium research are incomprehensible in light of the known facts about calcium, and in particular the fact that no condition has ever been diagnosed as a calcium deficiency. Rather, all calcium misuse within the living body is the result of deficiencies or misappropriations of other vitamins and minerals. Calcium is obviously a very important and basic necessity for physical, biological life. As such, nature has devised an almost bewildering number of ways to assure that no living thing goes without its vital calcium. The living body seems to be able to transmute three other minerals into calcium: potassium, magnesium, and silicon.

Potassium is the first basic source of calcium within the living body. Two of the potassium isotopes can be transmuted into calcium: potassium^{39} and potassium^{41}, as follows:

potassium^{39}	plus hydrogen^1	yields calcium^{40}
potassium^{41}	plus hydrogen^1	yields calcium^{42}

Silicon is the second basic source of calcium within the living body. Three silicon isotopes are transmutable into calcium in the following four reactions:

silicon^{28}	plus carbon^{12}	yields calcium^{40}
silicon^{30}	plus carbon^{12}	yields calcium^{42}
silicon^{29}	plus carbon^{13}	yields calcium^{42}
silicon^{30}	plus carbon^{13}	yields calcium^{43}

The primary source of calcium seems to be magnesium, since there are six verified transmutations from magnesium to calcium:

magnesium^{24}	plus oxygen^{16}	yields calcium^{40}
magnesium^{26}	plus oxygen^{16}	yields calcium^{42}
magnesium^{25}	plus oxygen^{17}	yields calcium^{42}
magnesium^{25}	plus oxygen^{18}	yields calcium^{43}
magnesium^{24}	plus oxygen^{18}	yields calcium^{42}
magnesium^{26}	plus oxygen^{18}	yields calcium^{44}

239

Note that in all of these potassium, silicon, and magnesium transmutations to calcium, calcium[44] can come only from magnesium. Since the shells of many sea animals are formed by such transmutations, and the creatures transmute only magnesium from sea water into calcium, there should be a larger portion of the calcium[44] isotope in their shells than occurs in land creatures. With chemical analysis of the shell, this proves to be true, further strengthening our basis of knowledge of these puzzling but proven transmutations.

PHOSPHORUS

Evidence of biological transmutation to create or transmute this mineral also exists. The living organism can combine magnesium and lithium to produce phosphorus, or in a reversible reaction combine phosphorus with hydrogen to produce sulfur. The first transmutation is further confirmed by giving a magnesium overdose to test animals. When this is done, both the calcium and phosphorus levels in the body will rise. It is also probable that carbon[12] plus fluorine[19] can be joined to produce phosphorus[31].

Any test will clearly demonstrate that cows excrete and give daily in milk far more phosphorus than they ingest. Yet, a deficiency of phosphorus in either cows or humans is unknown. Phosphorus is far too important to biological life for nature to take a chance on a deficiency which might result from a low phosphorus supply in dietary sources alone.   Thus, the natural physical development of life has assured that phosphorus deficiency cannot occur under any normal conditions by developing the ability to transmute other elements into phosphorus whenever they are needed in the body.

POTASSIUM

Much of the conventional knowledge of potassium activities in the body is flatly contradictory. Though it is a vital bulk element, there is little information on minimal needs – researchers are rarely able to induce a deficiency state. Also, deficiencies seldom occur from inadequate potassium intake in the diet. Even in low protein and low potassium diets, even to starvation, animals may grow very slowly, but do not show a potassium deficiency. The kidneys continue to secrete potassium in large amounts even when test diets deficient in potassium are fed for several weeks. Since potassium has been proven to be neither retained nor resorbed in the body, this contradiction taxes the average person's credulity.

Only Louis C. Kervran's explanations of the biological transmutations involving potassium can adequately explain what is occurring within the body in a logical sequence. The body apparently can create potassium in the following transmutation:

$$\text{Sodium}^{23} \qquad \text{plus oxygen}^{16} \qquad \text{yields potassium}^{39}$$

For this reason, the amounts of sodium and oxygen available are at least as critical to potassium metabolism as is the dietary content of potassium. The presence of potassium depends upon the availability of oxygen. This trans-mutation is an endothermal reaction in that it absorbs heat. This enables the body to exist in reasonable health and comfort in dry climates where the air temperatures are consistently well above the body temperature, when perspiration alone could not lower the body temperature sufficiently. The requirement then is for a bountiful supply of sodium and oxygen to be transmuted into potassium, thus soaking up a large amount of excess heat. One only needs to review the importance placed on salt in the Bible to realize that sodium chloride is vastly more than just a food flavoring or preservative. Fresh sodium that is injected into the body will be transmuted immediately into potassium.

Should potassium become too abundant in the body, it can be transmuted into calcium in the following transmutations:

$$\text{potassium}^{39} \qquad \text{plus hydrogen}^{1} \qquad \text{yields calcium}^{40}$$
$$\text{potassium}^{41} \qquad \text{plus hydrogen}^{1} \qquad \text{yields calcium}^{42}$$

In these two transmutations, potassium is the agent of equilibrium. By removing acidic hydrogen and creating alkaline calcium, potassium helps to maintain the body's acid-alkaline balance. The body controls excess potassium so efficiently through kidney excretion and transmutation that there is no known potassium toxicity, even when kidney failure causes an excessive buildup.

In experiments with potassium transmutation in chickens, hens that were deprived of calcium to the point at which they are producing only soft-shelled eggs will begin producing calcium-rich eggshells only twenty hours after being fed mica. Mica is a potassium aluminum silicate. It contains no calcium, but it does contain potassium, which the hen's body transmutes into calcium very efficiently. The silicon in mica is also transmuted into calcium, as discussed in the section on silicon.

In further tests with guinea fowl under the same conditions, removing the mica from the diet resulted again in soft-shelled eggs. Since potassium is not stored in the body to any extent, the transmutation of potassium and silicon into calcium is the only logical explanation.

In transmuting potassium[39] plus hydrogen[1] into calcium[40], the body has a ready source of calcium whenever needed. This transmutation is also reversible with calcium[40] minus hydrogen[1] giving potassium[39]. The study of biological transmutation helps to explain how a hen is able to produce calcium-rich eggshells continuously, even when no attention is paid to the calcium content in the hen's diet.

This also satisfactorily explains how my Society Finches fed on diets exclusively of whole white proso millet and shelled sunflower seed with water have been able to lay clutches of eggs with calcium-rich shells, far more than their diet or body reserves could provide, even though both of these foods contain only one one-hundredth of one percent calcium content. Millet has a high 0.43% potassium content, while sunflower seed is 0.06% potassium, resulting in an adequate amount of potassium for transmutation into the necessary calcium for the formation of perfect eggshells.

SULFUR

In his review of biological transmutations, Louis C. Kervran states that plants, animals, and bacteria can all create sulfur by merging two oxygen atoms into one sulfur atom. He refers to sulfur as a condensate of oxygen. In addition, phosphorus plus hydrogen will yield sulfur in a reversible reaction. It is interesting to note that no sulfur deficiency has ever been noted in plants, though some soils contain none. The only sulfur source for these plants is biological transmutation. Farming activities are continually removing sulfur from the land as a constituent of the amino acids in crops, so the only conceivable source for all of this sulfur is through transmutation. Fortunately, oxygen is always available to plants through the air for the transmutational formation of sulfur as needed.

SODIUM

Sodium's role in biological transmutations has been outlined in the section on potassium. The body apparently can create potassium in the following transmutation:

Sodium^{23} plus oxygen^{16} yields potassium^{39}

For this reason, the amounts of sodium and oxygen available are at least as critical to potassium metabolism as is the dietary content of potassium. In hot weather, sodium or salt is not excreted from the body, but instead is transmuted into potassium in a heat-absorbing reaction.

CHLORINE

Though the orphan science of biological transmutation has not yet delved deeply into the study of chlorine, Kervran feels that chlorine can be formed within the body by the combination of sodium and carbon to achieve the nuclear structure of chlorine. Two other possibilities exist, also. First, the formation of chlorine from carbon plus lithium and oxygen should be possible, or alternately, as a second possibility, silicon and lithium might be combined to create chlorine. No biological confirmation of these possible transmutations is yet known.

MAGNESIUM

The transmutation of calcium into magnesium within the living body is now solidly confirmed. Though plants use vast quantities of magnesium in the manufacture of chlorophyll, magnesium deficiency is never found unless a calcium deficiency also exists. Plants that are cultured in water that is magnesium-free form chlorophyll normally as they grow, indicating an adequate supply of magnesium. The transmutation involved is one atom of calcium minus one atom of oxygen to yield one atom of magnesium. The more calcium added for the plant's absorption, the more magnesium will be found in the plant tissues. If magnesium is missing in the living plant tissues, calcium can replace it and be transmuted to magnesium, but the reverse does not hold true in plants.

In the animal kingdom, the transmutation of magnesium and oxygen into calcium does occur regularly. Both animals and birds secrete more calcium than they ingest. This indicates a reverse transmutation in these groups from that existing in the plants. Shellfish, for example, can make calcium-rich shells with no calcium resources available, only an abundant supply of magnesium, as occurs in sea water. The transmutation involved here is the combination of magnesium plus oxygen to yield calcium. Refer to the section on calcium for the exact isotopes involved in this transmutation. In addition, in some germinating seeds the content of magnesium decreases while the calcium content increases, indicating a similar transmutation within these seeds.

Kervran states that the sodium in blood plasma is the source of magnesium production by transmutation in animals. The transmutation involved is sodium plus hydrogen to yield magnesium. Experiments with men in the Sahara Desert proved conclusively that during great dry heat a living organism secretes 80% more magnesium than it ingests. Kervran further estimates that at this rate, the body would have exhausted all of the magnesium that could be mobilized from tissue storage in only eight days. Yet, the subjects remained in fine health over the eight month period of the experiment. Since more sodium was ingested than excreted during the same period with no sodium accumulation observed, the conclusion is inescapable that the living body is able to transmute sodium into magnesium routinely whenever the need arises.

In addition, as previously mentioned, the primary source of calcium in the living body seems to be magnesium, since there are six verified transmutations from magnesium to calcium:

$$\text{magnesium}^{24} \quad \text{plus oxygen}^{16} \quad \text{yields calcium}^{40}$$
$$\text{magnesium}^{26} \quad \text{plus oxygen}^{16} \quad \text{yields calcium}^{42}$$
$$\text{magnesium}^{25} \quad \text{plus oxygen}^{17} \quad \text{yields calcium}^{42}$$
$$\text{magnesium}^{25} \quad \text{plus oxygen}^{18} \quad \text{yields calcium}^{43}$$
$$\text{magnesium}^{24} \quad \text{plus oxygen}^{18} \quad \text{yields calcium}^{42}$$
$$\text{magnesium}^{26} \quad \text{plus oxygen}^{18} \quad \text{yields calcium}^{44}$$

Refer to the section on calcium for further information on these calcium transmutations.

SILICON

Louis Kervran's studies of biological transmutations have offered an alternate theory as to the real uses of silicon in the living body. This explanation of silicon's use in bone formation involves the transmutation of silicon plus carbon to make calcium. There are three isotopes of silicon that the body uses in this transmutation, and these yield three different calcium isotopes, as indicated in the following examples:

$silicon^{28}$ plus $carbon^{12}$ yields $calcium^{40}$
$silicon^{30}$ plus $carbon^{12}$ yields $calcium^{42}$
$silicon^{29}$ plus $carbon^{13}$ yields $calcium^{42}$
$silicon^{30}$ plus $carbon^{13}$ yields $calcium^{43}$

Since ancient times, the knowledge of the use of horsetail *(Equisetum)* for recalcification has been a part of medical knowledge and folklore. This plant is extremely high in organic silica, a silicon and oxygen compound. Fractures are repaired and healed much faster with organic silica extracts than with the administration of calcium. Experimentation and x-ray examination of bone healing have proven that organic silica is a vastly more successful healing agent for bones than is calcium. However, for reasons not yet understood, mineral silica will decalcify the bones.

The phenomenon of biological transmutation also explains why at hatching a chick contains four times more calcium than the yolk and white of the egg together will contain. The fact that this increase in calcium is not coming from the shell has been conclusively proven, despite the claim by Romanoff and Romanoff in *The Avian Egg* that it originates in the calcium bicarbonate of the shell. However, the shell membrane contains 0.5% organic silica. The chick embryo's growing body transmutes this organic silica into calcium as it matures. A chicken egg will contain slightly more than half a milligram of silicon, which makes it the eighth most abundant mineral in the chicken egg.

IRON

Experimentation in biological transmutations has left no doubt that iron can be transmuted into manganese by microorganisms. Actinomycetes and some bacteria can perform this transmutation routinely. Isotope iron[56] can lose one proton in this biological transmutation and become manganese. Louis Kervran states that one of the best sources of iron for humans is in the manganese content of whole wheat, rice, and other cereal grains. The human body will transmute this manganese into iron by the addition of one atom of hydrogen. With sufficient organically bound manganese included in the diet, iron deficiency will never occur. Whether this transmutation is performed by intestinal bacteria or by one of the body's organs is unsure at this time.

MANGANESE

As discussed in the section on iron, manganese can be biologically transmuted into iron, and the opposite transmutation also occurs. Actino-mycetes and bacteria can transmute iron, Fe^{56}, into manganese Mn^{55}, by withdrawing one proton, in effect one hydrogen atom. This process occurs in the ruins of the ancient temples in Cambodia, where surface microorganisms transmute the iron content of the rock into a dark coating which contains 5% manganese. In controlled testing, these bacteria can be cultured on ferrous sulfate and will produce manganese by transmuting the iron in the ferrous sulfate. During seed germination, the opposite transmutation occurs; manganese will disappear while an equal amount of iron appears. Neither transmutation has yet been observed in birds, to the best of my knowledge.

"Biological life seems to have been blessed by the
Creator with the ability to transmute basic elements
internally with virtually no release of energy and with
a great deal of benefit to the organism."

CHAPTER 14

CONCLUDING COMMENTS

Anyone who has waded through the nutritional quagmire up to this point deserves a word of commendation. Yet, with all of the information that has been outlined already, there are still a number of loose ends that need to be covered. Some of these subjects should serve to open the mind and to feed the imagination. Much remains to be discovered in nutrition, and not all that remains is in the realm of the five physical senses. This chapter will present a number of interesting developments that have a bearing on nutrition. Also, a number of the items presented here are from my general knowledge and are not traceable to the books listed in the bibliography.

Much of our knowledge of nutrition is a by-product of the nuclear age. By tagging the nutrients with a radioactive element, researchers can trace them through digestion, absorption, circulation, and eventual utilization. This tool of research has been of inestimable value in piecing together the nutritional puzzle. Both fortunately for research and unfortunately for long term health, the body does not seem to discriminate between a natural isotope and a radioactive isotope. For this reason, radioactive isotopes are ideally suited to the task of following nutrients to their eventual utilization point within the body.

Still within the field of radioactivity, we are well aware of the damage that the emissions of radioactive substances can do to living bodies. The study of biochemical individuality shows that individuals within a species show a wide variance in their ability to withstand radioactive bombardment without any significant physical damage or illness. This dosage amount was formerly measured in roentgens, and a dose of 500 roentgens in the older radioactivity measurement is generally considered to be fatal for humans. However, in 1958, a species of happy, proliferating bacteria was discovered within the water of a nuclear reactor at Los Alamos. It not only lived, but reproduced every twenty minutes in an environment that was previously thought to be instantly deadly to

249

any living species. These bacteria were of the *Pseudomonas* family. They were tested extensively and were found to be able to tolerate for eight hours a dosage rate of 20,000,000 roentgens. This is twenty million roentgens, when 500 roentgens is deadly to a human being. What more can I say except hooray for the tenacity of life?

As you read further into the known information on nutrition, you will encounter the research terms 'in vivo' and 'in vitro' in your reading. These terms describe the laboratory conditions under which a nutritional experiment was conducted. An experiment in vivo was conducted within a living body, on a living bird or animal. An experiment in vitro was conducted in an artificial environment, such as in a test tube or other laboratory apparatus.

Many avicultural works warn of the danger of genetic faults in a strain of birds and the danger of perpetuating such faults by injudicious inbreeding. I have called this into question before, and though there may be no doubt that something is being reinforced, it does not always seem to be a genetic fault for physical deformity. Rather, the problem seems frequently to lie with the reinforcement of high genetic requirements for particular nutrients, the lack of which is bound to result in the physical deformity symptoms of deficiency. Though physical defects may well be a result of inheritance, never discount the possibility of deficiency symptoms caused by a high nutrient requirement.

The enrichment of refined foods has become common practice in the United States. This undoubtedly helps out nutrition by providing the minimum of nutrients necessary for health, but it certainly does not replace all that are lost in processing. Enrichment does not even replace one-quarter of the nutrients that have been lost. Too many people have looked upon the enrichment of refined foods as a panacea. It is not. If anything, this process has lulled everyone into a false sense of security while nutritional disaster overwhelms us. Review the introduction to vitamins for a recap of the vitamin losses from processing. The mineral losses are as bad or worse, and they are covered in the sections on minerals.

If the diet for either birds or people contains a large amount of processed or cooked foods, supplementation with vitamins and minerals that are in short supply is the only way for you to assure freedom from deficiency symptoms. There are a variety of vitamin-mineral supplements on the market, but I do not recommend mixing them with either seed or water for reasons listed in the introduction to vitamins. A full range supplement can be a great convenience and reassuring comfort to the aviculturist trying to make sure that the birds are getting all of the nutrients necessary. Supplements are not a substitute for good, basic feeding, however, Nothing will replace nature's perfect balances as found in seeds, fruits, nuts, insects, and fresh greens.

Though it should be obvious, I must forcefully point out that any cooked food is a dead food. The living fruits, vegetables and nuts are totally killed by cooking, down to the last cell. Most people never stop to think that what they eat is dead matter, if it has been cooked in any way. If this is not in the mind for human nutrition, it certainly will not be in the mind where the nutrition of cage birds and other birds raised in captivity is concerned. No other creature cooks food before eating it, and few even bother to kill their food first. If the total organism, such as an insect, is killed, the cells making up that organism still live on for a considerable time.

The fact that astounds most observers is that an invisible part of the total organism remains alive and well even after the physical part is completely removed. This used to be an esoteric teaching exclusively, but now it can easily be physically proven every day through the development called Kirlian photography. Actually, this process is not that new, since the technique dates back to the 1880's and the early days of photography. But it was the dedicated work of Semyon D. and Valentina Kh. Kirlian of Alma-Ata, Kazakhstan, that will be remembered as long as scientific study exists. Their perfection of this process of photography earned them the highest honor mankind can bestow — the process was named after them and today is known throughout the world as Kirlian photography.

The exact force that this process is photographing is still in doubt, but the technique is solid and the results are inspiring. When a portion of a leaf is removed and the electrophotograph still shows the forces emanating from the missing area as well as from the intact leaf, the ramifications are interesting, to say the least. As was mentioned in the foreword to this volume, only the Rosicrucian philosophy, as outlined in the Rosicrucian Cosmo-Conception by Max Heindel has explained such phenomena to my satisfaction.

The point to be made is that cooking will completely destroy these unidentified life forces. What role they may play in the nutritional process and in the maintenance of life in both birds and humans is completely unknown at this time. Nevertheless, I can safely assume that such strong life emanations cannot be without effect on the receiving body when eaten. I anxiously await further information and developments in this field.

A basic law of nature is that perfect nutrition means perfect health and total immunity from all disease. Very gradually, the realization is growing that germs are only part of the problem of disease. There is no way any microbe can get a foothold in the body if nutrition and health are in top shape. This might be called the toxemia theory, for it holds that germs can cause disease only where toxic waste products accumulate for them to live on. The accumulation of toxic wastes implies a state of less than perfect health. Experiments with human volunteers have proven that the healthy body is completely unaffected by the injection of living cancer cells. Even living cancer cells are almost instantly overwhelmed by the healthy body's normal defenses. The same will apply to all other microscopic foreign life forms entering the body.

The human body contains a hidden electrical system. Ages ago, the Chinese tapped this system and designed a science called acupuncture to use it to medical advantage. A German doctor has now used this system as a basis and devised an electronic machine that can monitor these micro-volts of power coursing through the body. The reading produced by this electronic device will pinpoint the location of body dysfunction, and when mated to a properly programmed computer, it will dictate the exact cure. This is similar in principle to the automotive diagnostic machines used in most large garages in this country. However, only a handful of medical doctors are yet using this system. Presumably, of course, the same sort of hidden electrical system exists in the avian body.

If you are an average or skeptical reader, by now you're ready to exhibit your disbelief of this new invention in the strongest of terms. Only the few will be open-minded and inquisitive enough to accept the possibility of such a diagnostic revolution. Such is human nature. However, it now appears that this will be the wave of the future, much as the first orbited satellite was the wave of the future. This system of diagnosis is only now beginning to be used. Perhaps one day in the future the office of every medical doctor will be equipped with this blessing of technology. Only time will tell.

An interesting controversy was floating around the avicultural field for a number of years, and still deserves mention. This concerns the use of sunflower seed in the avian diet. Opponents of its use claim a narcotic effect resulting from the natural content of a substance called papaverine in the sunflower seed. Papaverine is defined as a non-addictive antispasmodic and nerve relaxant. It is a salt of a lesser alkaloid of opium. Opium has among its contents one percent papaverine. It is still doubtful whether papaverine actually exists in sunflower seeds, or if it is just a similar compound. Personally, I do not feel that this substance, even if it exists in sunflower seeds, is a problem in avian nutrition. The outstanding nutritional value of sunflower seeds far outweighs any slight disadvantage that such a substance might have as a part of the contents of a sunflower seed.

Another field that has great promise for the future is that of biological transmutation. Through several dozen years of study and observation of nutrition, I have become firmly convinced of the solid foundation upon which this knowledge rests. The impossible contradictions that occur in the standard nutritional texts where minerals are concerned are fully explained and cleared up by the information already learned in the study of biological transmutations. Obviously such a radically different view of life and science will require many more years to be fully accepted, but the precedent is already established. Naturally radioactive minerals are continuously and naturally transmuted, as in the example of radium gradually being transmuted into lead. Living organisms routinely combine nitrogen with oxygen at room temperature, while the same process in a laboratory takes electric arc temperature or a very high temperate and pressure to accomplish the same end. The discoveries of Louis Pasteur required many years for full acceptance, and the work of Louis C. Kervran will certainly take no less time. Nevertheless, I feel certain that the future will regard Kervran in the same manner that we now regard Newton, Mendeleev, and Pasteur. When confronted with this possibility, Kervran stated, "I simply point out what has always existed." How true, and what more has any other scientist in history ever done?

All of the birds and the other surface dwelling creatures of our planet developed under the balance of light wavelengths emitted continuously by our sun. As these light waves strike the earth's atmosphere, the length of the light waves is modified. Some of the harmful rays are filtered out by the atmosphere. The greater depth or area of the atmosphere that the rays go through, the more they are changed towards the red and infrared end of the visible spectrum. This is why the setting sun is so orange in color; its light must pass through hundreds of miles of atmosphere before it reaches our eyes. The light from the sun when it is directly overhead passes through only a few miles of atmosphere, allowing the greatest amount of unmodified light to reach the surface.

When this normal balance of light in which birds evolved is altered, as by indoor artificial lighting, there are short- and long-term effects on the birds' lives, health, and reproduction. Some few of these more noticeable effects are now known, but most are still completely unknown. It can now be physically proven, for example, that unbalanced light that strikes the human eye will result in vastly reduced muscle power and physical ability. This unbalanced light will also affect the muscle strength of birds, and this is one reason why birds indoors under artificial light tire more easily and are easier to catch than those maintained in outdoor aviaries.

There are a wide variety of artificial light bulbs and fluorescent tubes now available, and most of these produce a balance of light wavelengths that is far different from that of natural sunlight. Some of them give off lightwaves that are heavily into the red and infrared end of the spectrum, such as the standard incandescent light bulb, while others are overly rich in the green, blue, or yellow wavelengths. The ultraviolet 'black light' tubes that are used in discos radiate predominantly beyond the visible violet in the invisible ultraviolet range, at the opposite end of the visible spectrum from the infrared area.

The old standard incandescent light bulbs, as already mentioned, produce light that is heavily in the red and invisible infrared wavelengths. Though we cannot see infrared radiation, we can feel it as heat. An incandescent bulb radiates a lot of infrared or heat radiation. In a small, enclosed room, one light bulb will rapidly raise the temperature of the room through its large output of heat. When used in brooders and other small enclosed places, a small bulb produces enough heat to keep the temperature of a small area very warm for young gallinaceous birds, or baby psittacines that are being hand-fed. A bulb that is too large can put out so much heat that it will dehydrate, burn and kill sensitive baby birds. A small, 7-watt bulb can even be used as a temporary incubator in a pinch when nothing else is available. These incandescent light bulbs do not emit any light in the ultraviolet wavelengths.

The commonly used fluorescent lighting tubes are made to emit more blue or other colors of light, depending on their purpose. Unless they are specifically manufactured to do so, they emit little or no light in the red or infrared ranges of the spectrum, and little or no ultraviolet light. Those that are manufactured as 'daylight' fluorescent tubes have a better balance of the light colors of the spectrum. The commercial tubes that go by the brand names Vita-Lite® and Kiva® have a good balance of the light wavelengths that are nearest to the balance of natural sunlight, but they range from two to ten times the cost of the standard fluorescent tubes.

A report published in the November, 1971, monthly issue of the *American Cage-Bird Magazine* illustrates the importance of full-spectrum lighting in maintaining any birds in captivity. The Bronx Zoo had for four years maintained a group of Tufted Puffins under artificial lights. During this time, there had been no breeding attempts. However, when the Zoo installed full-spectrum lighting, the puffins produced a fertile egg for the first time in captivity.

The basis for the observed effects of various wavelengths of light on living things is not yet understood. We do know from solid research that light affects the development of the body's hormone-producing glands. We also know that under the stimulation of light, the pineal gland controls the synthesis and release of hormones and enzymes into the bloodstream. Perhaps most important, light received through the eye will stimulate the pituitary gland. Since the pituitary gland is the master balance gland of the glandular system and of the body, light in this indirect manner will influence all of the glands in the body. Though research has not yet pinpointed many of the physical affects of this glandular light influence, there can be no doubt that these effects are profound and far-reaching.

All of the available research now indicates strongly that light is a basic, natural regulator of many body processes and physical activities in both birds and mammals. Research by William Rowan as long ago as 1925 showed that Slate-colored Juncos could be made to migrate northward rather than towards the south in the fall by varying the light-dark cycle they were exposed to before their release. Also, experience with ducks many years ago showed that hooding them to close off light to the eyes definitely prevents the stimulation of the male sex glands.

Canary breeders have known for probably hundreds of years that the gradual lengthening days of spring are a primary factor in bringing the canaries into breeding condition. It has also been proven that the red wavelengths of the spectrum are a decisive influence in bringing birds into breeding condition. As a consequence, if you have birds that are failing to come into breeding condition at the appropriate time, you might try installing a red light bulb to increase the concentration of these wavelengths to which your birds are being exposed. Do this in addition to gradually lengthening the daylight hours for the birds.

The ultraviolet wavelengths are of particular importance for the health and breeding of cage birds. These ultraviolet wavelengths of light are invisible to our eyes and are classified into two general groups, called the long wavelength ultraviolet and the short wavelength ultraviolet. The natural sunlight striking the earth is rich in long wavelength ultraviolet, which is closer to visible light. It is also called 'near ultraviolet', since it is the nearest to the visible light. This long wavelength ultraviolet alone will cause pigment darkening in the skin without burning. The commercial black lights give off light in the long wavelength range of ultraviolet. Ultraviolet light will not pass through glass, but will pass through most clear plastics, and it will pass through quartz glass.

The short wavelength ultraviolet, also called 'far ultraviolet', is farther away from visible light. It can be dangerous, and it is the form of ultraviolet

255

that causes sunburn with overexposure. The germicidal lamps used in hospitals to kill microorganisms emit ultraviolet light in the short wavelengths. And yet, this short wavelength ultraviolet is not all bad, for it is this area of the ultraviolet wavelengths striking the skin that allows the formation of vitamin D_3.

Another proven way in which ultraviolet light affects our birds is in the sex of the offspring of your breeding efforts. The long wavelength ultraviolet seems to be the primary factor in this influence. Experiments with fish, chinchillas, and other animals showed that the addition of full spectrum lights used in place of the standard incandescent or fluorescent bulbs resulted in an enormous increase in the production of female offspring in breeding efforts under artificial light. In transferring this information to the frequent complaints from bird breeders that their Society Finches and Gouldian Finches are producing a vast majority of males in indoor breeding, it was only reasonable to assume that a similar lack of ultraviolet light was the cause of this common avicultural problem, also.

In my own cage breeding, I was getting from 75% to 90% males while breeding these finches under artificial lights indoors. After reading about the effects of ultraviolet light in increasing the production of female offspring in animal experiments, I installed one four-foot black light tube in my birdroom, placed so that it would shine directly into all of the cages.

This one, simple change was sufficient to restore a normal 50/50 sex ratio to the offspring of all of the species in my birdroom, beginning with the next clutches laid under the new lighting system. Even the overabundant production of males in the Society Finches and Cutthroat Finches changed with the next nests of eggs laid so that the breeding birds produced an equal amount of males and females among their offspring.

Though an excess of males when breeding the canaries, budgerigars, and cockatiels may be highly desirable, since males are always in greater demand as pets and singers, a large excess of males can be a minor disaster in breeding such birds as doves and finches, which are usually maintained in pairs. Should your own birds be producing a large excess of unwanted males, you need to review your lighting conditions carefully. And keep in mind that any glass between the birds and the natural light will filter out all of the ultraviolet wavelengths. The natural light in open outdoor aviaries will provide the necessary ultraviolet wavelengths which have been proven to be so important in determining the sex ratio of the offspring. A simple four-foot fluorescent black light tube in your indoor birdroom will accomplish the same result.

Since this initial experimentation with a black light in balancing the sex ratio of the offspring was so successful, I have frequently recommended this change to other aviculturists who were also producing an unwanted excess of males. The feedback I have received has indicated that this is a solid and safe way of balancing the lighting in an indoor birdroom, which will invariably result in the production of a more balanced sex ratio in the offspring of any avian species.

For a thorough coverage of the subject of light in relation to living things, I would recommend that you read the detailed works of John N. Ott. He became interested in the effects of light through his work as a time-lapse photographer, and the information he gathered in this profession resulted in the publication of several books on this important subject matter. One that should be on your 'must read as soon as possible' list is his book, *Health and Light*.

Though chicken breeders and egg farm managers have known for many years that days lengthened with artificial lighting will cause the hens to lay more eggs, the importance of lighting has not been stressed sufficiently to bird breeders in particular and the avicultural community in general. The lighting that you supply your birds will affect their disposition, their health, and their breeding. Your own indoor lighting conditions may well spell the difference between success and failure in the maintenance and breeding of cage birds.

In their natural environments, all birds and animals have a number of protections against the development of any nutritional deficiency. The sheer variety of their natural diets is the most basic of these protections. In addition, the birds can apparently transmute a number of elements within their own bodies. The mechanism of craving is yet another means for assuring an ample supply of nutritional substances. The body instinctively craves certain foods that are rich in the nutrients needed. This replenishes the supply of any nutrient that is approaching a deficiency state. Last, in order to assure species survival, biochemical individuality has been developed as the emergency mechanism.

Finches and other small birds with their high rate of metabolism will show symptoms of any deficiency far faster than human beings. A severe deficiency of any nutrient will cause physical symptoms in a small bird within days or weeks, at most. In humans, this same deficiency may take months or years to manifest itself as definite, physical, deficiency symptoms. For this reason alone, all aviculturists must pay close attention to the birds in their care and to the nutritional content of their diets.

When maintaining and breeding any finches or other birds in captivity, two factors are vital. These are nutrition and environment. The most ideal plan for achieving perfection on both areas is worthless if the materials used are poor.

The best materials available are useless without a good plan for their logical, efficient use. Success with birds involves a sincere desire and a plan. The last item required is knowledge, and I hope that the material presented in this book has given you a part of that vitally necessary knowledge.

The items included in the following short section have come to the author in a very special way. Many are not at the point where they can yet accept the idea of more planes of existence than this physical one we inhabit, let alone the idea of communication between and among the many planes of existence. Yet, this information did come directly from the finer planes of the Creation. This information is included in this volume, followed by two special messages that were transmitted from the finest plane to our physical plane, as it has a bearing on your own nutrition, and your own future.

*   *   *   *   *   *   *   *   *   *   *   *   *   *   *

"Many times you have been told to lay up your treasures in Heaven; we must also remind you that the physical body must be fed and clothed, warmed and protected, else it is of no use to the spirit within and will be abandoned. Once the body is cared for, then the excess may be given to all in need with much spiritual profit. But he who mistreats and defiles his own physical body gains no blessing in Heaven, but rather a time of reflection to assure that in the next physical existence the body will be honored and well cared for. The body is provided through the love of the Creator, the All That Is, and you may not purposefully destroy it without enduring the consequences.

Never, never are you given more than you can bear at any time, no matter how intense the lessons and the experience. Suicide is not, not ever an open option to those enmeshed in the physical form. Though always He will forgive, also will He demand repayment from those who seek to and succeed in abandoning their lessons through ending the life of the physical body. Yes, in truth your body is the temple of the living God, and those who deny its needs and ignore its health must learn the lesson of adequate care for the body sooner or later.

As you have seen, the 'refined' foods have caused a precipitous decline in the health of the human body. Too much is removed in the refining that is vital

258

for the health of the body. As the cells weaken and die from lack of these nutritional forces, the vitamins and minerals and the life force itself which is consumed in the living foods, the spirit's hold on the body weakens. Thus are caused all of the various diseases that mankind has now begun to endure. Again the Law of Cause and Effect has come into play, as so few pay any attention to the nutritional knowledge that has been made available to you.

As the connection between the spirit and the malnourished body breaks down, the mental faculties appear to become weak, the memory lapses, and often the spirit is more in the higher planes than in the physical. It saddens us on these planes to see such suffering caused by lack of care for the physical body, for we see that we also may fall into this trap when next we enter a physical body.

Sickness is not the natural state of the human body; it is a perfect creation of the Perfect Creator. Though injuries must come to balance the wheel of destiny, sickness is a self-imposed torture that should not be. Through the triple powers of right thinking, nutrition, and joy in all that you do, the body should always be in perfect health. Any of the Creator's microorganisms are thrown off and repelled by the perfectly balanced physical body. The fact that no one has achieved this perfect health shows us that one of these three factors is out of balance."

* * * * * * * * * * * * * * *

"Long and in sadness have you heard and read of the extinction of the Passenger Pigeon in the North American continent. Yet this was also for a purpose, nay for several purposes. The species had become an evolutionary dead end, abandoning their young to predators and even unable to breed unless thousands of pairs were together. This was not a species of value for the spread of biological life throughout the galaxy and the Universe. As you have guessed, the spirits that enlivened those bodies, the Passenger Pigeons, are now enlivening the physical bodies of the commercial poultry. They now experience the cosmic law of balance, the Law of Cause and Effect: those who will not care for their young must understand what it is to have no chance to love and tend their young – their every egg is taken away, their young hatched and raised by the impersonal and unloving hand of man.

Think not that these birds fail to understand and learn the lesson. They do understand, and they do learn the lesson that most of the avian spirits have already learned. Other species have yet to learn this lesson, as you perceive, the cowbirds and the whydahs as examples. None may fail to learn the lessons that this physical Earth can teach so well. In time, all must learn to nurture their

259

young, to love and protect them, to feed and warm them, for only those who have well learned this lesson may go forth to populate the Universe.

Yes, a complicated existence is this on the physical plane, but still it is the greatest and fastest teacher of the Law of Cause and Effect, the basic foundation of God's Universe. Be gentle with those who have not yet learned this lesson, for all will learn it in time. You have been given the opportunity to learn your lessons, and all eternity in which to learn them. What more could you ask? You know that the Creator will always forgive your mistakes and that the Universe of His Creation lies before you. Yes, you are thrice blessed – in the opportunity, in the actual learning, and in the great path lying open to you once the lessons are learned. Joy in your opportunities, give thanks for your lessons, and bless the road along which you struggle towards a glorious future – a future so filled with love, opportunity and accomplishment that you cannot now imagine it. Feel now the love of the Creator as it surrounds and enfolds you. Understand that He would have you succeed no matter how long it takes, nor how difficult the road you travel. For this accomplishment, this success, this opportunity, is your destiny, the destiny of each spirit in human form, and no power in the Universe can keep you from this appointed destiny. The future is bright beyond imagining, and you will succeed, you must succeed, for this is your destiny."

"*My beloved people, for now you learn, for now you suffer, for now you experience all that will enable you to become the creators of the future. For it is My will that each will in time learn to create in perfection through your own developing abilities. See how well you are already progressing, to create the wondrous computers from only the on and off flow of electricity.*

Far more wondrous things will you discover in the years to come, as each of you prepares to travel to the stars. This also I have willed, but few can yet be trusted to travel the stars with only love. No thought of hatred or greed must leave the Earth, for the spirit worlds about the other stars are far more fragile than this dense physical Earth. Thoughts of hate do only minimal damage to the Earth, but would wreck My more fragile creations. So, My children, here you must stay until all hate and intolerance are transmuted into love. As the thoughts mature into love unending, so will the technology appear that will allow you to traverse the stars.

Learn solidly, and learn well, for your future is limitless. I have made more stars than human spirits, more planets than all of the cells in your bodies, more variety than you can yet imagine, even in your science fiction. And all this I have done for you, My beloved people. Yet not for you alone, for others grow and learn to share the cosmos with you, others that you will one day meet. Others that you must work with in love and understanding.

Learn each lesson with joy, strive for perfection, and know that the greatest of futures awaits you. All are My creations; therefore, all are your brothers. In brotherly love must you meet them in all their forms. Learn your lessons well, My children, and a new dawn on a million new worlds awaits you. All of My Creation awaits you with love."

"Blessed are you, my special children, for upon you will fall the responsibility for spreading and sharing what you have learned here on your beautiful Mother Earth. For I chose this one to nurture your learning, your growth, and your physical existence. Well did I know the immense patience, love, and fortitude this long journey of creation would require. And well did I also know that your Mother Earth was the best chosen to fulfill this task. Blessed is your Mother Earth for the great service she has performed in nurturing these millions of varieties of physical life forms. Great will be her reward as she sees her children go forth to spread life to My Universe. And great will be your reward, My Children, as you joyfully share all that has been learned here in the enfolding love of Mother Earth. All of My other children eagerly await your coming and rejoice at the speed in which you learn your lessons.

Think not that the rest of My children stand still, while only you of Earth progress. Such is not the case. All progress in different areas, along different lines, in different forms. All that you meet in time will be able to teach you much of their experience, as you will teach them of your physical ways. All learn, all progress, all are different. And all are My beloved children, created in love, nurtured in faith and hope, maturing in ability and blessed with opportunity. For all have the opportunity to do as much as they can, as do you, My beloved human children. Know that your destiny lies before you, your learning nears its end, and soon you will go forth to seed My Universe, to spread your special love, so perfectly taught by your Mother Earth. All is possible for you, My children, for you are destined to be creators. This have I promised; this have I planned; this I ordain to be. Be faithful in your lessons; be faithful in your learning, and once your learning is through, the time will be at hand for you to begin sharing and teaching. Even now you practice – even now you prepare for the glorious future awaiting you. And it will come; it will come. This is My promise; this is My Will. This is your destiny."

GLOSSARY

Abdominal – Referring to that area of the body located between the ribs and pelvis, which contains the intestines.

Absorption – The process of absorbing, taking up or soaking up a substance.

Acetylcholine – A white, alkaloid, crystalline compound necessary for the transmission of nerve impulses from one nerve fiber to the next.

Acid – A compound capable of acting with a base to form a salt.

Actinomycetes – A family of soil microorganisms resembling both bacteria and fungi, some having the capability to synthesize cobalamin, vitamin B_{12}.

Adenosine triphosphate – A high energy compound that serves in the body to soak up excess heat energy from glucose and fat breakdown and then stores this energy.

Adipose tissues – The body cell groups that contain the stored cellular fat.

Adrenal glands – A pair of small glands, one located above each kidney.

Adrenalin – A hormone secretion of the adrenal glands, which is also called epinephrine. It stimulates rapid breakdown of glycogen in the liver, giving an immediate energy boost for meeting higher, emergency body needs.

Alanine – One of the non-essential amino acids that make up proteins. Alanine is a part of the pantothenic acid molecule.

Albinism – A genetic characteristic that causes the total absence of normal color in any bird or animal, resulting in white fur or feathers and pink eyes.

Albumen – The nutrient-containing substance which surrounds a developing embryo, such as the white of an egg.

Albumin – Any of a group of water soluble proteins that are coagulated by heat, such as are found in egg white and in many other animal and plant sources.

Alcohol – Any of a large group of compounds which contains a hydroxyl group.

Aldehyde oxidase – An enzyme which contains molybdenum and which is an essential catalyst for the oxidation of a number of substances in the body.

Aldosterone – A hormone secreted by the adrenal glands which controls the regulation of sodium in the blood.

Algae – Primitive, one-celled or multi-celled plants that lack true roots, stems, and leaves, but usually contain chlorophyll.

Alkali – A substance which is basic as opposed to acidic.

Alkaloid – An organic basic substance that is derived from plants, such as nicotine, quinine, atropine, and morphine.

All-rac-alpha-tocopherol – A new designation for dl-alpha-tocopherol, the synthetic form of vitamin E. This designation was proposed many years ago, but is not in general use at this time.

Alpha-tocopherol – The chemical name for vitamin E, which has been used to designate both the natural and synthetic forms of this vitamin.

Alphitobius diaperinus – The scientific name for the Lesser Mealworm, found in North America in grain derived products and used in Europe where it is called the Buffalo worm.

Aluminum – A metallic element, atomic number 13, symbol Al, found consistently in body tissues, but with no known nor suspected nutritional function.

Amadina fasciata – The scientific name for the Cutthroat Finch or Ribbon Finch, native to Africa. This species is on the CITES Appendix III, and is no longer imported into the United States.

Amandava amandava – The scientific name for the Strawberry Finch, native to India and nearby areas.

Amines – Substances which contain Nitrogen.

Amino acid – Any organic compound containing both an amino group and a carboxylic acid group.

Amino group – A compound of hydrogen and nitrogen that is a characteristic component of amino acids.

Amygdalin – A substance that is claimed to be a vitamin, alternately called vitamin B_{17} or Laetrile.

Anemia – Any of a number of diseases characterized by a deficiency of the oxygen-carrying material of the blood.

Aneurin – An old name for thiamin or vitamin B_1.

Angina pectoris – the severe chest pain caused by insufficient blood supply, especially to the heart, and characterized by feelings of apprehension and suffocation.

Animal starch – Another name for glycogen, which is the storage form of carbohydrate within the avian and animal body.

Anions – Negatively charged ions.

Anorexia – Loss of appetite.

Antagonist – In nutrition, any substance that competes with a necessary nutrient for the same space.

Antibodies – Any proteins in the blood that are formed in reaction to foreign proteins, that serve to neutralize the foreign proteins, and by this action produce immunity against foreign microbes or their poisons.

Antihistamine – A substance that is used to reduce the effects on the body associated with histamine production.

Antimony – A metallic element, atomic number 51, symbol Sb, that is found consistently in the body with no known nor suspected biological function.

Antioxidant – Any chemical compound that prevents the combination of oxygen with a third substance.

Antirachitic factor – An outdated designation for vitamin D.

Antispasmodic – A substance which will ease or prevent a muscle spasm.

Aorta – The main artery leading from the heart.

Arachic acid – An alternate name for arachidic acid.

Arachidic acid – An extra-long chain saturated fatty acid with twenty carbon atoms in its chain.

Arachidonic acid – A polyunsaturated essential fatty acid with 20 carbon atoms in its chain.

Arginine – An essential amino acid.

Ariboflavinosis – A deficiency of riboflavin in the body.

Arsenic – A non-metallic element, atomic number 33, symbol As, an essential trace element in nutrition.

Arsenic trioxide – A poisonous compound of arsenic and oxygen.

Artificial – Not natural, synthetic or man-made.

Arteriosclerosis – A chronic disease in which thickening and hardening of the arterial walls interferes with blood circulation.

Ascorbic acid – The chemical name for vitamin C.

Aspartic acid – One of the non-essential amino acids.

Ataxia – Loss of muscular coordination.

Atherosclerosis – The deposit of lipid-containing materials, usually on the walls of the arteries.

Atom – The smallest unit of an element, consisting of a nucleus of protons and neutrons, surrounded by a system of electrons.

Atomic – Concerning the basic, elemental structure of any substance and its component atoms.

Atrophy – The wasting away of the body or its tissues and organs.

Aureomycin – A trademark for chlortetracycline, an antibiotic.

Aviculture – The science, hobby, and profession of maintaining and breeding birds in captivity.

Aviculturist – A person who maintains and breeds exotic birds.

Avidin – A protein substance found in raw egg white which binds biotin and makes it nutritionally unavailable. The heat of cooking inactivates avidin.

Bacteria – The one-celled microorganisms that live either free or as parasites, found everywhere in nature.

Barium – A metallic element, atomic number 56, symbol Ba, which is found consistently in the body, but not known nor suspected to be essential in nutrition.

Base – Any compound that is alkaline in nature as opposed to acidic.

Behenic acid – An extra-long chain saturated fatty acid with twenty-two carbon atoms in its chain.

Benzoic acid – An acid compound which the body cannot metabolize.

Beriberi – A severe deficiency disease caused by thiamine deficiency.

Beryllium – A metallic element, atomic number 4, symbol Be, with no known nor suspected nutritional function, but which will replace magnesium in its biological functions.

Beryllium phosphate – An unabsorbable compound composed of beryllium and phosphorus.

Betaine – A compound formed by the oxidation of choline in the body, which acts as a methyl donor.

Beta-lipoic acid – A water soluble form of lipoic acid.

Bicarbonate – An anion group containing hydrogen, carbon, and oxygen.

Bile – An alkaline liquid secreted by the liver, held in the gallbladder, and discharged into the intestine to aid in digestion.

Biochemical tissue salts – A group of twelve chemical compounds required for the proper functioning of the body, also called cell salts.

Biochemical individuality – The basic internal, biological differences in nutrient requirement and body function fond among individuals within the same species.

Biochemistry – The study of the use and reactions of elements and compounds within the living body.

Bioflavonoid – A member of a group of biologically active substances found in plants, including hesperidin, quercetin and rutin.

Biological – Concerning living things.

Biological transmutation – The ability of living things to change one basic element into another through internal biochemical processes.

Biosynthesis – The production of complex compounds from more simple ones within the living body.

Biotin – One of the B complex vitamins.

Bismuth – A metallic element, atomic number 83, symbol Bi, found consistently in the body, but not suspected of any nutritional function.

Black light – A commercially available fluorescent tube that emits light only in the violet and ultraviolet range of the spectrum. Incandescent bulbs are also available, but they are much lower in ultraviolet emissions.

Black tongue disease – The acute niacin deficiency disease in dogs, called pellagra in humans.

Boron – A non-metallic element, atomic number 5, symbol B, which is vital in the nutrition of plants, and now considered to be needed for optimal health in animals, also.

Bromine – A non-metallic element, atomic number 35, symbol Br, found consistently in living bodies, but not known to be essential in nutrition.

Budgerigar – The formal and Australian name for the common grass parakeet, *Melopsittacus undulatus*.

Bulk elements – Those inorganic elements that are needed daily in fairly large amounts as nutrients for the body, usually in amounts of over one gram in humans, and in corresponding amounts in birds and animals.

Bulk minerals – Those inorganic mineral elements that are needed by the human body for optimal nutrition in amounts of over one gram daily, and in corresponding amounts in birds and animals.

Butyric acid – A short-chain saturated fatty acid with only four carbon atoms. It occurs in the butterfat of milk.

Cadmium – A toxic, heavy metallic element, atomic number 48, symbol Cd, poisonous in any quantity, but suspected of essential functions in the body in trace amounts.

Calcification – Hardening of tissues of the body by the deposit of calcium salts.

Calcium – A metallic element, atomic number 20, symbol Ca, an essential bulk element in nutrition.

Calcium bicarbonate – A white compound of calcium, carbon, and oxygen that forms parts of bones, teeth, and shells. In most writing, it is usually called calcium carbonate.

Calcium fluoride – One of the twelve tissue salts. One of the primary forms in which fluorine occurs in the body.

Calcium orotate – The supplement form of orotic acid.

Calcium oxalate – The insoluble combination of calcium and oxalic acid.

Calcium pantothenate – The calcium salt of pantothenic acid, still with biological activity as a vitamin.

Calcium phosphate – One of the twelve tissue salts or cell salts. Calcium phosphate accounts for up to 90% of the body's phosphorus content.

Calcium sulfate – One of the twelve tissue salts or cell salts.

Calorie – The amount of heat needed to raise the temperature of one kilogram of water by one degree Centigrade at one atmosphere of pressure.

Canary seed – The seed of a grass native to Europe, *Phalaris canariensis*, widely used as a food for seed-eating birds.

Cannibalism – The act of feeding upon others of the same species.

Capric acid – A saturated fatty acid having ten carbon atoms in its chain.

Caproic acid – A saturated, short-chain fatty acid having six carbon atoms in its chain.

Caprylic acid – A saturated fatty acid having eight carbon atoms in its chain.

Carbohydrate – A large group of carbon, hydrogen, and oxygen compounds used by the body for energy, including all sugars and starches.

Carbon – A non-metallic element, atomic number 6, symbol C, a basic component of all proteins, fats, and carbohydrates.

Carbon dioxide – A gaseous carbon and oxygen compound that is the waste product of complete combustion, along with water.

Carbon monoxide – A gaseous carbon and oxygen compound that is absorbed in the bloodstream much faster than oxygen and is fatal in excess.

Carbonate – A salt or ester of carbonic acid.

Carbonic acid – A weak, unstable acid that forms from carbon dioxide and water.

Carbonic anhydrase – A enzyme containing zinc that is necessary in the body for the breakdown of carbonic acid.

Carboxyl group – A carbon, hydrogen, and oxygen compound present in all organic acids.

Cardiac muscle – The muscles of the heart.

Carotene – A term used to designate the precursors of vitamin A in plant products.

Carotenoids – Vitamin A precursors found in plant sources, usually as yellow or orange pigments.

Carrion – Dead or decaying flesh.

Casein – A white, tasteless protein found in milk.

Catalyst – A compound which increases the rate of a chemical reaction or causes a reaction by its presence, but is not changed by this function.

Catamblyrhynchidae – A traditional avian family classification for the Plush-capped Finch, now classified in the Sibley-Monroe family Fringillidae.

Cataract – Opacity of the lens of the eye, causing partial or total blindness.

Cations – Positively charged ions.

Cell – The smallest structural unit of an organism that is able to function independently.

Cell salts – A group of twelve chemical compounds deemed vital to proper body functioning, also called tissue salts.

Cellulase – An enzyme which breaks down cellulose in the digestive system.

Cellulose – A carbohydrate compound which is the main constituent of all plant tissues and fibers.

Centigrade – Also referred to as Celsius, a temperature scale with the freezing point of water at a standard atmospheric pressure taking place at 0°, and its boiling point at 100°.

Cerebellum – The portion of the brain responsible for the regulation and coordination of voluntary muscular movement.

Cerebrum – The large, rounded portion of the brain taking up most of the cranial cavity.

Cerotic acid – An extra-long chain saturated fatty acid with twenty-six carbon atoms in its chain.

Ceruloplasmin – A protein which contains copper in the body and stores copper in the blood.

Cesium – A metallic element, atomic number 55, symbol Cs, found consistently in body tissues, but which has no known nor suspected biological functions.

Chelate – To form a compound by joining an active substance to a metal ion, or the compound so formed.

Chelator – Any substance that attaches itself to a mineral to transport it in the body, also called a ligand.

Chemical energy – The energy stored in molecules of food.

Chemistry – The science which studies the structure, composition, properties, and reactions of matter, usually in its atomic or molecular forms.

Chitin – A semi-transparent, horny compound which forms the biggest part of crustacean shells and insect exoskeletons.

Chloebia gouldiae – The scientific name for the Lady Gouldian Finch, native to Australia, and found widely in aviculture throughout the world.

Chloride – A nutritionally essential anion of chlorine.

Chlorine – A non-metallic element, atomic number 17, symbol Cl, which is a vital bulk element in nutrition.

Chlorophyll – Any of a group of related green pigments containing carbon, hydrogen, oxygen, nitrogen, and magnesium, used by the green plants for photosynthesis.

Chlorosis – Bleaching, as of the leaves of plants deficient in manganese.

Cholecalciferol – Vitamin D_3, found only in animal sources, and formed on the skin of birds and animals through the action of ultraviolet light on a substance on the skin, 7-dehydrocholesterol.

Cholesterol – A glistening white, soapy substance which acts as a precursor of vitamin D and is a constituent of all body tissues.

Choline – A compound generally considered as a member of the B vitamin complex, but required in such large amounts that it is often called a basic nutrient rather than a vitamin.

Chondrodystrophy – A deficiency disease resulting in a deformed embryo within the egg, caused by manganese deficiency in the diet when the egg was formed.

Chromic acid – A corrosive, oxidizing acid which contains hydrogen, oxygen and chromium.

Chromium – A metallic element, atomic number 24, symbol Cr, which is a vital trace element in nutrition.

Chromosomes – The DNA-containing portion of the cell nuclei in plants and animals, responsible for the determination and transmission of hereditary characteristics.

Cilia – A microscopic, hairlike growth extending from a cell's surface and often capable of rhythmic motion.

Cirrhosis – A chronic liver disease characterized by progressive destruction and regeneration of liver cells with an increase of connective tissue that eventually causes liver failure and death.

Cirruline – One of the non-essential amino acids.

Citrovorum factor – An alternate name for folinic acid, the biologically active form of folacin.

Clupanodonic acid – A non-essential, extra-long chain polyunsaturated fatty acid with 22 carbon atoms in its chain.

Coagulation – The change from a liquid into a soft, semi-solid or solid mass.

Cobalamin – An alternate name for vitamin B_{12}.

Cobalt – A transitional, metallic element, atomic number 27, symbol Co, a vital trace element in nutrition as the base of the cobalamin molecule.

Cobalt chloride – A compound used therapeutically to stimulate red blood cell production. It is toxic in any quantity.

Coenzyme – An organic molecule that must be loosely associated with an enzyme for the enzyme to perform its function.

Coenzyme A – A substance containing pantothenic acid and several other compounds. It is the form in which pantothenic acid is used in most biological reactions.

Coenzyme Q – A compound synthesized in the body which is an essential link in the chain of events which releases energy from energy-yielding nutrients; also called ubiquinone.

Coerebidae – A traditional avian family used for classifying the conebills, bananaquit, flowerpiercers, dacnis, and others, now included within the Sibley-Monroe family Fringillidae.

270

Collagen – The fibrous material making up parts of bone, cartilage, and connective tissue.

Colostrum – The first milk produced after the birth of mammalian offspring, differing substantially in nutritional composition from later milk.

Comb – A fleshy, usually colorful crest or ridge growing on the top of the head, most prominently in the male.

Complete protein – A protein complex which contains all of the essential amino acids in adequate quantities.

Compound lipid – A triglyceride fat with a glycerol base, two fatty acids, and the third available position filled with another chemical group.

Congenital – Existing at birth, but not hereditary.

Constipation – Inability to expel waste products from the intestine.

Contaminant – A substance which makes another substance impure or corrupt, or anything 'what don't belong to be there!'

Convulsive seizures – Intense involuntary muscular contractions caused by a variety of nutritional deficiencies and other factors.

Copper – A transitional metallic element, atomic number 29, symbol Cu, a vital trace element in nutrition.

Copper sulfide – A relatively insoluble compound of sulfur and copper.

Coprophagy – The eating of excreted waste material in birds or animals; the consumption of droppings.

Cornea – The transparent covering of the pupil and lens of the eye.

Cowbird – One of a number of avian species in the genus *Molothrus*, which is classified in the traditional family Icteridae and the Sibley-Monroe family Fringillidae.

Craving – A desire or longing for a particular food item.

'Crazy chick disease' – A vitamin E deficiency disease in chicks, also called encephalomalacia.

Cretinism – An iodine deficiency syndrome characterized by arrested physical and mental development and complete idiocy.

Crop – The widened area of the esophagus in birds which serves as a storage area for food, technically called the diverticulum.

Crotonic acid – A monounsaturated fatty acid which has only four carbon atoms in its chain.

Crude protein – All of the protein content of a substance, whether it is digestible or not.

Crystalline – Constructed of identically made up molecules repeated in a pattern.

Cyanide – A group of poisonous compounds which contain a cyanide group, consisting of carbon and nitrogen.

Cyanide group – A compound of carbon and nitrogen which is highly poisonous when combined with sodium or potassium.

Cyanocobalamin – A form of vitamin B_{12} or cobalamin, which has an attached cyanide group.

Cysteine – One of the non-essential amino acids.

Cystine – One of the non-essential amino acids

d-alpha-tocopherol – The scientific name used for the natural form of vitamin E, to differentiate it from the synthetic form, which is dl-alpha-tocopherol.

Death – The transfer of the higher-vibration physical forms from the physical body to the finer planes of existence, with a resulting breakdown of the denser parts of the physical body into their component elements.

Decalcification – The process of breaking down and removal of calcium and phosphorus from the bones.

Deficiency – An inadequate supply of a nutrient in the diet, when one is referring to nutrition.

Deficient – Having an inadequate supply.

Degeneration – The deterioration of cells or tissues of the body, causing a loss of the function of those tissues.

Dehydration – The loss of water from the tissues.

Dementia – Depression and mental imbalance, which can be caused by niacin deficiency, among other causes.

Deoxyribonucleic acid – A long, spiral-appearing molecule that is the storage point for hereditary characteristics within the cell.

Depigmentation – The loss of color.

Dermatitis – Inflammation of the skin.

Diabetes – One of a number of diseases characterized by an excessive discharge of urine and persistent thirst.

Diarrhea – In birds, the constant evacuation of very watery droppings, which may be caused by a variety of factors, including enteritis.

Diffusion – The gradual scattering and mixing of one type of substance into another.

Digestion – The process of food breakdown in preparation for absorption which occurs in the crop, stomach, gizzard, and intestines of birds.

Diglyceride – A glycerol molecule with two fatty acids attached.

Dimethylglycine – The active ingredient in pangamic acid or vitamin $B_{15,}$ also called DMG.

Disaccharide – A compound sugar consisting of two simple monosaccharide molecules.

Disease – Any condition of abnormality in the health of an organism that is brought on by malnutrition or invading microorganisms.

Diverticulum – The scientific name for the bird's crop.

dl-alpha-tocopherol – The synthetic form of vitamin E, used to differentiate the synthetic form from the natural form, which is d-alpha-tocopherol.

DNA – A commonly used shortened form for the hereditary storage molecules within the cells, with the full name of deoxyribonucleic acid.

DNA-DNA hybridization – A process for comparing the genetic material of two species to determine their genetic similarities and differences.

Double bond – An open bond on two adjacent atoms that can be filled by other atoms, usually applied in nutrition to mean the open bonds on two adjacent carbon atoms, as in the structure of unsaturated fatty acids.

Drepanididae – A traditional avian family classification used for classifying the Hawaiian finches, which are now classified in the Sibley-Monroe family Fringillidae.

Duodenum – The first section of the small intestine.

Edema – Accumulation of fluids in the body tissues; swelling.

Eggbinding – A condition in which the hen cannot expel the egg from the oviduct and will die from the attempt; this is a common and often fatal symptom of nutritional deficiencies in the avian diet.

Eicosanoic acid – An alternate name for arachidic acid.

Elastin – A strong, flexible connective tissue in the body, found in the walls of the blood vessels.

Electrolytes – The salts of minerals which circulate in the blood and in solution separate into their component electrically charged ions.

Electron shell – One of the paths around an atomic nucleus on which the negatively charged electron particles travel.

Electrophoresis – The process of running an electric current through a liquid in order to charge the particles of the liquid to determine their characteristics.

Electrophotograph – A photograph taken of living material using the Kirlian method of photography to record the energy emanations of all life forms and living tissue that are invisible to normal human vision.

Element – A fundamental physical material composed of atoms which all have the same number of protons.

Eleostearic acid – An unsaturated fatty acid having the open double bond on the opposite side of the molecule from the vast majority of the fatty acids.

Emaciation – A condition of thinness, leanness, and wasting away of the body tissues.

Embryo – An organism in its early stages of development, still within the seed, egg, or womb.

Encephalomalacia – A deficiency disease in chickens which is caused by a deficiency of vitamin E in the diet.

Enrichment – The addition of vital nutrients to food products that have lost them in the refining process.

Enzyme – A protein substance which functions as a biochemical catalyst in living organisms.

Epinephrine – A hormone secretion of the adrenal glands, also called adrenalin, which stimulates rapid breakdown of glycogen in the liver.

Epithelial cell – A cell on the surface, such as a skin cell.

Equisetum – Botanical name for horsetail, a common plant of the forest floor, which is one of the richest known sources for organically bound silicon.

Ergocalciferol – The technical and scientific name for vitamin D2, which is found in plant sources.

Ergosterol – A provitamin used to form vitamin D2, ergocalciferol, through irradiation with ultraviolet light.

Erucic acid – A monounsaturated fatty acid that contains twenty-two carbon atoms in its chain.

Esophagus – The tube for passage of food from the mouth to the stomach.

Esoteric – Referring to a study that is not publicly known and is intended for and understood by only a small group.

Essential amino acid – An amino acid that cannot be synthesized by the cells of the body and which must come from the diet.

Essential fatty acids – The fatty acids that cannot be synthesized by the cells of the body and which must be taken in by way of the diet.

Ester – The combination of an alcohol and an acid.

Estrildidae – A traditional family classification used for classifying the waxbills, munias, grassfinches and others, which are now classified within the Sibley-Monroe family Passeridae.

Estrogen – A group of several female hormones that are produced mainly in the ovaries.

Extracellular – Outside of the cells.

Exudative diathesis – A deficiency disease in chickens especially, caused by a deficiency of vitamin E and selenium in the diet.

Factor R – An outdated designation for folacin.

Factor U – An outdated designation for folacin.

Fahrenheit – A temperature scale registering the freezing point of water at 32° and the boiling point at 212° under standard atmospheric pressure.

Far ultraviolet – The portion of the ultraviolet spectrum with the shorter wavelength ultraviolet rays.

Fast – A period during which an organism ceases to eat any food.

Fat – Any glyceride ester of a fatty acid, including all animal or vegetable fats and oils.

Fat soluble vitamins – The vitamins which are not soluble in water – A, D, E, K, and F (the essential fatty acids).

Fatty acids – A large group of chemical compounds characterized by a chain of carbon atoms with a methyl group at one end and a carboxyl or acid group at the other end.

Fatty degeneration – The accumulation of excess deposits of fat in the liver or other organs, which interferes with their normal functions in the body.

Ferritin – A brown protein which stores iron in the liver.

Ferrous sulfate – An iron salt which can be toxic and fatal in overdose.

Fertility – The capability of reproducing.

Flavonoid – Referring to any of a group of compounds found in the higher plants, many of them occurring as yellow or orange pigments, also called bioflavonoids.

Flavoprotein – A compound of a protein and riboflavin found in the tissues.

Flax – Plants of the genus *Linum* that yield flaxseed, linseed oil and linen fiber.

Fluorescent – Producing light by the emission of electromagnetic radiation.

Fluorescent bulb – A lamp that produces light by electromagnetic radiation when stimulated by an electric current.

Fluorides – The compound forms in which fluorine occurs in the body.

Fluorine – A non-metallic element, atomic number 9, symbol F, an essential trace element in nutrition.

Folacin – A water soluble vitamin in the B complex.

Folates – A group of substances with folacin activity.

Folic acid – An alternate name for the vitamin folacin.

Folinic acid – Also called the citrovorum factor, it is the biologically active form of folacin.

Follicles – Groups of cells arranged in a circle, containing a cavity, such as that at the base of a feather or hair.

Fontanels – The soft spots in the skull of an infant.

Free radical – An atom or group of atoms having at least one unpaired electron.

Frijoles – The Spanish word for beans.

Fringillidae – [1] A traditional avian family classification for the serins, siskins, linnets, rosefinches, bullfinches, and others, now included within the expanded Sibley-Monroe family Fringillidae. [2] A Sibley-Monroe avian family classification for the avian species that were formerly included within the traditional families Coerebidae, Parulidae, Drepanididae, Emberizidae, Fringillidae, Icteridae, Thraupidae, and the three monotypic families Catamblyrhynchidae, Tersinidae, and Zeledoniidae.

Fructose – A simple sugar or monosaccharide, found primarily in fruits.

Fungus – Plural is fungi; any of the yeast-, mold-, smut-, or mushroom-type plants lacking chlorophyll.

Gadeloic acid – A monounsaturated fatty acid that has twenty carbon atoms in its chain.

Galactose – A simple sugar or monosaccharide, found especially in the lactose content of milk.

Gallinaceous – Any bird in the order Galliformes, including domestic chickens and turkeys, pheasants, grouse, and quail, all having precocial young.

Gastrointestinal tract – The digestive tract, including the stomach and the intestines.

Gelatin – A protein substance extracted from animal collagen by boiling it in water or acid.

Gene – A functioning hereditary unit that is located on a chromosome.

Germanium – A metallic element, atomic number 32, symbol Ge, found consistently in the body, but with no known nor suspected biological function.

Gizzard – The organ, especially in seed-eating birds, which grinds seeds together with grit to break down the seeds into digestible form.

Glucose – A monosaccharide, the most important sugar in nutrition, which provides the energy for body heat and muscular movement in the physical body.

Glucose Tolerance Factor – A nutritional compound with a chromium base which acts as a vitamin in the body.

Glutamic acid – One of the non-essential amino acids.

Glutathione peroxidase – An enzyme containing selenium, which destroys peroxides formed within the cells.

Glyceride – A lipid with a glycerol base and at least one fatty acid attached.

Glycerin – An alternate name for glycerol.

Glycerol – An alcohol which serves as the base for cell fats and oils.

Glycine – One of the non-essential amino acids, which becomes essential in some embryonic and immature birds.

Glycogen – The storage form of carbohydrates within the body.

Glycogen phosphorylase – A body enzyme that stores pyridoxine and aids in the release of glycogen from the muscle tissues.

Goiter – The swelling in the throat produced by an expanding thyroid gland, which is usually caused by a deficiency of iodine in the diet.

Gold – A transitional metal, atomic number 79, symbol Au, found consistently in the body, with no known nor suspected biological function.

Gram – A unit of metric weight measurement, which is one one-thousandth of a kilogram or one thousand milligrams. There are 28.35 grams to the ounce.

Grit – Any small hard rock or shell ingested by seed-eating birds to assist the gizzard function in the crushing and grinding of the food.

GTF – The short name for the Glucose Tolerance Factor, a vitamin with a base of chromium.

Hatchability – The ability of an egg to support the full development of the embryo to maturity, enabling it to hatch when placed in incubation.

Heme – The iron chelate portion of the hemoglobin molecule

Hemoglobin – The iron-containing protein found in the red blood cells of the blood, giving the blood its characteristic color.

Hemorrhaging – Uncontrolled bleeding.

Hemosiderin – A brownish-yellow phosphate which stores iron in the body.

Hepatitis – Any disease which causes inflammation of the liver.

Heptoflavin – An outdated name for riboflavin.

Hereditary – concerning the transferring of characteristics from parents to offspring.

Hesperidin – The most active of the bioflavonoids.

Histaminase – An enzyme in the digestive system which changes histidine into histamine.

Histamine – A compound formed from histidine, usually by bacterial or enzyme action.

Histidine – One of the essential amino acids.

Hocks – The joints connecting the leg to the foot.

Homeostatic mechanisms – The body's ways and methods for regulating the levels of minerals within the body.

Homocysteine – A chemical which is present in the body and which is known to cause seizures.

Hormones – Secretions of one body gland or organ which are conveyed by the blood to stimulate another organ by means of their chemical activity.

Horsetail – A common forest plant, botanical name *Equisetum*, which has a high content of organic silica.

Hydrochloric acid – A colorless, clear chemical which is excreted by the stomach for the breakdown of proteins.

Hydrocortisone – A hormone which is secreted by the adrenal glands.

Hydrogen – A gaseous element, atomic number 1, symbol H, which is a basic component of all fats, proteins, and carbohydrates.

Hydrogenation – The act of combining with hydrogen, as in forcing hydrogen through an unsaturated fat to fill the double bonds of the fatty acids and create a less unsaturated fat or a saturated fat.

Hydrogen sulfide – A foul-smelling, colorless gas formed by the combination of hydrogen and sulfur.

Hydrolize – To break down a chemical compound by reaction with water.

Hydrolysis – The breakdown of a chemical compound by reaction with water.

Hydrolytic rancidity – The action of microorganisms which causes fats to turn rancid. This type of rancidity does not interfere with their nutritional value of the fats.

Hydroxyglutamic acid – One of the non-essential amino acids.

Hyperglycemia – High blood sugar.

Hypervitaminosis A – A toxic excess of vitamin A.

Hypervitaminosis D – A toxic, excessive intake of vitamin D.

Hypoascorbemia – The inherited inability of an organism to manufacture its own ascorbic acid or vitamin C.

Hypogeic acid – An unsaturated fatty acid with sixteen carbon atoms in its chain.

Hypoglycemia – Low blood sugar.

Hypothyroidism – Lowered activity of the thyroid gland.

Icteridae – A traditional family classification used for classifying the orioles, blackbirds, meadowlarks, cowbirds and others that are now classified in the Sibley-Monroe family Fringillidae.

Incandescent bulb – An electric light in which a filament is heated by the electric current to the point at which it gives off visible light.

Incomplete protein – A protein which lacks one or more of the essential amino acids in sufficient quantity.

Injection – The forcing of fluid into the skin, muscles, or blood by syringe or other similar means.

Inorganic – Consisting exclusively of mineral material, not composed of any organic matter.

Inositol – A vitamin in the B complex, sometimes considered as a nutrient rather than a vitamin, since it is required in such relatively large amounts.

Insulin – A hormone produced by the pancreas, which stimulates the entry of glucose into the cells of the tissues.

International Units – A measurement of weight of vitamins A & D, with one unit equal to 0.3 micrograms of retinol or 0.25 micrograms of vitamin D. One milligram contains 40,000 International Units.

Intestinal microbial synthesis – The manufacture of a substance by bacteria that are found within the body's digestive tract.

Intestine – The portion of the digestive tract that extends from the stomach to the anus.

Intrinsic factor – A secretion of the cells of the stomach wall which is necessary for the intestinal absorption of the vitamin cobalamin.

Invertase – An alternate name for sucrase, an enzyme which is necessary for the breakdown of the sucrose molecule.

In vitro – Refers to experimentation done in an artificial environment, such as a test-tube.

In vivo – Refers to experimentation with the living body.

Iodide – A nutritionally essential anion, the form in which iodine usually occurs in foods.

Iodine – A non-metallic element, atomic number 53, symbol I, a vital trace element in nutrition.

Ion – An atom or group of atoms with a net electrical charge, which is caused by the gain or loss of electrons.

Iris – The colored, muscular tissue surrounding the pupil of the eye, which controls the size of the pupil and the amount of light admitted.

Iron – A transitional metallic element, atomic number 26, symbol Fe, vital in nutrition in trace amounts.

Iron phosphate – One of the twelve tissue salts.

Irradiation – Exposure to bombardment by rays or particles.

Isoleucine – One of the essential amino acids.

Isotope – A form of a basic element which has a different amount of neutrons in the nucleus. As an example, Hydrogen has one proton and no neutrons; deuterium has one proton and one neutron; tritium has one proton and two neutrons. All have the physical characteristics of hydrogen.

Isovaleric acid – An unusual fatty acid with 5 carbon atoms in its chain.

IU – *see* International Units.

Kalium – The Latin name for potassium.

Keloids – Scar tissue which develops while an injury is healing.

Keratin – A strong, fibrous protein which forms hair, horns, hoofs, nails, scales, and feathers.

Ketones – Short-chain acids that are a by-product of incomplete fat oxidation.

Kidneys – A pair of organs located in back of the lower abdominal cavity, which maintain the body's water balance, regulate acid-base equilibrium, and filter out and excrete metabolic wastes as urine.

Kinetic energy – Active energy, as in the action of muscles.

Kirlian photography – A system of taking pictures under special conditions of electromagnetic stimulation to show the life force emanations that come from any living thing.

Kwashiorkor – A severe malnutrition disease marked by anemia, edema, potbelly, depigmentation of the skin, and loss of hair or change in hair color.

Lactase – The enzyme needed to break down the disaccharide lactose in the digestive tract.

Lactation – The formation and secretion of milk in humans and mammals.

Lactic Acid – A compound formed in the muscles as a waste product of carbohydrate breakdown.

Lactoflavin – An original, but now outdated name for riboflavin, resulting from its isolation from milk.

Lactose – Milk sugar, a disaccharide composed of one glucose molecule and one galactose molecule.

Laetrile – The name used for amygdalin in therapeutic doses, which is also called vitamin B_{17}.

Lauric Acid – A non-essential saturated fatty acid with 12 carbon atoms in the carbon chain.

Laxative – Any substance that stimulates the rapid movement of the food mass through the intestines.

Lead – A highly toxic metallic element, atomic number 82, symbol Pb, found consistently in body tissues, but with no known nor suspected biological functions.

Lecithin – A compound lipid consisting of glycerol, two fatty acids, and choline linked with them through phosphoric acid.

Legumes – Any plant of the family Leguminosae, which bears pods of seeds, such as beans, peas and alfalfa.

Lens – The transparent organ of the eye behind the iris which focuses the light rays entering through the pupil onto the retina.

Lesion – Any wound, injury, or sore.

Lesser mealworm – The larva stage of the beetle *Alphitobius diaperinus*, about one-half inch long when mature.

Leucine – An essential amino acid.

Ligand – A chelator.

Lignoceric acid – An extra-long chain saturated fatty acid with twenty-four carbon atoms in its chain.

Limiting amino acid – In an incomplete protein, the essential amino acid that is in insufficient supply and therefore makes that protein incomplete for nutritional purposes.

Linguistics – The study of the structure and theory of human languages.

Linoleic acid – An essential polyunsaturated fatty acid with 18 carbon atoms in its chain.

Linolenic acid – An essential polyunsaturated fatty acid with 18 carbon atoms in its chain.

Linolic acid – An alternate name occasionally seen for linoleic acid.

Lipid – A term used to indicate the fats and oils as a unit.

Lipochrome – An alternate, older name for the carotenoid pigments.

Lipogenesis – The process by which the body manufactures fat from excess carbohydrates in the diet.

Lipoic acid – A vitamin of the B complex not yet proven essential for birds, animals, or humans, and possibly supplied by synthesis in the body's cells.

Lipoprotein – The combination of a fat and a protein.

Lipositol – The phospholipid form of inositol in animal cells.

Lithium – A metallic element, atomic number 3, symbol Li, found consistently in body tissues and now presumed to be a vital trace element in nutrition.

Liver – The largest gland in the body, which is the body's chemical factory. It performs a wide variety of chemical functions.

Lonchura striata – The scientific name for the wild Striated Finch, and also for the domesticated variety, the Society Finch.

Lungs – The body organs that inhale air, extract oxygen from it, and exhale carbon dioxide gas and other waste products.

Lycopene – The carotene pigment that is found in tomatoes.

Lysine – One of the essential amino acids.

Macrocytic anemia – A deficiency disease which is caused by a deficiency of folacin in the diet.

Macro-minerals – Those mineral nutrients needed in large amounts; in the human body, those needed in amounts of over one gram daily.

Magnesium – A metallic element, atomic number 12, symbol Mg, an essential bulk element in nutrition.

Magnesium fluoride – A fluorine and magnesium compound, one of the primary compounds in which fluorine occurs in the body.

Magnesium phosphate – One of the twelve tissue salts.

Mal de la Rosa – The Spanish name for pellagra, which is the severe nutritional deficiency disease, caused by a deficiency of the vitamin niacin in the diet.

Maltase – An enzyme that catalyzes the splitting of maltose, a disaccharide, into two glucose molecules.

Maltose – A disaccharide composed of two joined molecules of glucose.

Mammary glands – The milk-producing glands in female mammals.

Manganese – A transitional metallic element, atomic number 25, symbol Mn, an essential trace element in nutrition.

Mango – A tropical, leafy evergreen tree native to Asia, or its sweet, juicy, yellow-orange fruit.

Mannose – One of the simple sugars or monosaccharides.

Mealworm – The larva of any of several beetles of the genus Tenebrio; the most often seen is Tenebrio molitor.

Megaloblastic anemia – A deficiency disease caused by a deficiency of folacin in the diet.

Melanin – A dark pigment found in skin, hair and feathers.

Melissic acid – An extra-long chain saturated fatty acid with thirty carbon atoms in its chain.

Membrane – A thin, elastic layer of tissue that covers, separates, or connects the organs of the body.

Menadione – A synthetic vitamin K compound in the K_3 group, also called menaquinone.

Menaquinone – A synthetic vitamin K compound in the K_3 group, also called menadione.

Mercury – A metallic element, atomic number 80, symbol Hg, with no known nor suspected nutritional function.

Messenger RNA – A form of ribonucleic acid which transfers information from the gene to the cell's protein making machinery, also written mRNA.

Metabolism – The physical and chemical processes involved in the maintenance of life.

Metabolize – To change and utilize in the cells for the maintenance of life.

Methionine – One of the essential amino acids.

Methyl donor – A molecule that contains a loosely bound methyl group that can be detached to perform necessary functions in the body.

Methyl group – A group of one carbon atom and three hydrogen atoms, loosely bound to a larger molecule.

Metric system – A decimal system of weights and measures based on the meter as a unit of length and the gram as a unit of weight.

Mica – Any of a group of complex silicates that crystallize in translucent or transparent layers.

Microbial synthesis – Manufacture by one-celled organisms.

Microgram – In metric weight, one one-thousandth of a milligram.

Microorganism – Any small, one-celled creature too small to be seen with the naked eye without magnification.

Microscopic – Invisible to the naked eye and able to be seen only with the use of a microscope.

Millet – Any of the seeds of the grass varieties in the genus *Panicum*.

Milligram – In metric weight, one one-thousandth of a gram.

Mineral – A naturally occurring inorganic element with a crystalline structure, or a compound of such substances.

Mineral oil – A clear, liquid, petroleum by-product.

Mineralization – The deposit of mineral elements into a tissue in the body.

Molecular energy – The conversion of chemical energy stored in the molecules of food into kinetic energy for muscle action.

Molecule – The combination of atoms of different elements to form the smallest possible unit of a compound.

Mollusk – Any of a large group of marine invertebrates, such as shellfish.

Molt – The gradual shedding of old feathers and regrowth of new feathers in birds.

Molybdate – A nutritionally essential anion which has a base of the element molybdenum.

Molybdenum – A transitional metallic element, atomic number 42, symbol Mo, an essential trace element in nutrition.

Money – A powerful force used in the human sphere, which is designed to serve as both a medium of exchange and a store of value.

Monoglycerides – Glycerol molecules that have only one fatty acid attached.

Monosaccharide – A simple sugar, such as glucose, which cannot be broken down into any smaller form of sugar.

Monounsaturated fatty acid – A fatty acid in which only one double bond is open and unfilled.

Montanic acid – An extra-long chain saturated fatty acid with twenty-eight carbon atoms in its chain.

Motacillidae – A traditional avian family classification used for classifying the wagtails, pipits and longclaws, which are now classified within the Sibley-Monroe family Passeridae.

Mucous membranes – The wet tissues lining all body channels which are exposed to the air, designed to filter out and trap any dust or invading microorganisms.

Multiple sclerosis – A disease of the central nervous system characterized by hardening and degeneration of the tissues.

Muscular atrophy – A condition in which the muscles waste away.

Muscular dystrophy – A non-contagious deficiency disease in which muscles deteriorate and complete incapacitation is the end result. Vitamin E and trace element deficiencies in the diet are closely linked with this disease.

Musophagidae – An avian family name used to classify the turacos, which are unique in their ability to form the iron-based turacoverdin pigment and the copper-based turacin pigment.

Myelin – A white, fatty material which encloses the nerve fibers.

Myoglobin – A protein which contains iron, found in the muscles, which carries oxygen in the muscle cells.

Myopathy – Any disease of a muscle.

Myristic acid – A non-essential saturated fatty acid with 14 carbon atoms in its chain.

Myxedema – A disease caused by severely decreased thyroid activity.

Nausea – The feeling of stomach upset and the need to vomit.

Near ultraviolet – The portion of the ultraviolet spectrum with the longer wavelength ultraviolet rays, closer to visible violet light.

Necrosis – The death of living tissues.

Neochmia ruficauda – The scientific name for the Star Finch, which is native to Australia.

Nervonic acid – A monounsaturated fatty acid which has twenty-four carbon atoms in its chain.

Nestling – An immature altricial bird that is still being cared for by the parent birds in the nest.

Neuromuscular – Having to do with both nerve tissue and muscle tissue.

Neutrons – The particles in the nucleus of an atom with no electrical charge. Differing numbers of neutrons result in the different isotopes of the elements.

Niacin – A vitamin in the B complex, also called vitamin B_3.

Niacinamide – The form of niacin found in animal tissues, and also called nicotinamide.

Nickel – A transitional metallic element, atomic number 28, symbol Ni, an essential trace element in nutrition.

Nicotinamide – The form of niacin found in animal tissues, which is also called niacinamide.

Nicotinic acid – The form in which niacin is present in plants.

Niobium – A transitional metallic element, atomic number 41, symbol Nb, with no known nor suspected biological functions. However, niobium can displace vanadium in biological reactions.

Nitrates – Compounds of nitrogen and oxygen.

Nitrogen – A gaseous element, atomic number 7, symbol N, the most abundant gas in the air, and a component of proteins.

Nitrogen fixing bacteria – Any of numerous soil bacteria that are associated with legume plants and are able to change gaseous nitrogen into a form which plants can absorb and utilize.

Norleucine – A non-essential amino acid.

Nucleic acids – Any of two groups of complex compounds found in all living cells, necessary for the production of cell proteins and for cell reproduction.

Nucleus – [1] The central part of the atom, consisting of the protons and neutrons. [2] The central part of a living cell which controls heredity, metabolism, and reproduction of the cell.

Nutrient – Any item from the food supply that the body needs for health, metabolism, or reproduction.

Nutrition – The nourishment or feeding of the physical body.

Nutritionist – A person who specializes in the study of the body's food and nutrient needs.

Nyoinositol – One of nine closely related six-carbon atoms, the only one biologically active as the vitamin inositol.

Obesity – Extreme fatness.

Oils – Any of a large group of substances that are slippery, combustible, viscous, liquid or liquifiable at room temperatures, and insoluble in water.

Oleic acid – A non-essential, monounsaturated, fatty acid, which has 18 carbon atoms in its chain.

Oligosaccharide – A complex sugar containing from three to six simple sugars or monosaccharides. The term polysaccharide usually replaces this term for any molecule containing three or more monosaccharides.

Ophthalmologist – A physician specializing in the treatment of the eyes.

Opsin – A protein in the eye which combines with retinal to form the compound called visual purple.

Optic Nerve – A sensory nerve that connects the retina of the eye to the brain, which allows the transformation of light entering the eye into usable sight.

Organic acids – By-products of the incomplete breakdown of glucose, other carbohydrates and amino acids.

Organic matrix – The protein framework around which crystals of bone are formed.

Organism – A cell or group of cells functioning as an independent living unit which is capable of reproduction.

Orotic acid – A substance that is claimed by some to be a vitamin with the designation vitamin B_{13}.

Osmosis – The passing of fluid through a membrane.

Osmotic pressure – The force that enables liquid substances to pass through a membrane until pressure on the both sides of the membrane is equalized.

Osteoporosis – A disease characterized by the abnormal removal of calcium and phosphorus from the bones, resulting in very porous and weak bone structure.

Oviduct – A tube through which the egg travels during formation within the hen's body.

Ovoflavin – An old and outdated name for riboflavin, resulting from its isolation from eggs.

Oxalic acid – A substance found in spinach, rhubarb, and certain other vegetables, which binds calcium in an insoluble form.

Oxidation – Burning in any form. In nutrition, it is a very slow, controlled process that provides body heat and energy.

Oxidative rancidity – The decomposition of fats caused by the addition of oxygen, which destroys the nutritional value of the fats.

Oxygen – A gaseous element, the most common element on earth, atomic number 8, symbol O, which is a component of all water, proteins, fats, and carbohydrates.

PABA – Para-aminobenzoic acid, a part of folacin that was formerly considered to be a separate vitamin.

Palmitic acid – A saturated, non-essential fatty acid which has 10 carbon atoms in its chain.

Palmitoleic acid – a monounsaturated fatty acid which has 16 carbon atoms in its chain.

Panacea – A cure-all, such as a nutritional substance or remedy that will cure all ills.

Pancreas – A gland behind the stomach which secretes digestive juices into the duodenum and also produces insulin.

Pangamic acid – A compound whose basis is dimethylglycine or DMG. Many researchers classify this substance as vitamin B_{15}.

Pantoic Acid – One of the two component parts of pantothenic acid. The other is alanine.

Pantothenic acid – One of the B complex vitamins, occasionally referred to as vitamin B_5.

Papaverine – A white, crystalline, non-addictive alkaloid found in opium, and used to relax muscle spasms and as a local anesthetic.

Para-aminobenzoic acid – Commonly called PABA, it is a part of folacin and was formerly considered as a separate vitamin.

Paralysis – Loss of the ability to move a part of the body voluntarily.

Paranoia – A baseless feeling characterized by delusions of persecution or grandeur.

Parathyroid – Any of four small glands located in the throat by the thyroid gland that secrete a hormone that is necessary for the metabolism of calcium and phosphorus.

Parkinsonism – A chronic nerve disease characterized by tremors, muscular rigidity, and impaired motor control.

Paroaria coronata – The scientific name for the Brazilian Red-crested Cardinal, native from Brazil to Bolivia and central Argentina.

Parulidae – A traditional avian family classification used to classify the warblers that are now classified in the Sibley-Monroe family Fringillidae.

Passenger Pigeon – An extinct avian species of North America, *Ectopistes migratorius*, of the family Columbidae.

Passeridae – An avian family classification which Sibley and Monroe used to classify the passerine birds formerly placed in the traditional avian families Estrildidae, Ploceidae, Prunellidae and Motacillidae.

Passerine – Describing the perching birds and songbirds such as finches, warblers, jays, blackbirds, sparrows, and others.

Pasteurization – The process of heating to a certain temperature and holding that temperature for a certain period of time to destroy disease microorganisms.

Pellagra – The severe nutritional deficiency disease caused by a deficiency of niacin in the diet.

Pelvic bones – The bones making up that part of the skeleton between the lower limbs and the spinal column.

Penicillin – An antibiotic compound which inhibits the growth of disease-causing bacteria.

Pepsin – A digestive enzyme secreted by the stomach which catalyzes the breakdown of protein into peptides.

Peptide linkage – The primary chemical bond between amino acids that results in the formation of complex proteins.

Pericardium – The membrane tissue which surrounds the heart.

Periodic group – A group of elements with similar properties on the periodic chart of the elements.

Permeability – The ability to let something pass through, as water through a cell membrane.

Pernicious anemia – A nutritional deficiency disease caused by a deficiency of cobalamin in the diet.

Perosis – A disease, especially in chickens, which is characterized by pinpoint hemorrhages, slight puffiness around the hock joint, and leg bones twisting out of alignment, unable to support the weight of the bird.

Peroxide – A compound containing oxygen in which two atoms of oxygen are linked by a single bond.

pH – Potential hydrogen, a measure of the acidity or alkalinity of a solution.

Phenylalanine – One of the essential amino acids.

Phlebitis – Inflammation of a vein.

Phosphate – A compound of phosphorus and oxygen which occurs in combination with other elements, such as calcium, to form calcium phosphate.

Phospholipid – A compound of a fat or oil with phosphorus.

Phosphoric acid – A colorless liquid containing hydrogen, phosphorus, and oxygen.

Phosphorus – A non-metallic element, atomic number 15, symbol P, which is a vital bulk element in nutrition.

Photoreceptor – A nerve that is sensitive to light.

Photosynthesis – The process by which chlorophyll-containing plants produce carbohydrates and other organic compounds from inorganic elements and sunlight.

Phylloquinone – Any component with vitamin K activity in the K_1 group.

Physetoleic acid – An unsaturated fatty acid that has sixteen carbon atoms in its chain.

Physiology – The vital processes of an organism, or the study of those vital processes.

Phytates – Compounds composed of phytic acid and phosphorus which inhibit calcium absorption.

Phytic acid – A substance found in some plants, particularly cereal grains, which binds minerals into an unabsorbable form.

Phytoquinone – Any compound with vitamin K activity in the K_1 group. Also called phylloquinone.

Pigment – A deposit of colored compound.

Pignolias – Pine nuts, the edible seeds of certain pine trees.

Pine nuts – Pignolias, the edible seeds of certain pine trees.

Pituitary – A small endocrine gland attached to the base of the brain, whose secretions control other endocrine glands.

Placenta – An organ in female mammals that lines the uterine wall, to which the fetus is attached by an umbilical cord.

Planes of existence – The levels of the Creation, as taught by esoteric schools, most holding that there are seven planes of existence, each divided into seven levels, the highest plane being the Creator, the All That Is, and the lowest being the physical.

Plantain-eaters – An alternate common name for the turacos of the avian family Musophagidae.

Platelets – Blood cells smaller than the red blood cell and associated with the clotting of the blood.

Ploceidae – A traditional avian family classification for the weavers and some of the sparrows, now included within the Sibley-Monroe family Passeridae.

Poison – Any substance that reacts in the body to cause positive harm to the cells and tissues.

Polarized light – Light that travels in a uniform straight path rather than in the random straight path follow by most light.

Politburo – The chief political and executive committee of a communist party.

Pollutant – Any substance that contaminates another substance.

Polycythemia – A disease characterized by a great excess of red blood cells, caused by a toxic excess of cobalt.

Polyneuritis – Inflammation of many nerves simultaneously.

Polysaccharide – A compound sugar composed of at least three and usually more than six simple sugar or monosaccharide molecules.

Polyunsaturated fatty acid – A fatty acid with more than one open double bond available in its carbon chain.

Potassium – A metallic element, atomic number 19, symbol K, which is a vital bulk element in nutrition.

Potassium chloride – One of the twelve tissue salts.

Potassium iodide – The compound that is most commonly used as an iodine supplement for humans, birds, and animals.

Potassium phosphate – One of the twelve tissue salts.

Potassium sulfate – One of the twelve tissue salts.

Potential Hydrogen – A measurement of the acidity or alkalinity of a solution, usually shortened to pH.

Precursor – A substance that body processes are able to chemically change into a vitamin.

Pregnancy – The condition of a female mammal carrying a developing fetus or fetuses.

Prenylmenaquinones – Compounds in the K_2 group that have vitamin K activity.

Progne subis – The scientific name for the Purple Martin, native to North America.

Proline – A non-essential amino acid.

Proso – The Russian term for millet, most frequently seen in the description of large millets, such as those in parakeet mixes, e. g., white proso millet.

Prostate – The gland in male mammals located just before the neck of the bladder which produces an alkaline fluid which is discharged with the sperm.

Protein – A very complex combination of amino acids, which consist of carbon, hydrogen, oxygen and nitrogen.

Protons – The positively charged particles in the nucleus of an atom which dictate the characteristics of the atom.

Proventriculus – The true glandular stomach of birds, located between the crop and the gizzard.

Provitamin – A substance that can be transformed into a vitamin by a process in the living body.

Prunellidae – A traditional avian family classification used for classifying the accentors which are now classified in the Sibley-Monroe family Passeridae.

Pseudomonas – A genus or group of short, rod-shaped bacteria.

Psittacidae – The family classification in ornithology used for the parrots.

Psittacines – Birds of the parrot family.

Pterin – A compound that forms folates in the food supply together with para-aminobenzoic acid.

Purified diet – A planned system of food intake for experimental animals, containing known amounts of the necessary nutrients in pure form for control and testing purposes.

Pycnonotidae – An avian family classification used to classify the bulbuls.

Pyridoxal – A form of pyridoxine, vitamin B_6, which is found primarily in animal tissues.

Pyridoxal phosphate – A coenzyme form of the vitamin pyridoxine which functions in many biological reactions.

Pyridoxamine – A form of pyridoxine, vitamin B_6, found primarily in animal tissue.

Pyridoxic acid – The form in which excess pyridoxine is excreted in the urine.

Pyridoxine – A vitamin of the B complex, also called vitamin B_6.

Pyridoxol – The primary form of pyridoxine, which occurs in plant material.

Quercetin – One of the more common bioflavonoids.

Quinones – A group of aromatic compounds found in many plants.

Radiation – The emission of rays or particles.

Radium – A rare, radioactive, metallic element, atomic number 88, symbol Ra, with no known nor suspected function in nutrition, though it is found consistently in body tissues.

Rancid – Unpleasant in odor and taste, as is true when oxygen causes the decomposition of fats and oils.

Rancidity – The decomposition of oils and fats which results in unpleasant odor and taste.

Rapeseed – The seed of a Eurasian plant, botanical name *Brassica napus*, usually called simply rape in aviculture.

Rapic acid – An unsaturated fatty acid with eighteen carbon atoms in its chain.

Recessive – Concerning and describing a latent genetic trait, a trait which cannot appear visually or physically unless both parents possess the gene for that trait.

Red blood cell – An erythrocyte, the disc-shaped cell in the blood lacking a nucleus, which holds hemoglobin and gives the blood its color.

Regeneration – The regrowth of a dead or damaged portion of tissue in the body.

Reproduction – The process by which members of a species create others of their own kind.

Residual ash – The dry mineral remainder after all organic material is burned away or otherwise removed.

Resorption – The process of absorbing, soaking up or taking up again for a second time.

Retina – The light-sensitive membrane lining the interior of the eyeball and connected through the optic nerve to the brain.

Retinal – An aldehyde form of vitamin A, also called vitamin A aldehyde.

Retinoic acid – An acid form of vitamin A, also called vitamin A acid.

Retinol – An alcohol form of vitamin A, also called vitamin A alcohol.

Rheumatoid arthritis – A chronic nutritional deficiency disease characterized by inflammation of the joints, with stiffness, weakness, deformity and loss of mobility.

Rhodanese – An enzyme which breaks down cyanide in the cells of animals and bacteria.

Rhodium – A metallic element, atomic number 45, symbol Rh, with no known nor suspected need in nutrition. However, rhodium will displace cobalt in its metabolic functions.

Rhodopsin – An alternate name for visual purple.

Riboflavin – A vitamin in the B complex, also called vitamin B_2.

Ribonucleic acid – Any of the complex compounds found in all living cells, whose structure determines protein synthesis within the cell. Usually it is called simply RNA.

Ribose – A simple sugar or monosaccharide, important as the base of riboflavin and the nucleic acids.

Ribosomal RNA – A form of ribonucleic acid which is the machinery for the synthesis of proteins within the cell, also written rRNA.

Ricinoleic acid – An unsaturated fatty acid with eighteen carbon atoms in its chain.

Rickets – A vitamin deficiency disease caused by lack of sufficient vitamin D in the diet. It can also result from an abnormality in the calcium:phosphorus balance in the body.

RNA – Ribonucleic acid.

Rod cells – The cells of the retina of the eye that respond to dim light.

Roentgen – A unit of radiation dosage, now rarely used.

Rosicrucian Fellowship – A philosophically oriented group headquartered in Oceanside, California, whose students hold that all living things have higher spiritual bodies invisible to normal human vision, and that rebirth is continued through many lifetimes until the individual achieves perfection, as Christ personified.

RRR-alpha-tocopherol – A newer name for d-alpha tocopherol, the natural form of vitamin E, which has not been generally accepted in the labeling of supplemental forms of this vitamin.

Rubidium – A metallic element, atomic number 37, symbol Rb, that will displace potassium in metabolic functions. It is suspected to be a necessary trace element in nutrition, but not yet proven to be.

Rutin – One of the bioflavonoids which is found in especially large amounts in buckwheat.

Safflower seed – The seeds of the safflower plant, *Carthamus tinctorius*.

'Salt sick' – A wasting disease of ruminants caused by a deficiency of the element cobalt in the diet.

Saturated fatty acid – A fatty acid which has all available bonds in its carbon chain filled.

Sciatic nerve – The main nerve in the region of the hip.

Scurvy – An acute nutritional deficiency disease caused by a deficiency of vitamin C or ascorbic acid in the diet.

Sea squirt – A member of the family of sea creatures called Ascidians, unique in using vanadium as an oxygen carrier in the blood.

Selenite – A nutritionally essential anion with a selenium base.

Selenium – A non-metallic element, atomic number 34, symbol Se, vital in nutrition in trace amounts.

Selenium oxides – Highly toxic compounds of selenium, which is in other forms a vital trace mineral in nutrition.

Seminal fluid – The fluid which carries the sperm cells.

Serine – One of the non-essential amino acids.

Serinus mozambicus – The scientific name for the Yellow-fronted Canary or Green Singing Finch, native to Africa.

7-dehydrocholesterol – The provitamin which is irradiated to form vitamin D_3, cholecalciferol.

Shen-nung – A legendary Chinese emperor who lived about 4,700 years ago. He is remembered for a treatise on herbal medicine.

Siderosis – A disease caused by excess iron in the body.

Silica – A silicon and oxygen compound.

Silicic oxide – One of the twelve tissue salts.

Silicon – A non-metallic element, atomic number 14, symbol Si, essential in nutrition in quantities larger than trace minerals.

Silver – A transitional, metallic element, atomic number 47, symbol Ag, found consistently in body tissues, but with no known nor suspected biological function. It is a copper antagonist in the diet.

Silver sulfide – A compound of silver and sulfur which causes the dark stains on silverware used for eggs.

Skeletal muscles – The muscles attached to the bones which allow movement of the body from one location to another.

Slipped tendon – A manganese deficiency symptom in birds in which the tendon slides out of place.

Smooth muscles – The involuntary muscles of the internal organs, such as those controlling intestinal rhythm.

Society Finch – An alternate name for the Bengalese Finch, whose Asian origins as a domesticated bird probably began in either China or Japan. Most bird breeders and ornithologists presume this bird to be a domesticated form of the Striated Munia, *Lonchura striata*.

Sodium – A metallic element, atomic number 11, symbol Na, which is vital as a bulk element in nutrition.

Sodium chloride – A compound that supplies a substantial amount of both sodium and chlorine in the diet. It is one of the twelve tissue salts.

Sodium fluoride – The compound in which fluorine occurs in sea water.

Sodium phosphate – One of the twelve tissue salts.

Sodium sulfate – One of the twelve tissue salts.

Softbill – Any bird whose primary diet consists of insects, fruits and berries.

Soybean – The seed of a legume native to Asia which is very nutritious and high in protein.

Species – A particular kind or variety of bird, or of any other living thing.

Spermatozoa – Usually called sperm or sperm cells, they are the male cell which fertilizes the egg. The singular term is spermatozoon.

Spine – The backbone.

Stannic sulfate – A compound of tin, sulfur and oxygen which can be used as a dietary tin supplement.

Starch – A polysaccharide, the only one that the avian metabolism can use efficiently. It is the most important carbohydrate in nutrition.

Starvation – Suffering and dying from extreme or prolonged lack of food.

Stearic acid – A non-essential saturated fatty acid which has 18 carbon atoms in its chain.

Sterile – Infertile or incapable of reproducing sexually.

Sterna antillarum – The scientific name for the Least Tern, native to North America and the West Indies.

'Stiff lamb disease' – A fatal disease of newborn lambs which is caused by a deficiency of vitamin E in the diet.

Strain – A group of birds or other organisms of the same species that have a distinctive set of inherited characteristics.

Streptomyces bacteria – A family of one-celled mold organisms that produce the antibiotic streptomycin and the vitamin cobalamin as a by-product.

Stress – Any distress or a mental or emotional influence which disrupts normal biological functioning.

Strontium – A metallic element, atomic number 38, symbol Sr, which is found consistently in the body, but with no proven essential nutritional function.

Strontium[90] – The radioactive isotope of strontium.

Sub-clinical scurvy – Severe vitamin C deficiency with symptoms just below the level which would be diagnosed and defined as scurvy.

Sucrase – The enzyme which as a catalyst splits the glucose and fructose molecules of sucrose apart. It is also called invertase.

Sucrose – A disaccharide which is composed of one glucose molecule and one fructose molecule.

Sugar – A general term used for any of the monosaccharides or disaccharides.

Sulfa compounds – Any of a group of synthetic organic compounds which are capable of inhibiting bacterial activity and growth.

Sulfur – A non-metallic element, atomic number 16, Symbol S, which is an essential bulk element in nutrition.

Sulfur-containing amino acid – A group of amino acids which contain sulfur in their composition. The three most important in nutrition are methionine, cystine, and cysteine. Taurine is another.

Sunflower seed – Any seeds from commercially grown plant varieties of the genus *Helianthus*.

Sunshine vitamin – Vitamin D.

Supplement – An additional substance added to the diet to supply a nutrient or group of nutrients that may be deficient in the diet.

Synthesis – The manufacture and building within the cells of the body, when referring to nutrients.

Syphilis – A chronic venereal disease usually transmitted by sexual contact.

Taeniopygia guttata – The scientific name for the Zebra Finch, which is native to Australia and nearby islands.

Tannic acid – An acid compound, also called tannin, which the body cannot metabolize. It is derived from many species of plants.

Tauraco corythaix – The scientific name for the Knysna Turaco of the avian family Musophagidae.

Taurine – A amino acid which contains sulfur and which is not essential as a component of the diet.

Taxonomy – The science of classifying and naming the living species of the world, both plant and animal.

Tenebrio molitor – The scientific name for the mealworm, the larva of a black beetle which is often called the darkling beetle.

Tersinidae – A traditional avian family classification used for classifying a single species, the swallow-tanager, which is now classified in the Sibley-Monroe family Fringillidae.

Testicle – A male reproductive gland, which produces spermatozoa and the androgen hormones, and which normally occur in pairs.

Theralin – A commercial vitamin-mineral supplement marketed by Lambert Kay.

Thiamin – A water soluble vitamin in the B complex, also called vitamin B_1.

Thiamin hydrochloride – A more stable chemical form of thiamin.

Thiamin mononitrate – A more stable chemical form of thiamin.

Thiaminase – An enzyme found in certain raw fish that splits and destroys thiamin. Thiaminase is inactivated by heat.

Thioctic acid – An alternate name for lipoic acid.

Thraupidae – A traditional avian family classification used for classifying the tanagers, euphonias, chlorophonias and other birds which are now classified in the Sibley-Monroe family Fringillidae.

Threonine – One of the essential amino acids.

Thyroid gland – A gland located in the throat which requires iodine for the production of thyroxine, which controls body growth and metabolism.

Thyroxine – The thyroid hormone formed from iodide and tyrosine.

Tibiometatarsal joint – The foot joint in birds where the toes join to the leg.

Timnodonic acid – A non-essential polyunsaturated fatty acid which has 20 carbon atoms in its chain.

Tin – A metallic element, atomic number 50, symbol Sn, an essential trace element for the nutrition of rats and probably for all birds and animals.

Tissue – A group of cells functioning as a collective unit in the body.

Titanium – A transitional, metallic element, atomic number 22, symbol Ti, which is found consistently in body tissues, but with no known nor suspected biological function.

Titmice – A group of small, passerine birds classified in the avian family Paridae, and the genus *Parus*.

Tissue salts – A group of twelve compounds which are necessary for the proper health and functioning of body tissues.

Tocopherol – The chemical name for vitamin E and its close chemical relatives.

Tortilla – A corn-based, thin, unleavened pancake, characteristic of Mexican food preparation and used in a variety of ways.

Toucans – A group of large birds native to Central and South America, characterized by their huge beaks, which are classified in the avian family Ramphastidae.

Toxemia – A condition in which toxins or poisons are not eliminated from the body, but provide fertile ground for the existence and multiplication of disease microorganisms.

Toxic – Harmful or poisonous.

Toxicity – The condition of being poisonous.

Trace elements – Those elements essential in nutrition in trace amounts, usually in quantities of milligrams or micrograms daily.

Trace minerals – Those elements essential in nutrition in trace amounts, usually a few milligrams or less daily. Many are needed only in quantities of micrograms.

Transcobalamines – Blood proteins that bind and transport cobalamin in the bloodstream.

Transfer RNA – A type of ribonucleic acid that serves as an adaptor, often written tRNA.

Transitional metals – Those metals having an incomplete or unfilled outer electron shell, and are thus reactive in nature.

Transmutation – The change from one basic element to another through the addition or removal of protons from the nucleus of the element.

Triacontanoic acid – An alternate name for melissic acid, an extra-long chain fatty acid with 30 carbon atoms in its chain.

Triglyceride – A glycerol base with three fatty acids attached.

Tripalmitin – A simple triglyceride with all three of the available positions filled with palmitic acid.

Trivalent chromium – The type of chromium that forms the basis of the Glucose Tolerance Factor.

Trypsin – An enzyme produced in the pancreas for food breakdown in the small intestine.

Tryptophan – One of the essential amino acids that must come from the diet.

Tungsten – Also called wolfram, a transitional metallic element, atomic number 74, symbol W, with no known nor suspected biological function. It is a molybdenum antagonist.

Turacin – A unique color pigment, neither melanin nor lipochrome, with a copper salt base, found only in the feathers of certain turacos of the avian family Musophagidae.

Turaco – A family of African birds related to the cuckoos, also called plantain-eaters, and classified in the family Musophagidae.

Turacoverdin – An iron-containing pigment unique to the turacos of the avian family Musophagidae.

Tyrosinase – An enzyme needed for the conversion of the amino acid tyrosine into melanin.

Tyrosine – A non-essential amino acid used by the body to form melanin and thyroxine.

Ubiquinone – An alternate name for coenzyme Q.

Ultraviolet light – Light rays just beyond the violet of the visible spectrum. They are invisible to the normal eye. The longer wavelength or near ultraviolet is closest to the visible violet, while the shorter wavelengths or far ultraviolet is farther from the visible spectrum.

Unsaturated fatty acid – Any fatty acid that has any of its double bonds open and unfilled.

Uraeginthus bengalus – The scientific name for the Red-cheeked Cordon Bleu, native to Africa.

Uranium – A metallic element, atomic number 92, symbol U, found consistently in body tissues, but with no known nor suspected biological function.

Uric acid – A nutritional waste product of metabolism, excreted through the urine.

Urine – A fluid containing dissolved waste products excreted as a liquid in mammals and primarily as a white semi-solid material in birds.

Uroflavin – An old, now outdated term for riboflavin, derived from its source of isolation, the urine.

U. S. Pharmacopaeia Unit – A measurement unit equal to an International Unit, used to measure vitamin A. One unit is 0.3 micrograms of retinol.

Utilization – When referring to nutrition, the use within the body of a particular nutrient.

Vaccenic acid – An unsaturated fatty acid having the open double bond on the opposite side of the molecule from the vast majority of the fatty acids.

Valine – One of the essential amino acids that must come from the diet.

Vanadium – A transitional metallic element, atomic number 23, symbol V, which is an essential trace element in nutrition.

Varicose veins – Blood or lymph vessels that are abnormally dilated, knotted, and winding.

Vascular – Concerning the vessels for the circulation of plant and animal fluids such as blood, lymph or sap.

Verdoflavin – An old name for riboflavin, resulting from its extraction from grass.

Vertebra – One of the bones forming the spinal column.

Vionate – A commercially available vitamin-mineral supplement.

Viosterol – An alternative name for ergocalciferol, vitamin D_2.

Viral infection – Any manifestation of disease caused by the invasion of viruses into the cells.

Visual purple – Rhodopsin, a compound which enables the eye to see in dim light.

Visual yellow – A chemical compound formed when light strikes rhodopsin.

Vitamin – Any of numerous complex chemical compounds essential in small amounts for the control of metabolic processes.

Vitamin A – A group of fat soluble substances vital for life in humans, birds and animals.

Vitamin A acid – Retinoic acid.

Vitamin A alcohol – Retinol

Vitamin A aldehyde – Retinal

Vitamin A palmitate – A combination of vitamin A and palmitic acid in which form vitamin A occurs in animal sources in the food supply.

Vitamin B_1 – An alternate designation for thiamin.

Vitamin B_2 – An alternate designation for riboflavin.

Vitamin B_3 – An alternate name for niacin.

Vitamin B_5 – An alternate, infrequently used designation for pantothenic acid.

Vitamin B_6 – An alternate name for pyridoxine, a group of water soluble substances that are essential for nutrition.

Vitamin B_{12} – Cobalamin or cyanocobalamin, a water soluble substance containing cobalt, essential for life in birds, animals, and humans.

Vitamin B_{13} – An alternate name for orotic acid.

Vitamin B_{15} – An alternate designation for pangamic acid.

Vitamin B_{17} – An unofficial, popular designation for amygdalin, also called Laetrile.

Vitamin C – Ascorbic acid, a vital, water soluble nutrient.

Vitamin D – The fat soluble substances cholecalciferol and ergocalciferol, which perform vital biological functions in humans, animals and birds.

Vitamin D_2 – Ergocalciferol, found in vegetable sources.

Vitamin D_3 – Cholecalciferol, found only in animal sources and essential in the nutrition of birds.

Vitamin E – A fat soluble vitamin, chemically known as d-alpha-tocopherol.

Vitamin E acetate – The more stable form of vitamin E.

Vitamin F – An alternate term for the essential fatty acids, used especially in Europe.

Vitamin G – An old, now outdated name for riboflavin.

Vitamin H – A seldom used designation for biotin.

Vitamin K – A group of fat soluble substances with essential metabolic functions.

Vitamin L – A presumed essential nutrient derived from yeast and liver and necessary for lactation in animals.

Vitamin M – An essential factor from the folacin group.

Vitamin P – The bioflavonoids.

Vitiligo – A skin disorder characterized by irregular spots of white, totally lacking in pigment, appearing on the skin.

Wasting disease – A disease of ruminants caused by cobalt deficiency.

Water soluble vitamins – The vital vitamin compounds not synthesized in the body, which are soluble in water and insoluble in fats.

Wattles – Fleshy folds of skin hanging from the neck or throat, often brightly colored.

Wax – Any ester formed by the combination of any alcohol other than glycerol with fatty acids.

White proso millet – A form of large, white millet, normally used in parakeet mixes and wild bird feeds.

Wilson's disease – An inherited disease characterized by chronic, long-term copper toxicity.

Xanthine oxidase – An enzyme containing molybdenum which is an essential catalyst for the oxidation of a number of substances in the body.

Yaws – A tropical skin disease characterized by multiple red pimples.

Yellow fat disease – A fatal disease of mink caused by vitamin E deficiency.

Zein – A protein found in corn.

Zeledoniidae – A traditional avian family classification used for classifying one species, the wren-thrush, which is now classified in the Sibley-Monroe family Fringillidae.

Zinc – A metallic element, atomic number 30, symbol Zn, vital in trace amounts for the nutrition of birds, animals, and humans.

Zirconium – A transitional metallic element, atomic number 40, symbol Zr, found consistently in body tissues, with no known nor suspected biological function.

"Nutrition is the single most important factor
for maintaining birds in good health and condition."

BIBLIOGRAPHY

Arnall, L. & Keymer, I. F. *Bird Diseases*. T.F.H. Publications, Inc. 1975

Chaney, Margaret S., Ross, Margaret L., and Witschi, Jelia C. *Nutrition*, 9th Edition, Houghton Mifflin company, 1979

Davis, Adelle. *Let's Get Well*. Harcourt Brace Javonovich, Inc. 1965

Ellis, John M. *The Doctor Who Looked at Hands*. Vantage press, Inc. 1966

Guthrie, Helen Andrews. *Introductory Nutrition*, 2nd Edition. C. V. Mosby Company, 1971

Harper, H. A., Rodwell, V. W., and Mayes, P. A. *Review of Physiological Chemistry*, 17th Edition, Lange Medical Publications. 1979

Kervran, Louis. *Biological Transmutations*. Swan House Publishing Company. 1972

Krippner, Stanley, and Rubin, Daniel. *The Kirlian Aura*. Anchor books/ Doubleday. 1974

Mertz, Walter, Editor – *Trace Elements in Human and Animal Nutrition*, Fifth Edition. Academic Press, Inc. 1987

Morris, William, Editor. *The American Heritage Dictionary of the English Language*. American Heritage Publishing Company, Inc. 1969

Morrison, F. B. *Feeds and Feeding*. 20th Edition. The Morrison Publishing Company. 1944

Nutrition Search, Inc. *Nutrition Almanac*. McGraw Hill Book Company. 1975.

Pais, István & Jones, J. Benton. *The Handbook of Trace Elements*. St. Lucie Press. 1997

Pfeiffer, Carl C. *Mental and Elemental Nutrients*. Keats Publishing Company. 1975

Pfeiffer, Carl C. *Zinc and Other Micro-Nutrients*. Keats publishing company. 1978

Random House, numerous editors. *The World Atlas of Birds*. Random House. 1974.

Rodale, J. I. *The Complete Book of Minerals for Health*. Rodale Books, Inc. 1972

Rodale, J. I. *The Complete Book of Vitamins*. Rodale Books, Inc. 1974

Schroeder, Henry A. *The Trace Elements and Man.* The Devin-Adair Company. 1973

Scott, Milton, L., Nesheim, Malden C., and Young, Robert J. *Nutrition of the Chicken*, 2nd Edition. M. L. Scott & Associates. 1976

Sibley, Charles G. and Monroe, Burt L., Jr. *Distribution and Taxonomy of Birds of the World*. Yale University Press. 1990

Sturkie, P. D., editor. *Avian Physiology*, 3rd Edition. Springer-Verlag. 1976

Underwood, Eric J. *Trace elements in Human and Animal Nutrition*, 4th edition. Academic Press. 1977

United States Department of Agriculture. *Food, The Yearbook of Agriculture.* U. S. Government Printing Office. 1959

United States Department of Agriculture. *Handbook of the Nutritional Contents of Foods.* Dover Publications, Inc. 1975.

Voitkevich, A. A. *The Feathers and Plumage of Birds.* Sidgwick & Jackson. 1966

Williams, Roger J. *Biochemical Individuality.* University of Texas Press. 1956

INDEX

For items with multiple references, the page numbers entered in **bold-faced type** will indicate the primary coverage in the text. *Italicized bold page numbers* indicate a glossary entry.

H

I

M

Termites, 44, 45
Tern, Least, 23
Tersinidae, 163, *294*
Testicle degeneration, 108
Testicles, 108, 213, *294*
Thiamin, 84, 85, 121, 138, **150-153**, 182,
    214, *294*
Thiamin hydrochloride, 150, *294*
Thiamin mononitrate, 150, *294*
Thiaminase, 153, *294*
Thioctic acid, 136, *295*
Thirst, 184
Thraupidae, 163, *295*
Threonine, 38, *295*
Thyroid gland, 39, 127, 204, 205, 206, 212,
    231, *295*
Thyroxine, 39, 205, 206, 212, *295*
Tibiometatarsal joint, 213, *295*
Tin, 222-223, *295*
Tingling in fingers and toes, 100
Tissue salts, 235-236, *295*
Titanium, 234, *295*
Titmice, 46, *295*
Tits, 49
Tocopherols, 102-109, *295*, *see* d-alpha-
    tocopherol *and* dl-alpha-tocopherol,
    also vitamin E
Toenails, 35
Toes, 100, 108, 121, 141, 149, 152, 228
Tomatoes, 29
Tongue, 137, 148, 225
Tooth decay, 143, *see also* teeth
Tortillas, 37, 138, *295*
Toucans, 210, *295*
Toxemia, 251
Toxic compounds, 31, 66, 72, 110, 252

Toxicity, 93, 94, 100, 106, 114, 132, 147,
    151, 159, 193, 198, 201, 202, 203,
    206, 209, 210, 215, 216, 218, 220,
    223, 224, 229, 230, 231, 232, 233,
    295
Toxins, 14, 32, 81
Trace elements, 24, 168, 225
Trace minerals, 88, 118, **191-234**, 235, *295*
Transcobalamines, 127, *295*
Transfer RNA, 161, *295*
Transitional metals, 169, *296*

Transmutation, *296*, *see* biological
    transmutation
Tree leaves, 88
Triacontanoic acid, 64
Triglycerides, 67-68, 224, *296*
Tripalmitin, 67
Tritium, 279
Trivalent chromium, *296*, *see also*
    chromium
tRNA, 161
Tropical fish, 44
Trypsin, 158, *296*
Tryptophan, 38, 40, 50, **83-84**, 138, 143,
    147, *296*
Tubers, 74
Tuna liver oil, 94
Tungsten, 216, *296*
Turacin, 199-200, *296*
Turacos, 199, 209, *296*
Turacoverdin, 209, *296*
Turdus migratorius, 44
Turkeys, 107, 123, 124, 139, 145, 181, 192
Turnip greens, 33
Tyrosinase, 199, *296*
Tyrosine, 38, 39, 51, 164, 199, 205, *296*

U

Ubiquinone, 164, *296*
Ultraviolet intensity, 97
Ultraviolet light, 88, 96-97, 100, 103, 142,
    146, 254-257, *296*
U. S. Department of Agriculture, 119
Unity of Nature, 13
Universe, 259-260
Unsaturated fatty acids, 56-70, 88, 204,
    296, *see also* fatty acids *and* essential
    fatty acids.
Uraeginthus bengalus, *296*, see Cordon
    Bleu Finches
Uranium, 234, *296*
Uric acid, 37, 51, *297*
Urine, 67, 75, 76, 98, 121, 127, 144, 159,
    164, 170, 180, 184, 187, 191, 193,
    194, 197, 203, 205, 216, 224, 231,
    297
Uroflavin, 146, *297*, *see* riboflavin

V

W

X

Y

Z